Aminadab

# Contents

*French Modernist Library*

*Series Editors:*

*Mary Ann Caws*

*Richard Howard*

*Patricia Terry*

BY MAURICE BLANCHOT

Translated and with an introduction by Jeff Fort

University of Nebraska Press : Lincoln & London

Publication of this translation
     was assisted by a grant from the
French Ministry of Culture
     National Center for the Book.

Library of Congress Cataloging-in-Publication-Data
Blanchot, Maurice.  [Aminadab. English]
Aminadab / Maurice Blanchot; translated by Jeff Fort.
p. cm. – (French modernist library)
Includes bibliographical references.
ISBN 0-8032-1313-1 (cloth: alkaline paper) –
ISBN 0-8032-6176-4 (paperback: alkaline paper)
I. Fort, Jeff, 1966-  II. Title.  III. Series.
PQ2603.L3343 A713 2002  843'.912–dc21  2001053460

Experience itself is authority (but authority expiates itself).
MAURICE BLANCHOT,
quoted by Georges Bataille in *L'expérience intérieure*

But if I am not the same, the next question is "Who in the world am I?" Ah, *that's* the great puzzle!
LEWIS CARROLL, *Alice's Adventures in Wonderland*

*Aminadab is a novel not récits*

THIS IS A STRANGE BOOK. For readers familiar with Blanchot's narrative works, such a statement goes without saying. Strangeness is the very
element in which these works move and unfold; it is their single most constant "effect" and has the status of a deliberate, if elusive, method.

*Aminadab* is Blanchot's second novel. Published in 1942, it appeared
only a year after his first novel, the first version of *Thomas l'obscur*. With
the exception of the latter (which has long been out of print in France),
*Aminadab* is the last of his narrative works to be translated into English;
its appearance makes it possible for the reader of English to survey very
nearly the entirety of Blanchot's fiction.[1] One interesting feature that marks
this work is the shift from the novel to what Blanchot would later designate
as *récits,* a term that is difficult to translate and whose ambiguity serves
well the "stories" that these later works never quite coalesce into. While
not completely devoid of features resembling characters and events, the
*récits* gradually dispense with all recognizable narrative conventions and
constantly verge toward the rarefied disappearance of the voice that prof-
fers them. *Aminadab,* on the other hand, is very much a novel and insists
on being one, as the designation *roman* (novel) on the cover of the original
edition informs us. It focuses on a single character and maintains a more
or less linear plot that can be summarized in fairly simple terms: Thomas
arrives in an unidentified village, and upon seeing a woman signal to him
(apparently) from one of the upper windows in a boardinghouse, he de-
cides to enter the building and look for her. The novel follows him through
the uncanny detours of his search and his efforts to reach the upper part
of the building. Such a plot can be seen as altogether conventional and
even in a way as very "classic"—the hero on a quest. By adopting it, Blanchot is attempting to confront the familiar genre with his own insistence
on strangeness and with a resolutely antirealist aesthetic, which he considered more urgently needed than ever, precisely for the sake of challenging
and renewing the contemporary novel.

We know that Blanchot was meditating a great deal on the nature of
the novel around the time of writing *Aminadab* because we have several
articles from this period in which he addresses the question. The situa-

tion in which these articles were written was remarkable, to say the least, and its contradictions shed light on Blanchot's thinking concerning the novel, as well as on the composition of *Aminadab:* Between 1941 and 1943 Blanchot, living in occupied Paris, was employed to write a weekly column for a pro-Pétain paper called *Journal des débats.* Having disengaged from his shrill pamphleteering of the 1930s, however, Blanchot did not write political articles (and had no interest in doing so); rather, his column fell under the rubric *Chronique de la vie intellectuelle* (Chronicle of intellectual life) and was devoted entirely to literary matters.[2] Oddly, he seems to have tried simply to ignore the political context of his venue (though it must have seemed very odd to see these often extremely refined literary meditations printed next to the crude political propaganda that characterized the paper). It is often said that the beginning of World War II, especially the surrender of France, marks for Blanchot a period of withdrawal from the political into the literary, and there certainly are grounds for locating here an important transformation in Blanchot's thought and writing. (It was also the period in which his friendship with Georges Bataille began, an event of great significance in Blanchot's life and work.) Indeed, the paradoxes of this situation are further sharpened by the extreme refusal of engagement—and of all forms of verisimilitude and realism—as well as the vindication of the novel's radical autonomy that Blanchot puts forth in these articles.[3]

Attacking "the facilities of realism" on the one hand and the servile observance of traditional forms on the other, Blanchot advocates a traditionalism (if it can be called that) that would remain faithful to the disruptive and creative aspects of tradition.[4] The tradition itself is not simply given but something that must be sought, and this search necessarily involves experimentation and risk—for example, the risk of arbitrariness that realism would avoid by depending on external circumstances for an appearance of necessity. But verisimilitude, Blanchot argues, cannot provide the necessity required by the inner workings of the novel, for, he says, the world itself cannot provide this. In one article entitled "The Pure Novel," Blanchot sums this up revealingly: "[T]he world, which should provide the creative self with raw material, today seems itself to be exhausted; it has lost its originality and its objective truth, it imposes itself only as an inconsistent and impure system whose appearance the mind feels tempted, even obliged to reject in order to reestablish its own interpretation of it and to express its own original experience." In this respect, Blanchot concludes, "the pure novel, whatever its failings, may deserve more attention than the accomplished works of objective narrative. It is in search of the unknown. It demands the inaccessible."[5] This search—which may well recall the one undertaken in *Aminadab*—is Blanchot's justification for withdrawing from, even "rejecting," the world when it comes to artistic creation and artistic experience. In search of the unknown, it sets up a world of its own. In the same essay Blanchot elaborates on this movement in terms that resonate clearly with the project pursued in *Aminadab:*

> Since the rule of verisimilitude has no value, the novel is free to transform reality: not just color it differently but change its structure, overturn its laws and extinguish the light of understanding. It secretes its own world. It is master of its own appearances. It arranges its figures and incidents into a new ensemble, around a unity of its own choosing and with no need to justify its frame of reference. This freedom can seem absolute, but it is none the less bound by a fundamental necessity to harmonize, without *trompe-l'oeil* effects, the inside and the outside of the novel's creation.[6]

The language of the novel leaves the world behind in order to search for its own reality and its own laws, which are not those of the familiar world that surrounds us. But in this separation from the world, it nevertheless maintains a strict relation to the "outside" of the novel—not a relation of representation, however, rather a linguistic relation, one which assumes, enigmatically, that the nature of the novelistic world, however "unreal," and the nature of the "real" world both have their common source in the most essential operations of language. The shadow of Stéphane Mallarmé falls heavily over these ruminations (one of the essays is entitled "Mallarmé and the Art of the Novel"), and the "purity" they invoke is closely related to the one sought in the poet's work. The refusal of the world, Blanchot claims, means attempting to find in language not a depiction of the world but "the essence of the world," the very principle of its constitution as a world.[7] Mallarmé, he says, takes seriously the notion that "language is an absolute, the very form of transcendence, and that it can none the less find its way into a human work." Blanchot the novelist, however, takes the poet's work as a precedent that "allows us to dream of a writer, a symbol of purity and pride, who would be for the novel what Mallarmé was for poetry, and to envisage that work with which Mallarmé sought to match the absolute."[8] With this dream in mind, Blanchot sketches out a pressing task for the novelist in which "he heads towards those strange tenebrous regions where he seems to awaken in the deepest sleep, towards that pure presence where things appear so bare and so reduced that no image is possible, towards that primordial spectacle where he never tires of contemplating what can be seen only after a complete self-transformation."[9]

I have dwelt on these essays and their extreme statements because of their unmistakable resonance with Blanchot's project in *Aminadab*. How can we not see the boardinghouse as an attempt to figure "those strange tenebrous regions" into which the novelist must sleepily tread? Is not Thomas's striving toward the heights, his search for the upper floors and for the woman who may have waved to him, not strictly analogous to the search for the law that dictates the inner necessity and coherence of the novel itself? This is true especially in that so much of Thomas's time is spent discussing and interpreting the law, attempting to position himself in relation to it, and trying to assume for himself its singular application to him and his destiny. Finally, where is it more obviously the case that a world is constituted by the risky fiat of language than in a novel? Indeed, it is difficult not to see the novelistic world conjured up in *Aminadab* as an allegory that is strangely coextensive with the adventure of writing that it would allegorize.

Of course, it is not solely in the wake of Mallarmé that Blanchot attempts to take up this challenge. The tradition of the novel itself had already confronted it, at least implicitly, in what I referred to above as its most "classical" structure from its roots in narratives like *The Odyssey*, to the medieval romances and quests, to *Don Quixote* and *Moby-Dick*, the novel form has always put into play, often ironically, the drifting and wandering search for the distant, the unknown, the inaccessible, and the otherwise enigmatic. It is clear that if Blanchot took on this form, it was in order to undo it from the inside, or rather to continue the undoing that was already well under way—a process that involves bringing more and more manifestly into the sphere of the narrative the linguistic origin of its existence.

One absolutely inevitable reference in this respect is Franz Kafka, whose work *Aminadab* resembles in ways that are surely meant to be obvious. *The Castle*, which it most closely resembles, falls (however obliquely) within the tradition of the novel as search, and Blanchot, in this early novel, is as it were taking up the thread left by Kafka's last great work. In his review of *Aminadab,* Jean-Paul Sartre reports that Blanchot claimed not to have read Kafka when he wrote the novel; but of course Sartre doesn't fall for this ruse and proceeds to accuse Blanchot of turning Kafka's effects into a cliché or commonplace (we hardly have Blanchot to thank for that).[10] And yet, in a sense, we could say that it is true he had not yet read Kafka and that *Aminadab* itself is Blanchot's (first) reading of Kafka.[11] Perhaps we could also apply to Blanchot the statement he himself used to describe Kafka's diary writings: "il fait son apprentissage," he is carrying out his apprenticeship.[12] In his diaries Kafka apprenticed himself to "masters" such as Goethe, Kleist, and Flaubert. In *Aminadab,* Blanchot (at thirty-four still a young writer) openly and unabashedly apprenticed himself to Kafka, not only by borrowing certain forms (the novel as wandering and as a series of conversations) and addressing some of the same essential concerns (the law, error, fiction itself) but also by actually repeating, practically verbatim, certain phrases from Kafka, and sometimes not the least well known.[13] It is clear that Blanchot more or less explicitly set out to write a novel under the guidance of an exemplary predecessor and, in his search for the unknown, to enter into the uncanny space in which the land surveyor had lost his way.

Blanchot later wrote of *The Castle* that its entire meaning might be carried by the wooden bridge where K. pauses to "stare up into the illusory emptiness" before crossing it into the village and initiating the novel's ambiguous adventure.[14] What he meant, I think, was that this movement of arrival and beginning enacts the radical leave-taking that the novel, in Blanchot's extreme conception of it, must perform. Even more than K., Thomas is a figure without a past, and his entry from the "broad daylight" of the village into the obscure spaces of the house seals his separation from the world of the familiar day. Blanchot would eventually speak a great deal about "literary space";[15] in *Aminadab,* the entry into this space is in some measure taken literally, in the sense that here this space is figured as a fictional place, enclosed by walls. The writer's entry into a literary space, a space made of *letters,* is thus doubled by the character's entry into a microcosm that takes the form of a house, and it is this doubling that gives *Aminadab* the aspect of an allegory and that causes it to resonate far beyond the fictional situation depicted. This movement is an exit into an outside that can never be inhabited and in which things are seen from across an irreducible distance even as they threaten to suffocate with too

to love the
way that
one brought
us to all to
love

great a proximity. As Michel Foucault emphasizes in his beautiful essay on Blanchot, "The Thought from the Outside," which refers a great deal to *Aminadab*, it is a distance opened by language and located in the simple but vertiginous "I speak" that has been deprived of all bearings and continues in a perfect coincidence with its own unmoored taking place.[16]

For his part, Sartre referred to *Aminadab* as "fantastic," but it is not at all certain that this term applies to *Aminadab*. If so, it is in the manner of a work like *Don Quixote*, that is, as the disenchanted space of a simulation sustained entirely by language. *Aminadab* begins and ends as a mirage of signs and significations, from the sign in the window to the enigmatic aphorisms on the lamps glowing in the endless twilight of the final scene. Blanchot makes it very clear in the opening pages that the strange world of *Aminadab* is constituted by signs whose manipulation it is. When Thomas first enters the building, he searches up and down a long corridor for a stairway, but in vain; until, that is, he suddenly notices a curtain with a sign above it on which is "written in crudely traced letters: *The entrance is here*." The conclusion is simple and direct: "So the entrance was there." If this is "fantastic," it is nevertheless far from magical and is closer to a mere manipulation of words whose only effects are empty simulations. One is reminded of Alice, whose fall down the rabbit hole is accompanied by a sleepily murmured interchange of letters ("do cats eat bats? . . . do bats eat cats?") and who upon landing finds herself in a situation strikingly similar to that of Thomas—searching a hallway for an open door, she's given instructions by signs that appear out of nowhere ("drink me"). Just as Alice's wonderland is not ruled by magic (not even within her "reality"; she has to take drugs to bring about her transformations) but rather by linguistic play, Thomas's adventures in the boardinghouse proceed according to laws that are first and foremost textual. The "fantastic" here does not consist in the immediate realization of thoughts or a dreamlike alternate world but in the empty effects of nomination. In this sense, literary space is one in which the name in no way creates the thing but rather, as Blanchot asserted in an early essay, the absence of the thing, its shimmering emptiness (an absence and emptiness that are prior to, and constitutive of, any presence and fullness).[17] Here enchantment is disabled by the rigor of fiction itself, the recognition that this gesture—creating something by naming it—remains empty and leaves only the residue of the name. Here everything is possible, but nothing actually happens except a fictional speech in search of its own law and origin.

One of the most important effects of this speech is precisely that of simulation and mimesis. Like K.'s "illusory emptiness," the space through which Thomas wanders is full of illusions and is itself an illusion. It is a world made up of crude but fascinating images that double the already artificial world containing them. This is made clear from the beginning with the proliferation of paintings and other types of doubling whose relation to—or difference from—Thomas's "reality" is disturbingly indistinct. He himself is painted not long after entering the building, and the artifice of the building is doubled in paintings that depict the rooms exactly. He is soon attached, by handcuffs, to a companion who remains his distorted double throughout most of the novel and whose voice in the end replaces his own. In an early scene this companion is described as having a tattoo on his face that duplicates the face itself. Thomas's intimate embraces of his tattooed companion present a mimicry of earlier literary adventures, a malodorous parody of Ishmael's affectionate encounter with Queequeg in the early chapters of *Moby-Dick* (a novel that has an important place in Blanchot's criticism). It is thus at every point and on multiple levels that the fictive nature of the novel is incorporated into the novelistic world itself, not as a narrator's ironic reflections but as the very law of the world that is in the process of unfolding. Thomas thinks at one point: "Was not everything here play-acting?" This question is echoed throughout Blanchot's fictional work, most explicitly in the *récit* entitled *The One Who Was Standing Apart from Me* where the first-person narrator asks several times: "Here where we are, everything is dissimulated, isn't it?"[18] Literary space presents itself as a "here" that is pure dissimulation, pure fiction and artifice. In this regard, the suspension of disbelief required by the fantastic is not relevant here, because belief is never solicited. Thomas himself does not believe, and in this he is the "doubting" figure his name evokes; indeed, he does not even believe in the illusoriness of the illusions: "I have reason to think that there is a bit too pronounced a tendency here to explain everything in terms of illusions." And yet he is irretrievably caught up in a movement driven by the attraction of this false world. His "quest" passes through illusions in search of an illusion and through a textual space that seeks its law in speech as a simulation of speech.

To carry out his search, Thomas must know the laws of the house. Everyone he encounters is deeply preoccupied with these laws, but no one really knows what they are. They remain inscrutable and arbitrary, contained in books that no one reads and that may not even exist. The result is that, together with this obscure and ubiquitous law, it is "carelessness that reigns in the house." No one knows who is part of the staff and who is a tenant, who is a servant and who is to be served. But this scrambling of relations does not do away with hierarchy; on the contrary, it makes of hierarchy a principle of delirium. For Thomas, the law points upward and is necessarily the law of ascent. Everything depends on reaching the upper floors. Along the way he encounters characters who both forbid him and bid him on, and each point he reaches is one to be passed, leading on and upward to the next one. In his long discussions with these characters, the law simultaneously opens and blocks his way, and each encounter throws up obstacles and points beyond itself. Thus the law invites its own transgression and transcendence, a passing beyond that leads, it would seem, to the distant origin of the law in which all these encounters would converge. But Thomas's upward trajectory is also, in another sense, a downward movement. At the end, Dom, his erstwhile companion, says to Thomas: "Your ambition was to reach the heights," but this is only to proclaim his failure. If he reaches the upper floors, it is only after falling into a vertiginous illness, after which he wakes to discover that he is treated as—and therefore effectively is—a servant.[19] If he approaches the uppermost point of the house, brilliant but invisible, it is only because he has been ordered to clean it. If he has reached his goal, it is only in order to expire in a twilight of weakness and debility that will never quite come to an end. In this regard one might recall Samuel Beckett, who wondered whether "the ascent to heaven and the descent to hell might be one and the same. How beautiful to believe that this were so."[20] But if this were so, then it might be that the movement of transcendence, leading into the upper regions, enjoined and forbidden by the law, is indistinguishable from a transgression, a stepping beyond, that lands one in an inexpiable hell of language.

If there is one thing that the characters in *Aminadab* do, it is talk. Their endless commentaries, their unreliable and conflicting clarifications, their meandering stories and legends—especially the long and remarkable monologue placed near the center of the novel—open within the narrative a series of impassioned and delirious voices. I would hazard to say that with these voices, carried away by forces that far exceed the fictional situation of which they speak, this novel enters into its most singular and proper mode. In them, Blanchot's prose takes on the mixture of rigor and lyricism that is characteristic of his most beautiful, enigmatic, and challenging writing. At the same time, these passages make it more clear than ever that we are dealing, in some sense, with an allegorical text, for they reveal the far-reaching dimensions of the experiences being related, resonating with broad domains that are equally historical, political, religious, and of course literary. But in their indeterminacy, they evoke allegorical associations that cannot be reduced to a single alternate set of meanings or to a particular, discernible referent. They introduce a "saying otherwise" (alle-gory) that overflows the fictional parameters and exceeds all reference, threatening to resolve, literally, into nothing. If *Aminadab* is an allegory, it is an allegory of nothing, and Thomas is told that if he were ever to reach the upper floors, he would find nothing because there is nothing.[21] In his ambiguous relation to the law, he strives upward toward this nothing; the voices that throw up their elaborate detours in his path also move toward the nothing that inhabits them as their most obscure compulsion. Driven beyond all figuration, they speak from an enigma located at the juncture of two questions that are repeated throughout *Aminadab*: Who are you? What do you want?

If *Aminadab*'s allegorical associations cannot be reduced to a single referent, the title itself does evoke one particular and very important set of associations. Blanchot's biographer, Christophe Bident, informs us that Aminadab was the name of Emmanuel Levinas's younger brother, who had been shot to death by the Nazis in Lithuania not long before the novel appeared.[22] In Hebrew the name means "my people are generous" or "wandering people."[23] These references are nowhere explicit in Blanchot's novel, in which Aminadab is not, properly speaking, a character but a legendary underground figure who is mentioned only toward the end. But one could claim that this peripheral position actually places the name and what it designates even more centrally within the texture of the novel, as though it were literally encrypted.

In fact, it is not difficult to see at least a suggestive, if not necessarily very clear, relation between the concerns of the novel and the Jewish existence to which its title points. Here again, Blanchot's critical writings are illuminating. In an essay written twenty years later entitled "Being Jewish," Blanchot speaks of the meaning of Jewish experience in terms that resonate clearly with some of his most constant preoccupations concerning literature and literary language. In this essay, Blanchot wants to insist that

the apparently negative forms of Jewish experience, such as exile and up-
rootedness, are not merely negative. To the questions (attributed to Boris
Pasternak) "What does being Jewish signify? Why does it exist?" Blanchot
responds: "It exists so that the idea of exodus and the idea of exile can exist
as a legitimate movement; it exists, through exile and through the initiative that is exodus, so that the experience of strangeness may affirm itself
close at hand as an irreducible relation; it exists so that, by the authority of
this experience, we might learn to speak." Emphasizing the radical exteriority of this experience and of the speech that it would teach us, Blanchot
elaborates on the nature of this speech:

> To speak to someone is to accept not introducing him into the system of
> things or of beings to be known; it is to recognize him as unknown and to
> receive him as foreign without obliging him to break with this difference.
> Speech, in this sense, is the Promised Land where exile fulfills itself in sojourn
> since it is not a matter of being at home there but of being always Outside,
> engaged in a movement wherein the Foreign offers itself, yet without dis-
> avowing itself. To speak, in a word, is to seek the source of meaning in the
> prefix that the words exile, exodus, existence, exteriority, and estrangement
> are committed to unfolding in various modes of experience; a prefix that for
> us designates distance and separation as the origin of all "positive value."[24]

If the name Aminadab means "my people are generous," Blanchot points
out that "the great gift of Israel [is] its teaching of the one God." But he
hastens to qualify this: "But I would rather say, brutally, that what we owe
to Jewish monotheism is not the revelation of the one God, but the revelation of speech as the place where men hold themselves in relation with
what excludes all relation: the infinitely Distant, the absolutely Foreign."[25]
The Distant and the Foreign cannot be equated with God as a transcendent
reality occupying another superior world; they are rather names for the
alterity and strangeness of what is always already in our midst, a strangeness closely bound up with language and with the partly unbridgeable relation to the other through language. To speak this strangeness (Paul Celan:
"the poem has always hoped . . . to speak on behalf of the strange,
on behalf of the other") is to address the otherness that makes familiarity,
and speech itself, possible; it is to approach the place where we are already
but which we cannot ever quite inhabit. As Blanchot puts it, in reference
again to Jewish experience: "The Jewish people become a people through
the exodus. And where does this night of exodus, renewed from year to

xvi

year, each time lead them? To a place that is not a place and where it is not possible to reside."[26]

Within the parameters of a novelistic fiction, *Aminadab* attempts to approach and to explore this place that is not a place. Like *The Castle*—whose author may well have had similar reflections in mind—it is a novel of wandering and speech, endless error and passionate commentary. Thomas is an exile with no abode who finds himself, however, in the promised land of speech. In this sense, *Aminadab* remains true to the exigency of exteriority and strangeness that Blanchot attributes to literary space, in which all movement is wandering and where speech bears the weight of the law—not as a legal corpus but as an ontological principle—the impossible but always shimmering mirage of a destiny and a destination. The task of literature, which Blanchot implies must in some sense "be Jewish,"[27] and which *Aminadab* emblematizes and enacts in its excessive allegories, is to maintain this passionate movement toward an intimate strangeness opened by language at the heart of the ordinary and familiar and to speak the language that would keep it open.

I would like to thank the editors at University of Nebraska Press for their support of Blanchot's work and of this novel in particular. I would also like to thank Susette Min for her encouragement and companionship. Lastly, I am pleased to have the occasion to express my gratitude to two important translators of Blanchot who have preceded me. Lydia Davis has been an inspiration and a generously supportive interlocutor. To Ann Smock I am especially indebted; her help as a teacher and a friend have been indispensable, and without it I could not have carried out this work. Both were among the first to recognize the importance of Blanchot's writing and the necessity of translating it; for their groundbreaking work they deserve our praise and thanks.

1. The first version of *Thomas l'obscur* was written throughout the 1930s and appeared in 1941. Later Blanchot excised almost two-thirds of this text and published it as a "second version" in 1950. *Thomas the Obscure* was one of the first texts of Blanchot's to be translated (trans. Robert Lamberton [Barrytown NY: Station Hill Press, 1973]) and was followed by the admirable translations by Lydia Davis of the largest part of Blanchot's fiction. These in turn were followed by others, including most recently *Le Très-haut,* published in 1948 (trans. Allan Stoekl as *The Most High* [Lincoln: University of Nebraska Press, 1996]), and *L'attente l'oubli,* Blanchot's last fictional work, published in 1962 (trans. John Gregg as *Awaiting Oblivion* [Lincoln: University of Nebraska Press, 1997]).

2. Roughly one-third of the 171 articles were later published as Blanchot's first collection of literary essays, *Faux pas* (Paris: Gallimard, 1943).

3. Several of these articles—those with the most general programmatic statements—can be found in English in *The Blanchot Reader,* ed. Michael Holland (London: Blackwell, 1995). I will be citing these translations.

4. "In Search of Tradition," *Blanchot Reader,* 31.

5. "The Pure Novel," *Blanchot Reader,* 42.

6. "The Pure Novel," *Blanchot Reader,* 39.

7. "Mallarmé and the Art of the Novel," *Blanchot Reader,* 44.

8. "The Recent Novel," *Blanchot Reader,* 37.

9. "Mallarmé and the Art of the Novel," *Blanchot Reader,* 47.

10. Jean-Paul Sartre, "Aminadab ou du fantastique considéré comme un langage," in *Situations* (Paris: Gallimard, 1947), 1: 122–42.

11. It is striking to note that there are no articles by Blanchot on Kafka before *Aminadab,* though several of his most important literary essays would later be devoted to Kafka's writing.

12. *La Part du feu* (Paris: Gallimard, 1949), 22.

13. Readers can find these for themselves. One unmistakable instance will suffice here: At one point Thomas's interlocutor says to him, "The house does not need the interest of those who inhabit it. It receives them when they come; it forgets them when they go." Such sentences appear like recognizable markers standing in territory that is being rediscovered from another direction.

14. "The Wooden Bridge (Repetition, the Neutral)," in *The Infinite Conversation,* trans. Susan Hanson (Minneapolis: University of Minnesota Press, 1993), 463 n.3.

15. Especially, of course, in *The Space of Literature,* trans. Ann Smock (Lincoln: University of Nebraska Press, 1982).

16. "Maurice Blanchot: The Thought from the Outside," in *Foucault/Blanchot,* trans. Brian Massumi and Jeffrey Mehlman (New York: Zone Books, 1987).

17. See "Literature and the Right to Death," in *The Gaze of Orpheus,* ed. P. Adams Sitney (Barrytown NY: Station Hill Press, 1981), 21–62.

18. *The One Who Was Standing Apart from Me,* trans. Lydia Davis (Barrytown NY: Station Hill Press, 1993), 50. I have slightly altered the translation to make it more clumsily literal. The published translation is also revealing: "Where we are, everything conceals itself, doesn't it?"

19. Recall K., who after all his tireless striving to reach the castle, ends up accepting an invitation secretly to inhabit the lowliest maid's quarters in the basement of the Herrenhof.

20. Samuel Beckett, *Disjecta* (New York: Grove Press, 1984), 172.

21. We may recall the passage in *The Writing of the Disaster* (trans. Ann Smock [Lincoln: University of Nebraska Press, 1986]) in which Blanchot writes (apparently autobiographically) of a child's shattering experience of realizing "that nothing is what there is, and first of all nothing beyond."

22. Christophe Bident, *Maurice Blanchot: Partenaire invisible* (Seyssel: Champ Vallon, 1998), 206.

23. Bident also points to other associations: Aminadab occurs in the Bible as the name of the father-in-law of Aaron (Exod. 6:23) and in the Davidian genealogy (1 Chron. 2:10, Luke 3:33), and it is the name of a demonic figure portrayed and commented on by St. John of the Cross (in *Spiritual Canticle*). It also appears in a story by Nathaniel Hawthorne entitled "The Birth-Mark." In Arabic, *Adab* is the term for a literary genre meant to entertain and instruct, emerging with the expansion of the Islamic empire and evoking the diversity of peoples and cultures.

24. "Being Jewish," *Infinite Conversation,* 128.

25. "Being Jewish," *Infinite Conversation,* 127.

26. "Being Jewish," *Infinite Conversation,* 125.

27. It is interesting to note that an anonymous reviewer of the first *Thomas l'obscur* accused it of being "as outmoded as the Jewish art that inspired it." Cited in Bident, *Maurice Blanchot,* 200 n.2.

IT WAS BROAD DAYLIGHT. Thomas, who had been alone until now, was pleased to see a robust-looking man quietly sweeping his doorway. The shop's metal curtain was raised halfway. Thomas bent down a little and saw a woman inside lying on a bed that took up all the space in the room not occupied by the other furniture. The woman's face was turned toward the wall, but it was not completely hidden: tender and feverish, tormented and yet already suffused with calm—that's how it was. Thomas straightened up. He had only to continue on his way. But the man who was sweeping called to him.

"Come in," he said, extending his arm toward the door to show him the way.

Thomas had no such thing in mind. Yet he approached to look more closely at this man who spoke to him with such authority. His clothes were especially remarkable. A black morning coat, gray-striped pants, a white shirt with slightly crumpled cuffs and collar: each item of his outfit deserved close examination. Thomas was struck by these details, and so as to linger a little longer with his neighbor, he reached out to shake his hand. This was not exactly the gesture he had meant to make, since he still intended to leave this place without forming any closer attachments. The man probably sensed this. He looked at the hand held out in front of him, and after addressing to him a vague sign of politeness, he took up his sweeping again, this time paying no attention to what was happening around him.

Thomas was cut to the quick. Soon the house opposite began to stir; the shutters banged, and the windows opened. He could see small rooms—bedrooms and kitchens apparently—that presented a filthy and disorderly sight. The shop seemed infinitely better maintained; it was pleasant and attractive and seemed to be a place where one could rest. Thomas walked directly toward the entrance. He looked around, then fastened his gaze on an object in the display window that had not caught his attention. It was a portrait with little artistic value, painted over another image that was still partly visible on the canvas. Its clumsily represented figure disappeared behind the monuments of a half-ruined city. A spindly tree on a green lawn was the best part of the picture, but unfortunately it ended up interfering with the other image, which—to the extent that one could imagine it by prolonging the constantly interrupted lines—was supposed to represent the beardless face of a man with common features and a scheming smile. Thomas examined the canvas patiently. He was able to make out some very tall houses with a great number of small windows, situated artlessly and with no attempt at symmetry, some of which were illuminated. There were also, in the distance, a bridge and a river, and perhaps—but here it became completely vague—a path leading into a mountainous landscape. In his thoughts he compared the village in which he had just arrived with these small houses, built so densely on top of one another that they formed one vast and solemn construction, rising up into a region through which no one passed. He pulled himself away from the image. On the other side of the street, shadowy figures approached one of the windows. It was difficult to see them, but someone opened a door leading into a more brightly lit vestibule, and the light shone on a couple of young people standing behind the curtains. Thomas watched them discreetly; the young man noticed that he was being scrutinized and leaned his elbow on the windowsill: he studied the newcomer openly and candidly. His face was youthful; the top of his head was wrapped in a bandage that covered his hair, giving him a sickly air that clashed oddly with his adolescent appearance. With his smiling look, he dispelled any suggestion of discouraging thoughts, and it seemed that neither pardon nor condemnation could touch anyone who stood before him. Thomas remained motionless. He enjoyed the restful atmosphere of the scene to the point of forgetting all other plans. But the smile did not satisfy him; he was waiting for something else. The girl, as if suddenly becoming aware of this expectation, made a quick sign with her hand, like an invitation; then she quickly closed the window, and the room was submerged again in darkness.

Thomas was quite perplexed. Could he consider this gesture truly as a call to him? It was rather a sign of friendship than an invitation. It was also a sort of dismissal. He hesitated. Looking again in the direction of the shop, he realized that the man who was sweeping had gone back inside as well. This reminded him of his first plan. But then he thought that he would always have time to carry it out later, and he decided to cross the street and enter the house.

He stepped into a long and spacious corridor and was surprised not to

2

see any stairs right away. According to his calculations, the room he was looking for would be on the fourth floor, perhaps even higher; he was anxious to search for it and to climb up as quickly as possible. The corridor seemed to have no way out. He went quickly down the length of it and then came back. When he had returned to his point of departure, he set out again, this time slowing his pace, sticking close to the wall and following its cracks and crevices. This second attempt was no more successful than the first. However, since his first inspection, he had noticed a door, covered with thick curtains, above which was written in crudely traced letters: *The entrance is here*. So the entrance was there. Thomas went back to it again, and reproaching himself for having overlooked it, he studied the massive door with an almost painful concentration; it was heavily set on iron hinges and was made of solid oak so thick as to defy any assault. It was a skillful piece of carpentry, ornamented with intricate sculptures, but it appeared no less rough and massive for all that and would have seemed in its proper place in an underground passage whose exit it would have hermetically sealed. Thomas moved closer to inspect the lock; he tried to move the bolt and saw that a simple piece of wood, wedged tightly into the stone, held the door in its slot. It would take nothing to push it in. But he remained no less undecided. It was no great matter to enter; he wanted also to be able to leave whenever he wished. After waiting patiently for a few moments, he was startled by the noise of a violent quarrel that seemed to have erupted on the other side of the wall. As far as he could judge, this incident was occurring in one of those ground floor rooms that sank below street level and were repulsively filthy. The noise soon began to annoy him—the shouts echoed oppressively, but he could not tell how they reached his ears with such force. He could not remember ever hearing cries at once so raucous, strident, and smothered. One would have thought that the quarrel had erupted in an atmosphere of harmony and friendship so perfect that it could be broken only by the most terrible curses.

At first Thomas found it irksome to be the witness of such a scene. He looked around and thought of how he could leave this place. But since the shouting was becoming more familiar, without losing any of its violence, he thought that it was too late. He raised his own voice in turn and asked through the din if he could enter. No one answered, but a silence fell, a strange silence in which accusations and anger were expressed even more sharply than in shouts and noise. Certain that he had been heard, he wondered how they would respond to his appeal. He had brought some supplies, and although he was not hungry, he ate a little to gain some strength. When he had finished, he took off his overcoat, folded it, and, stretching out on the floor, laid his head on it like a pillow. It was not long before his eyes were closed. He had no desire to sleep, but he rested in a feeling of calm that for him took the place of sleep and carried him far away from here. The same calm reigned outside. It was a tranquility so assured and disdainful that he felt he had behaved foolishly in thinking of nothing but his rest. Why did he remain where he was without doing anything? Why was he waiting for help that would never come? He began to feel a great nostalgia, but soon there was nothing greater than his fatigue, and he fell fast asleep.

When he woke, nothing had changed. Raising himself up, he leaned on his elbow and listened for a few moments. The silence was not unpleasant; neither hostile nor strange, it was simply impenetrable, that was all. Seeing that he was still forgotten inside the house, Thomas tried to sleep a second time. And yet, though he was still weary, he could not find sleep again. He fell into a momentary doze, then woke abruptly wondering whether indeed this really was sleep. No, it was not real sleep. It was a restfulness in which his worries fell out of sight but that nonetheless made him even more sad and anxious. He grew so tired that when he woke again, he was not at all happy to see a man with thick hair and troubled eyes waiting for him in the doorway. It was even a rather unpleasant surprise. "What's this?" he said to himself. "Is that the man they've sent for me?" Nevertheless, he stood up, shook out his coat, tried in vain to brush away its wrinkles, and, having taken all the time he needed, made as if to enter. The guardian let him take a few steps and seemed unaware of his intentions until Thomas was right up against him, about to knock him out of the way in order to get past. At that point, he placed his hand on Thomas's arm in a timid gesture. They were so close to each other that it was impossible to tell them apart. Thomas was the taller of the two. The guardian, seen up close, appeared even more abject and debilitated. His eyes trembled. His suit had been pieced together from odds and ends, and despite the skillful stitching and the proper appearance of the whole outfit, it left a disturbing impression of poverty and negligence. It was impossible to see these rags as a real uniform.

Thomas gently pulled himself away without meeting any resistance. The

4

door was only half open. Through this opening he could see the first steps of a stairway leading down into a more shadowy region. One, two, three steps were dimly visible, but the light went no farther. Thomas took from his pocket a few coins, passed them from one hand to the other, and looked out of the corner of his eye to see if this offer would be well received. It was difficult to read the thoughts of the guardian. "Should I speak to him?" he wondered. But before he could open his mouth or do anything more than outline a friendly gesture, his interlocutor reached out forcefully, grabbed the coins, and threw them into the only pocket still intact on his vest, a very wide and deep pocket trimmed with dirty gold braids. Thomas was surprised but did not take the incident badly. He looked hurriedly for the latch in order to push the door all the way open. The guardian stood before him. Something in his attitude had changed, but what? It was hard to tell. He still had a ragged and even humble look; it seemed that his anxiety had become sheer distress, and his eyes flashed with a spark that comes from fear. And yet he barred Thomas's way. He did so without authority, without conviction, but he held himself quite firmly in the doorframe so that, in order to pass, it now became necessary to use force. "What a nuisance," thought Thomas. How had such a transformation taken place? It was as if the guardian had had nothing to guard until now, as if Thomas had suddenly created new duties for him by buying his complicity.

This new obstacle was soon reduced to its proper proportions; the man still had the same modest attitude, and perhaps all he wanted was to be the first to walk the path they were about to take together. A word from Thomas cleared the way: "Is that," he said, "the stairway to the fourth floor?"

The guardian, after reflecting a moment, responded with an evasive gesture, then turned around and, opening the door all the way, stepped through to the top of the stairway. Thomas was intrigued by the gesture. Its meaning was not very clear. Did the porter, this everlasting porter, mean to acknowledge that he knew nothing about the house, that he could not give the least information about anything? Was he attempting to evade his responsibilities? Or did he know so much about it that he could only wave away his thoughts with a gesture of doubt and indifference? Thomas decided that his first duty, his only duty for now, was to get his companion to speak before it was too late. He called to him, and the other man took up his position again. He considered him anew. What could he expect from someone so wretched, so degraded? He was overcome with a feeling of solitude and by the anguish of his own destitution.

"Are you the porter?" he asked the man.

He answered yes with a nod. That was all. The response was definite, but it said nothing.

Seeing what meager help he was receiving from the guardian, he took a step back and realized that he was right up against the door. This was a surprise. The door did not look the same as before. The sculptures and designs, which appeared to be set in wood, were made up of the heads of extremely long nails whose threatening points stuck out several inches on the other side. On the side of the door facing the hallway, these designs were rather pleasing. They were not visible right away; it was necessary to give up trying to discover anything by looking too intently and to wait patiently to receive the emerging patterns, almost by force. Thomas looked at the other side as well. Was there any order in this crisscrossing of points and metal rods? He stared for a long time at the panel, but the craftsman must have neglected the backside of his work; the arrangement was completely random. But there was one detail at least that rendered the artist's thought: above the latch was a small sliding window, painted bright red, which a twisted and monstrous iron hinge seemed to bury in the thickness of the wood. The small piece of metal serving as a shutter had recently been covered with a thick layer of paint that stood out brilliantly from its pathetic and dilapidated surroundings; it seemed to promise a new sensation to anyone inclined to stoop to the level of the opening. Thomas prepared to find out how it would be. He tried to lift the iron slat from its wooden frame but was met with heavy resistance: the window opened only from the outside, and the opening was meant for the visitor who wished to look into the house from outside without opening the door. There was yet another oddity: by opening the window, one also bolted the door; when the metal rod reached the end of its slot, it slid into two metal hooks that held it in place, so that whoever wanted to look into the house had also to give up entering it for the moment. Although such details as these no longer held much interest for Thomas, he lingered over them for a long time. He would have liked to reverse his steps and peek through the little window into this dark vestibule at the first stairs he had to walk down. He thought that in this way he would have understood many things. But now it was too late; he had to keep moving forward. In itself the stairway was

6

not very pleasant. Its steps had been washed, and the stone, though worn down and marked in certain spots by deep imprints, was so shiny that it appeared to be new. On each side, and at a considerable distance, stood two walls between which the stairway passed like a ridiculously narrow path. This path was very short, six steps, perhaps ten, for the last ones were lost in obscurity, and it was impossible to tell if they led to another vestibule or if everything ended there. Thomas set off toward his goal with such enthusiasm that he did not at first hear the guardian call to him and did not stop until he was on the second step. And yet the voice he heard was extraordinary. It was marked by a gravity and sadness that made it difficult to believe everything it said. Certainly it was because of his voice that the guardian had been chosen to fulfill his function. Thomas remained motionless when he heard it. The guardian had to repeat what he had said; this time his voice was not so gentle.

"Where are you going?" he asked. "Are you looking for someone?"

Thomas did not answer. Although he was not surprised by this question, and although he was in fact rather relieved to notice that he was not being ignored, he suffered from a painful impression. Indeed, where was he going? How could he explain his presence here? He looked over at the wall from which he was separated by a veritable abyss. He was there, that was all he could say.

"Why are you questioning me?" he asked. "Is it forbidden to come and go in this house?"

The porter lifted his head in surprise. He was still a young man, and there was in his youth an inexplicable reflection of grandeur and dejection, of life and cruel endings, something that made one think of another world, but one that is wretched and inferior.

"Naturally," he answered in his grave voice, "anyone can enter here, if he has a reason for coming. Whoever is a tenant here can do what he wants and need not answer to anyone, on the condition, of course, that the rules be respected."

Thomas replied energetically: "I could become a tenant."

"Well then," said the guardian, "you're on the right track, for I'm the one in charge of tenancy."

So this porter was not so unimportant after all. At that moment, he pushed the door to and it gently closed. It was hard to see anything in the stairway now. It seemed that the steps were even narrower than before and that night had suddenly filled the vestibule, transforming it into a gloomy prison. What was the weather like outside? Thomas could hardly remember the impressions of his arrival at dawn; it all seemed so far away. The only thing he remembered—and it was as if he had lost everything he had—was the woman lying in the middle of the shop, her face turned toward the wall, calm and distant from everything. He felt lightheaded. The guardian, as though aware of his discomfort, slipped up to him and took his arm in a benevolent gesture.

"First of all," he said, "you must tell me your name."

He spoke politely—what kindness in his manners! Thomas leaned heavily on the arm offered to him and took a step forward. His companion gave him support; the steps came quickly to an end. They came to a circular room connecting several hallways and lit from above by a half-concealed lamp. Seats draped with dust cloths had been placed around an empty space so carefully and with such geometric precision that they seemed rather a mockery of order and propriety and human cares. No one was there. Thomas even had the impression that no one had ever been there before him, and even though he saw on one of the chairs a cap decorated with beautiful golden braids, this did nothing to change his conviction. The room was small and round, and the dim lamp, which emitted more shadow than light, revealed its rigorously designed shape. Thomas now thought that the house seemed more luxurious and comfortable than was apparent from its exterior; everything was clean and elegantly adorned. But this did not make one want to stay there. Pictures hung on the walls. They had been painted with such meticulous care that, although each one of them seemed rather large in such a small room, it was necessary to look very closely not only to distinguish the details but also to have a sense of the whole. It was difficult to see the images clearly, but they did not offer a subject of great interest. Although the precision of the execution suggested a certain skill, it was tedious always to find the same features over and over, the same tricks and inventions, the laborious effort of an incoherent, unsatisfied, obstinate mind. Thomas went from one to the other. They were all similar to one another, and if their confused character had not made it impossible to grasp anything more than fragments, he would have thought them all identical. It was very odd. He made an effort to understand what they represented, and once he managed to disregard the useless ornamentation—especially the acanthus leaves that were scattered profusely throughout—he discovered, amidst the disorder of these too carefully traced lines and figures, the image of a bedroom with its various pieces of furniture and its particular layout. Each picture represented a room or an apartment. In his naïveté, whoever had executed the drawing had substituted a vague and crude symbol for the direct representation of an object. In place of a lamp meant to burn during the night, there was a sun; there was no window, but everything visible through the window— the street, the shops across the way, and, farther in the distance, the trees of the public square—had been faithfully drawn on the wall. Because of the repugnance that had prevented the painter from showing certain figures in their true forms, the beds and couches had been replaced in all the rooms by whimsical constructions, such as a mattress laid on top of three chairs, or an alcove with no way in or out.

Thomas looked patiently at these details. How childish it all was!

"I see," said the guardian, "that you are interested in our rooms. Go ahead and choose the one you want."

So these were the rooms of the house. Out of politeness, Thomas pretended to examine the images with greater pleasure, now that he understood their significance. But either because he directed his curiosity to details without importance, and therefore seemed stupid and intolerable to someone more informed, or else because he ignored things worthy of admiration, and so gave away his lack of inclination to take the matter seriously, his goodwill did not seem to satisfy the guardian who approached certain paintings and abruptly turned them against the wall. Thomas was vexed and astonished. It was precisely the pictures he could no longer see that he would have liked to examine more closely.

"I believe," he said, "that you are pressing me unduly." And, pointing to the forbidden images, he added, "I have not yet decided against taking one of those rooms."

The incident did not stop there. As though to show how casually he regarded all these grave and formal proceedings, Thomas himself tried to turn one of the pictures around, and he would have done so if the guardian had not stopped him with a rapid gesture, yelling: "That one is rented!" Did he mean the picture or the apartment represented in the picture? There was no way to clarify this right now; Thomas barely had time to jump back to avoid a brutal blow. The shock, the sudden movements, and the bizarre emotion invading him now compelled him to sit down, without watching what he was doing, on a large armchair. He settled into it with a real sense of well-being. He rested his hands on the arms of the chair, sat up straight, put his legs squarely in front of him, and it seemed then that he was a powerful judge, that he had suddenly regained an authority that, however, he had never possessed. The guardian himself humbly approached, as if he wanted to ask for pardon, stopping and bowing a few steps in front of him so that he might receive from such a magnificent client the right to treat him as befitted his rank. Thomas glanced at him distractedly: "I have no use," he thought, "for this subordinate." Finally, the guardian turned around, and after picking up the cap with gold braids and putting it on, he walked toward a small wooden desk, opened it, and pulled out a notebook with a white label on it. "Now it's clear enough," thought Thomas. "All I have to do is sign my name and everything will be in order." The guardian opened the notebook with its blank pages and slowly leafed through it, though he more than anyone knew that he would find nothing there. He stopped occasionally on a certain page and followed unwritten lines with his finger, or else he went back to a page he had already read and seemed to compare it with a new passage that it clarified or contradicted. Thomas intended at first to let the guardian believe that he was taken in by this playacting and to do nothing to put a stop to it. Was not everything here playacting? So he remained where he was and sat back comfortably. It was out of sheer politeness that he said, addressing his words not to his present interlocutor but to others with whom he would have liked to make contact: "I will wait as long as it takes."

The wait, however, was very short. The little room soon seemed much less pleasant, and the lack of air, the absence of space, the painful impression made by the walls pressing in on all sides rapidly dissipated all the charm one might find in this neat but cramped room. Thomas had to unbutton his jacket. He tore off his collar. He slid down on the armchair, and despite some efforts to maintain a measure of dignity, he gave himself over to an attitude of misery.

The guardian rushed to help him, but he was so clumsy that in trying to prevent Thomas from falling, he lost his balance and had to cling to him, half crushing him and, with his arm now wrapped around his neck, on the verge of suffocating him completely. Never had Thomas felt his guardian so close to him, and the contact was in no way pleasant. The odor was especially unbearable; it gave the impression that his body was discharging itself, in a fit of humility, with effluvia that made one doubt its reality. After pushing away this suffocating presence—he did not know how he had come to this and had the impression of having struggled against an adversary who had latched onto him, who stubbornly refused to go away—he remained paralyzed and numb, not caring to straighten out his suit, which had been almost entirely stripped away during the struggle. At some point, he must have woken up. When he opened his eyes, he was surprised to see that one of the walls of the small room was the door of a cabinet, which the guardian had just opened and entered. Inside it there was a meticulously ordered row of suits of all colors hanging down to the floor. The guardian examined several pieces of clothing—he looked especially at the cut of the back—and he settled on a well-cut black suit, a little old fashioned but of good quality. The jacket—which was much longer than necessary—and the gray-striped pants were placed on a chair next to Thomas, who quickly took off all his clothes. Seeing how poor and worn out they were, he was pleased by the attention of the guardian, who was providing for him at little cost an extra suit that was almost new. First he put on the pants. The style was not current. All sorts of pockets and buttons, whose use escaped him, transformed these formal clothes into work clothes. Three crude-looking belts with enormous buckles closed around the waist. Folds ran here and there along the legs. The whole suit fit Thomas quite well; he appreciated the elegance of the jacket and was hardly bothered by the ungenerous armholes that felt too tight.

Immediately afterward, he made his way to the door, through which he entered a large room lit by a bright light. This room was completely different from the one he had just left. The light emitted by a spotlight attached to the ceiling shone with such brilliance that everything it illuminated seemed truly precious. A divan with beautifully reflective velvet was directly lit, but, with the exception of a chair and a small table that received their share of light, the rest of the room was almost completely dark. Nevertheless, a feeling of luxury and wealth permeated everything. An enormous painter's easel with a large canvas on it divided the room in two, and anyone entering had to wonder how he could ever cross through the network of ropes, the heap of stools, and various other random objects that formed the great central barricade. Thomas thought that this odd structure had been hastily put together so that the painter could execute an important commission, perhaps a grand historical scene. From one of the ropes hung several palettes of various sizes, each one showing the fragment of an image that was meticulously and pleasantly painted in thick layers of color. The figures were lovely, but Thomas did not take the time to look at them closely—he would have hesitated to do so anyway—and his gaze wandered toward the enormous brushes soaking in pools of black liquid that stained the carpet. The whole thing gave off an unpleasant odor of rancid oil. The impression it gave was not that of a lively disorder left by interrupted work but of something deliberately ruined, as if the task of the man working there was not to paint but to defile his work instruments and to create around himself a useless and unseemly décor.

Despite these traces of disorder and vulgarity, the room left an impression of wealth. What a fortune was spent on this setup! A mirror covered with a dirty sheet was attached to the easel, close to where the painter's face would be, as if he had planned to do his own portrait someday. On the other side, a sundial, chosen perhaps as an object of study for a future painting, was lit by a few rays from the spotlight. It was difficult to tell what in this arrangement was supposed to be used for painting and what was supposed to be painted. One had the impression that the painting was there, already finished, and that the artist, exhausting himself in a destructive effort of transcription, was the only one who did not know it. One could even wonder whether in distributing colors on a canvas he had not intended to destroy the painting whose existence shocked him. Thomas wanted to look at everything in detail. There were so many interesting things in the painter's paraphernalia. A crystal carafe of unusual dimensions was filled with liquid colors in a mixture that, under the brightness of the spotlight, shone like a single color, so pure and pleasing to the eye that it did not seem to be formed from the dirty residue of work. A twisting iron stopper sealed it, and a glass tube extended down into the colors. Thomas raised the implement to eye level. The liquid was naturally flat and dark, but some reflections floated on the surface resembling particles of metal, and one could well believe that thanks to the siphon a very pure mixture would be transferred onto the canvas.

In a corner of the room he picked out a stool. Taking it upon himself to place it in front of the easel, he sat down to appreciate the painter's work methods. The canvas stood directly in from of him now, and he saw that a painting had been sketched on it, representing, like all the others, a furnished room, precisely the one in which he found himself at that moment.

He could see the great concern for precision in the painter's work. Every detail was reproduced. This was still only a sketch, but every last object, with the exception, indeed, of the divan, was put in its place, such that one might well wonder what a more complete study would add to the faithfulness of the imitation: it would become impossible to distinguish the room from the painting. The only problem was that the color was lacking. Thomas noticed with a slight malaise that the stool on which he was sitting was represented on the canvas. Perhaps he had acted without thinking.

When he stood up, he almost knocked against the guardian. So he was still there. As soon as he saw him, Thomas could not help shouting: "Who are you?" for he was surprised and almost terrified by the change that had occurred in his person. The guardian had put on a large gray smock. Either because of the length of the overcoat, or else for a completely different reason, he seemed to cut a more towering figure, and the deformities of his body were no longer visible. On his face, which continued to be disfigured by the difficulty of seeing, there was a rather attractive and delicate expression. But Thomas was struck immediately by the disagreeable quality of the transformation. It was the same miserable man standing before him, but his misery was no longer humble. He took on the appearance of something tempting, toward which one felt irresistibly drawn, and although there was nothing noble in this attraction, it seemed that one was obliged to the man who inspired so much gratitude and admiration for it. Thomas thought he recognized his face. But when would he have seen him? Everything he had encountered outside was already so far away, and here he had not yet seen anyone else. Nevertheless, the guardian spoke to him in the same way as before. Only he was a little more talkative.

"There is the painting," he said. "We will begin it now. Do you wish to remain standing, or would you not prefer to lie down on the divan? The work will not take very long, but I have noticed that you are subject to weak spells."

Despite his fatigue, Thomas hesitated to follow this advice. He only moved back a little. The room was so cluttered that when he took a step back, he slipped on the puddles of oil and was able to stop himself from falling only by hanging onto the guardian's arm.

"You see there," said the latter. "You still need some rest. Let me help you over."

The path was incredibly complicated. They had to pass through ropes, slide zigzag between benches, and back up again in order to avoid stepping on the portraits that the painter had painted directly onto the floor. It seemed that the journey would never end. When they finally reached the divan, Thomas thought the obstacles were overcome and let himself fall rather than lie down on the velvet-covered cushions. It was a real fall; the divan was very low to the ground. The shock was so great that he lay there as if inanimate. The guardian held him under his arms and raised him up, only to sink him into a heap of pillows, which he arranged not for the comfort of the position but for the purposes of the décor. This position did not suit him in any case. He lifted his model up again so that the jacket would be more visible, unbuttoned his vest, and finally crossed his two hands on his chest in an attitude of quiet self-absorption. Thomas, who had begun by cursing this tormentor, was finally grateful to him for this attention. He felt a strange well-being, as if everything that was happening to him had already taken place sometime before. The rays from the spotlight gently bathed his body; it seemed that this light also gave him the form of a memory and that it made him lighter with the heaviest things, like marble and precious metals. Had all this not already happened? Had he not already once before witnessed this scene of crossing his hands, opening and closing his eyes, being plunged into darkness by light itself, and had it not then had a meaning that it would never have again? He tried to lower his eyelids, for the brilliant light falling on him was burning him, but the painter called out to him: "Are you as tired as all that? Can you not remain a few moments without turning your eyes away? You're not making my task any easier."

There was no pleasure in hearing this, but Thomas was not affected by it. He was no longer of a mind to be ruffled by harsh words, which, in this room, in any case, did not sound like threatening words but rather like true words before which one could only bow. So he looked directly at the painter. But the painter, who had so sternly demanded the attention of his model, seemed to have lost sight of him. His only thought now was to stir the contents of the carafe in which a horrid mixture of colored residues swirled around, and as he had not found the shade he desired, he began to spread onto the crystal a layer of dirty red that he scooped up from the puddles on the floor. "What a filthy worker," thought Thomas. "So this is the painter they have given me." All the same, he could not help looking with interest at these gestures; they recalled for him the childish behavior of great artists, steeped for too long in the seriousness of their task and intent on making the common world understand, by the frivolity of their distractions, the sublimity of the work that has drawn them into such foolish obsessions. In any case, the painter did not altogether neglect his painting. For brief moments he worked at it with great ardor, without for all that worrying much more about his model. Thomas had the impression of not being there, or, by the fact that he had been put in this spot, of already being a part of the painting, such that the reproduction of his features no longer had any importance. From time to time the painter pulled from his pocket a miniature, which he consulted with care and which he then shamelessly copied. Copying seemed to be his preferred artistic method. He worried always about forgetting certain details, and three-quarters of his time was spent in a feverish comparison that left him simultaneously satisfied and worried. Thomas had great difficulty in maintaining his pose. Added to his fatigue was the temptation to change his position slightly so as to be able to feel the intensity of the painter's attention. No one bothered about him, and yet he was not free to move as he pleased. He ended up falling into a light sleepy state, but he took care to keep his eyes open, fixing on his executioner an impassive gaze unmoved by any hope for rest.

"There, it's done!" cried the painter. "Now it's your turn. When you have said what you have to say, we'll be finished."

So they were consulting him. Benumbed and miserable, Thomas saw a few inches before his face the canvas that was being presented to him as finished. Finished? He noticed first of all that the sketch, so precise before, had been smeared in several spots and that the divan was quite clumsily represented. But this did not prevent the painter from being satisfied; he pointed with an extraordinary joviality at certain details, as if they were the expression of a unique artfulness. Thomas politely approved; the clothes were reproduced exactly; in fact, they were so faithfully drawn and painted that in studying this meticulous copy, one felt a bizarre and quite unpleasant sensation; were these clothes then so important? As for the face, Thomas wondered in vain how the painter could imagine passing it off as that of its model. There was not the slightest resemblance. It was a sad and aged face on which the blurry features, as though erased by time, had lost all significance. What still mattered was the gaze. The painter had given it a strange expression, in no way alive—for it seemed on the contrary to condemn existence—but bound to life by a reminiscence lost among rubble and ruins. This gaze did not appear to Thomas any stranger than the rest. Of whom did it remind him? He looked around. It reminded him naturally enough of the guardian, whose troubled eyes rested on things with an expression that held them at a distance; one might have thought that these eyes looked by virtue of an internal light whose gleam might be extinguished from one moment to the next and that continued only out of a perverse stubbornness. The painter did not grow tired of admiring his work. The joy he drew from this contemplation rejuvenated and fortified him. This did not make him any more beautiful to look at, but however inappropriate his conduct was, it had an exalted and feverish quality from which it was impossible to turn away.

Thomas watched him move about the room, carrying the painting in his outstretched arms, holding it under the light, placing it back in the darkness. From a distance the portrait did not conform to reality as vividly as he had thought; only the suit was visible, but the suit bore a striking resemblance. In any case, these details did not seem to him to be of any real importance. Only the painter's gestures and movements held any interest for him, an interest explained by his curious behavior. After a few moments, the painter regained his sense of seriousness. He placed the painting in a frame and covered it with a piece of cloth. Then he took off his smock and appeared again in the worn-out suit covered with decorations and tarnished braids in which he had first appeared. He went on arranging certain things in the room, poured the water from the carafe onto the floor, and stirred the brushes around in the puddles. He carried out this action as though it were perfectly natural, which was enough to explain the state of the room itself. This room lost the chaotic aspect that the light had made so pleasant. Darkness invaded it almost completely. The guardian spread a tightfitting cover over the divan, and by means of a curtain rod, he lowered a large drop cloth that covered the easel. The rest of the furniture disappeared beneath a few other covers. The last object to be concealed was a canvas hanging on the wall; then it was over.

Thomas saw that it was time to leave; the room was already empty. Still, he asked the guardian: "Can you give me some time?"

At that moment he heard a knock. The guardian answered by shouting: "I'm coming."

"I'm coming too," shouted Thomas, as if he had to put a word in as well.

The door did not open right away. The sound of jangling keys—there must have been a huge bunch of them—rang through the wall. One had the impression that the visitor was amusing himself with his keys but had no intention of using them. This game continued until the visitor dropped the mass of metal to the ground with a loud crash. Thomas opened the door and caught the man just as he was bending down to pick up the mass of iron instruments that had slipped away from him. He was a solid, hearty fellow, with a youthful and scheming air about him. He gave a look of annoyance, and, with quick and skillful movements, he took hold of Thomas's wrists, and the latter suddenly found himself bound in hand-cuffs. It was an unpleasant sensation to feel the coldness of the steel against his skin, but he offered no resistance. "This was bound to happen," he said to himself.

He followed the young man who, unhindered by the darkness, led him down a hallway at a rapid pace. On each side of the hallway there were doors that stood out in the darkness because of the black color that had been painted over them. Thomas could not see much of anything. One of his hands was bound to the left wrist of the newcomer who was pulling him along without paying much attention. After a few abrupt and halting steps, the hallway became so narrow that it was no longer possible to con-tinue. "Okay," thought Thomas, "this pause will give me an opportunity to question my companion." At this moment the sound of a bell made him look up. He had no reason to believe that this bell was meant for him, but when the sound died down, he saw the bell still swinging slightly over the door right next to him, and he approached it. Who could have rung it? The guardian gave him no time to reflect; in his hand was a key, which he slid into the lock. When the door was partly open, he pushed it with his foot and stood aside. Thomas looked in to see an ordinary bedroom, well lit and carefully furnished. Its only amenities were two armchairs and two beds arranged side by side. The colors of each set were different; the light falling on them brought out their nuances, and they seemed to comple-ment one another harmoniously. The carpet had not been so well chosen, but in the center of the wall there was a painting that Thomas liked and that he promised himself to examine more closely if he ever had the op-portunity. While he was glancing around at the room, the door closed; the guardian had left. He then took a few steps, carefully avoiding the stools, the almost miniature tables, the small shelves on the floor covered with worthless ceramics that made it difficult to walk around. The room seemed different according to whether one looked to the right or to the left, and it seemed to change again when one walked away from the door rather than toward the hallway. But these changes of perspective were not great. When facing the door, the only possible thought was to continue straight ahead, and the furniture no longer mattered. Unsatisfied with this tiring little stroll, Thomas stopped and sat down in one of the armchairs, while his companion timidly took a place in the other seat. They had not yet spoken to each other. Thomas continued to look directly in front of him, as if he could not take his eyes from the door that had closed on him. Seated or standing, he returned always to the same fascinating point.

It seemed to him that the light was growing dim or that, if the brightness was not in fact diminishing, there was something in the air that was absorbing the rays. It was as if the night had passed through the atmosphere and found itself there not because of the darkness whose traces could not be perceived but in the feeling to which darkness would give rise if it reigned. In truth, Thomas's eyes were growing tired and sleep lay heavy upon them. He rose with difficulty. Fortunately, the mattress was very close; he fell onto it, dragging with him the young man who tried for several minutes to regain his balance, either by twisting around so as to put his hand in a less contorted position, or else by trying to get to the second bed by flinging himself over Thomas's body. Finally he came to rest on his knees, his head buried in the covers.

To his own great surprise, Thomas could not fall asleep. Was it because of this foreign presence that he had to put up with? He closed his eyes, but he continued to see the room just as it was. He clearly perceived its every detail. He could see the curved back of his companion and had before his eyes the panel of the door and the light reflecting off it. This room was odd. In his insomnia, he had nothing to do but look around him mechanically, letting his eyes wander, and it seemed to him that what they saw did not belong to the order of visible things. Everything was so distant, so far outside! He tried to turn over on his side, but the man he was attached to made this nearly impossible. And him, how could he sleep? Yet he slept a heavy sleep and let out a gentle snore that was like a supplementary acquiescence to sleep. Violently shaking him, Thomas drew him out of his torpor, and while the poor man tried to untangle himself from the sheet that covered him, he asked him a question: "Which one of us is the prisoner?"

Then with his free hand, he helped pull off the cover. Once the man was

18

loose, he slowly emerged leaning on his forearms, as if he were about to jump; he moved his head closer, revealing his irregular features and withered skin. Thomas turned away at first, but he gradually became used to the face by focusing first of all on the ears, which seemed to be trying to hear once again the words that had just struck them. They stretched humbly toward him, and if he had not maintained a slight distance, they would have ended by sticking one after the other against his mouth, toward which they strained, the better to receive its breath. Thomas therefore repeated his words — he wanted to hear them a second time for himself anyway — but this was a mistake. Not only did he not receive a response right then, he also provoked in his interlocutor a sharp feeling of dissatisfaction, as if he had displayed his incomprehension in thinking that such organs needed something said to them in order to hear. He moved on to inspect his neck; the man's head seemed to emerge directly out of his shoulders, perhaps because of the billowy clothing that encircled it. As for the face, what he had taken to be bruises and scars were the lines of a second face drawn on as a tattoo, probably under the advice of an artist, in order to reconstruct a portrait of the face on the face itself. Under close scrutiny, the work appeared to be very skillful. There were some enormous errors in the drawing — for example, the eyes did not match; the one underneath the right eye seemed small and embryonic, whereas the other one spread across the left portion of the forehead in an exaggerated style — but he was struck by an intense lifelike impression. This second face was not superimposed on the first one, far from it. Considered directly, the face of the captive showed only crudely fashioned features, but by turning his head quickly from left to right, without taking his eyes off the mouth, Thomas distinguished some very fine features that were like the traces of a former beauty.

Thomas was absorbed in his contemplation. His own face was so close to this other one that he brushed against it and smelled its acrid and tepid odor. It would have suited him more to remain at a distance, but after some moments he gave in to his fatigue and pressed his cheek against the cheek that was offered to him. He thought that this way he would find rest, and since he was already halfway out of the bed, he leaned heavily on the shoulder of his companion. He was met with nothing but succor and goodwill. The young man was in a very uncomfortable position; half raised on the tips of his toes, his knees spread apart, his body bent forward, it was a miracle that he was able to maintain this posture. Thomas clung to him all the more tightly, and they were welded together into a single block. Such intimacy had its drawbacks. First of all, he had to put up with the nauseating odor that grew more unpleasant with each passing moment. Then there was something unnerving in this interweaving that forced them to mingle their breaths and that linked the two bodies in a wearisome union. Thomas was aware of all this, but he did not loosen his grip. In truth, it was not simply to ensure his protection that he lent himself to these embraces; he thought that such familiarity would lead to a conversation full of candor, and he was waiting for the right moment to ask questions. Thus he let time pass without changing his position, with a clammy face and a paralyzed body. He fixed his eyes on a point on the wall. After distinguishing a vague patch of color, he recognized the painting that had first attracted him.

"Tell me, what's that portrait?" he asked.

It was the portrait of a young woman; only half of her face was visible, for the other part was almost blotted out. The expression was sweet and gentle, and although it was not without sadness, one felt attached to the smile that brightened it. How to interpret this smile? This was the moment to lean forward and look more closely. But it was futile. Thomas could not release his own grip. He turned around and pressed his pouting lips against his companion. In this posture, which his fatigue forced him to accept, he drifted into sleep, enjoying as though in a dream the sensations that came over him. So he did not hear at first the groanings of the young man. The latter had to speak to him to arouse his attention.

"Could you not," he said, "give me some room? A little air, a little freshness; your company is not very pleasant."

Thomas had to listen with great care, for the voice was shaky and almost drowned out by the noisy buzzing sound that became louder when the young man's mouth was open. To hear better, he clamped himself with renewed force against the body he was squeezing. Then he said, "What's your name?"

"Why are you squeezing me like that?" said the voice in distress. "Let me catch my breath. Your only pleasure is inflicting torture."

"You think so?" said Thomas. He set little store by what he himself was saying but was interested in the responses. "How would you like me to position myself? Do you want us to share the bed?"

The young man did not like these words; nevertheless, he responded more calmly: "I see that they warned you about me."

Now they both fell silent. For fear of suddenly disturbing his companion, Thomas did not change his position, and he continued to smell the sweat that seeped through his clothes and penetrated him with the violent odor of another body.

"Why don't you tell me about the portrait?" he asked him.

He had to wait for a response; the young man raised his head and tried to gaze at Thomas, trying to read in his eyes the hidden meaning of his question.

"Naturally," he said, "you would like to leave."

Thomas did not respond directly. "You have no doubt been here for a long time," he said. "You must know the ways of the house. Can you not speak to me frankly? I am stronger and in better shape than you. I can help you."

The young man seemed shaken by this proposition. He asked Thomas again with insistence, as though to make this notion familiar to him, if he did not wish to leave.

"I will leave when the time comes," said Thomas, "but first I want to fulfill my obligations, although I can see that I will encounter more difficulties than I had foreseen."

At that moment he thought he heard the little bell that had called him into this room, and it terrified him. Was it already time to leave? Was he wrong to complain, and did they want to punish him? He listened carefully, but since everything was quiet, he wondered if he had not dreamt it.

"Didn't you hear something?" he asked. "Didn't the bell just ring out a warning? If there is a misunderstanding, I'm counting on you to tell me. But perhaps," he added, "you don't want to show me any kindness?"

Thomas spoke with his lips pressed to the cheek of his companion, while the latter tried to turn his head slightly so as to place his mouth against this mouth that was speaking to him; he seemed to be searching for a way to soothe his ills, but at the same time if by chance he touched this mouth he turned away violently, as if it would have awakened the suffering it was supposed to cure. Thomas waited a moment to see if he would receive a response; then he declared: "Since you don't want to speak, all I can do now is keep quiet."

But the situation was no longer the same since they had begun to speak to each other. Although he felt a repugnance at resorting to such measures, he bent down to the other's ear and shouted with all his strength: "You'll be alone now—I'm leaving."

Thomas was himself surprised at his violence. His voice seemed loud enough to be heard throughout the entire house; it was not confidence that made this voice so piercing, that pressed it entirely into one single shout, that made it disdain every obstacle, as if it were best to have done at once and for good. The voice must have passed through the entire house, but in the room itself it died down immediately. The young man decided to respond all the same: "I will tell you about the portrait," he said. "This room where we are now is much larger than you would think at first. It is one of the most beautiful rooms of the house, and you can never overestimate your good fortune at being able to stay here. The walls are bright; the furnishings are simple and comfortable. Everything is arranged to make one's stay here pleasant."

Thomas nodded in approval, but he said: "The portrait is of a young lady, isn't it?"

"Just a second, please," said the young man. "First I would like to point out to you some interesting pieces among the furnishings. The bed on which you are lying is new. No one has used it but you. The mattress was redone for your requirements. They have neglected nothing in making sure that you find true repose in it."

"And all these knickknacks?" asked Thomas, pointing to the shelves.

"They too have their use," answered the young man. "Would you like to see them one at a time? You haven't yet looked at them enough to know how useful they might be to you."

"Let's see them then," said Thomas.

"Wait," said the young man. "I have something to say about them first. Naturally," he added in a softer tone of voice, "there have been other guests here before you. You could never hope to be the first. Everything possible has been done to eliminate their traces, but there was not enough time to put everything back in order. So do not be surprised if these objects are jumbled and mismatched; each person has used them for his purposes, and so you will discover here the habits of your predecessors."

"Really?" said Thomas. "There were other guests. Are you sure you're not mistaken?"

"It doesn't matter," said the young man, with a superior air. "Now have a seat, I'll show you these little items. You can take a good look at them."

Thomas did not move. "Impossible," he said, shaking his head.

"Fine," said the young man. "Then I have nothing to add. Besides, it's better if you look at them later."

Thomas expected it to end this way, but he was no less irritated. It was not the meaning of the words that hurt him; the words themselves disgusted him. Should he place the blame on the intimacy of their two bodies? At first he had followed with his eyes the words coming from the mouth of his companion; then his attention had been so violently attracted that his own mouth imitated the movements and formed in turn the syllables and consonants, until finally his tongue could not help but search under its palate for the words that it brought up from their very source. He was perhaps somewhat confused by the unpleasant quality of certain expressions. Completely harmless words struck him as being shot through with horrible odors, as if they pointed for him to a sad and repugnant future. The phrases that followed were no better; something unassimilable had insinuated itself into the conversation and had prevented Thomas from appreciating all that was being said. As for the conclusion, he attached no importance to it in itself; it was there like the limit of what he could absorb, and the conversation might have ended on a more optimistic note without, however, bringing him any relief. For a few moments he stopped speaking to his companion. He turned away very slightly, and his gaze, which until then had been riveted on his face, floated about and stared into the distance. "That old portrait," he said to himself. Once he felt attracted by the portrait again, he no longer wanted to turn away. Who was it? He raised his hand, but the image became hazy and began to blur. Everything was much darker. The lamps seemed to be dying out. If the larger pieces of furniture were still visible, the small details that had so much importance began to disappear. With his free hand, Thomas struck his companion. "Why don't you keep the lamps burning?" he said angrily. The blow was not violent, it was meant to get his attention, not to hurt him. But the young man was beside himself. His face took on a dumbfounded expression.

"How you mistreat me!" he answered, his voice barely audible. "But all is not yet settled between us. If my company displeases you and makes you regret the burdens it imposes, you can call the guardian, and perhaps he will decide to separate you from me."

"I'll do without the guardian," replied Thomas. "I have no intention of begging him or anyone else. But," he added, "you are no doubt less free than I am."

"Everyone here is free," retorted the young man.

These replies made Thomas ill at ease. There was something pedantic in this way of understanding things. At one moment the young man seemed overwhelmed at being a captive, then he displayed great pride and derived his glory precisely from what had dragged him down. Despite his disgust, Thomas would have liked to satisfy his hunger for these words. They seemed to him so distant, so ungraspable; they were so foreign to any and every truth and at the same time so imperious. What was he doing here anyway? He thought again of the portrait and said to himself that the moment had come to lose heart. The light had gone out. The silence was impenetrable. And he was more alone than if he had never had a companion. He forced himself out of the embrace that had held him prisoner up to now and stretched out on the bed again. Another ring now encircled his left ankle, a finely wrought ring that was attached by a larger one to the young man's leg. Because of this hindrance his position was still uncomfortable, but he hardly noticed. He listened impatiently as his companion tried to revive the conversation by giving a report on the house. Should he pay any attention? At other times he would not have missed a word. But his experience had taught him already that the inhabitants of the building did not always tell the truth and that even when they were not lying, their words were rarely of any use. Besides, he could not have understood these words; they were spoken in a tone that stripped them of all sense; no meaning could correspond to an expression of such great sadness; for them to carry so much despair, they had to be deprived completely of the unburdened clarity contained in an intelligible word. What painful words! What a speech of endless distress! Thomas listened for a moment to the word *bedroom* and the word *reason*, then he struck his companion to make him shut up.

"What a bunch of chatter!" he said. "This has gone on long enough."

He threw a blanket over his head and was finally able to rest.

The next morning when he awoke from a heavy sleep, he saw that the lamps were burning. Even if he had not been disturbed, he would not have slept for much longer, since for him there was no more rest to be had. He heard a light knocking at the door. "Let's go in," said someone in the hallway.

The door opened violently, and in a single movement, three men tried to work their way in while fighting over space. Thomas saw them strike each other, half seriously and half in jest, without being able to under-stand if they were in a hurry to enter or if they were afraid of crossing the threshold. Finally they came to an agreement and slid into the room arm in arm.

"So you're the ones who were supposed to come," said Thomas, after taking a look at them.

They resembled each other very closely, though they had done every-thing they could to distinguish themselves. They all wore a number in the buttonholes of their jackets, and as if that were not enough, there was on each of their sleeves a thin white band with several words written on it. Thomas would have liked to decipher the inscription, but they never ceased to move around in a display of feverish activity. Hardly were they over the threshold when they let out a great cry, at once sharp and deep, and threw themselves on his companion, who was just then beginning to throw the covers off.

"Alright now, hands off!" they shouted.

A harsh punishment was to be expected, but as soon as they saw how the young man looked, they burst into hearty laughter and began to gesticu-late hilariously, pointing out to each other his face still puffy with sleep. Thomas did not take the scene lightly. The physiognomy of the three new-comers did not seem to him to be commensurate with these comic games. Their miniscule and piercing eyes turned on everything with an air of confrontation, and the insistence of their gaze, no matter what it fastened on, gave rise to suspicion, then to error. But neither was it a relief to es-cape from this gaze. Thomas could not long tolerate remaining aloof. He silently watched the three men who were dressed as maîtres d'hôtel, and seeing that they were not concerned with him, he reminded them that he was there: "I'm the new tenant," he declared. "Are you part of the staff?"

He had spoken very loudly, and when they heard him, they took a sud-den step back. They exchanged looks and seemed not to know what to do, but it was an indecision that might just as well have been related to the meaning of the words spoken as to the response they were about to give. "The house?" they said in concert.

"These may be people from the basement," thought Thomas. All three of them reflected for a few moments, their eyes half closed as if they were waiting for words that would be particularly difficult to understand. But then, after their interlocutor had said nothing more, they seemed to forget his presence altogether, imperceptibly taking on again, although with a little more restraint, their insouciant and jovial demeanor.

Thomas jumped to the bottom edge of the bed. Because of his companion, he was forced to bend down a little, but he tried nevertheless to stare fixedly at the three who had filed in one behind the other with the puerile, and no doubt ironic, desire to avoid exposing themselves to the view of the stranger. So it was the first one he saw almost the whole time, although the two others, slipping out of the line, showed themselves occasionally in a brief flash. He would have liked to consider them one at a time in order to see who they were. The one he could see wore an elegant but oversized jacket, and he slid his hands into its folds to show its defects. The other two seemed to be dressed in a much coarser material. Thomas stretched out his hand to grab one of the armchairs. He was immediately surrounded by the three maîtres d'hôtel, who jostled one another as they seized the chair and placed it at his disposal and then grabbed his companion, whom they pushed along with kicks and blows. Thomas found himself seated rather comfortably, but the young man had caught one leg in the arm of the other chair and could only keep his balance by supporting himself with one hand on the floor. He began to moan in pain.

"That's enough," said Thomas. "We have to talk now." The other men intervened as well. All they wanted was to reduce the prisoner to silence, but with their spastic gestures, they hit him so roughly that the moaning began again in earnest. The noise was unbearable. "Make him shut up!" shouted Thomas.

He was so close to the captive that this moaning voice seemed to be coming from his own breast, and it was difficult not to give in to the desire to lament for himself as well. One of the three men cautiously opened his jacket a little. He pulled out a handkerchief and folded it twice; then after looking inquiringly at his comrades, he fell upon the young man, threatening to gag him. "What a silly idea," thought Thomas. "That won't fix anything." He shook his head but was unable completely to prevent the plan from being carried out, for the handkerchief fell to the floor, and the maître d'hôtel finally placed his hand over the mouth of the bellowing wretch. The two others came closer, and for the first time Thomas saw them distinctly. He wondered how he could ever have compared them to this one who was now so close to him. They were much older; their hair was almost gray. Nor did they have the same sort of look on their faces, although wherever they looked, they too gave rise to an unpleasant sensation.

26

"I entered this house inadvertently," Thomas said to them. "I was passing by on the street outside when someone made a sign to me; I only wanted to stay for a moment. But now I'm in a predicament, for I don't know anyone, and no one is expecting me." He noticed that the two men listened attentively. This was already a comfort. "My situation," he continued, "has not yet been officially defined. To be a tenant would not seem to me to be a bad thing, but would I be admitted as such? Would I be able to fulfill the requirements? Would I have any guarantees? I arrived only a short time ago, but I have seen enough to make me fear entering into anything without due consideration." He addressed a cautious glance at his listeners, who nodded their heads. "I could also try to return to the outside. Outside there are difficulties, and it is not always pleasant to go by foot. But at least one knows where one is going. Have you been assigned to take me somewhere?" The two men looked at each other as if they wanted to prepare a response in common, but they remained silent. "I understand," said Thomas, who had hoped for an explanation. "You cannot answer me. My question is not one that should be addressed to you. From now on I will wait until I am questioned."

He fell silent; his words were so futile that he had to wonder whether they had really been spoken at all. Nevertheless, the two men were still standing motionless before him. "Are they not here to serve me?" he thought, and he could not help shouting: "Well who are you anyway?" They responded together by holding out their arms, which were encircled by an inscription in Gothic letters. It was a sort of motto. This time Thomas was able to decipher it. *I serve alone.* The third of the men, seeing that his comrades were making themselves known, did not want to be forgotten, so while maintaining his hold on the prisoner, whose face he hid with his arm, he offered his inscription to be read. It was the same, but instead of being embroidered, it was written carelessly in ink on a white band. "How can you be of any service?" asked Thomas.

"Service?" they replied in a single voice. One of them took from his pocket a small notepad, which he opened to a random page. He waited with a pencil at the ready.

"Now it's time for the interrogation," thought Thomas. It was a relief; now he had only to submit to the will of others. However, there was a long pause before one of them made up his mind to begin. Speaking was not their strong point. The number-two man, after standing for a while with his eyes lowered, began to move imperceptibly toward the door, as if he wanted to escape from a harrowing ordeal. But he bumped against a shelf and jumped back terrified by the noise of clanking saucers and cups. His acolytes rushed toward him. Thomas thought they were going to smash everything to pieces, and in fact, with their abrupt and clumsy movements, they knocked over two large vases, which shattered into pieces, spilling out all their water. They were unconcerned with this mishap. One of them triumphantly seized a cup and saucer and placed them on the table. Then they ran toward the door, yelling: "To the kitchen!"

The door closed so violently that the bell jingled overhead. Thomas was glad to be free of their presence, but he wondered whether he had really taken as much advantage of this visit as he had wished. Of course, they were from down below, so they knew nothing of the house, properly speaking, but the things that went on in the basement floors were sometimes the most important of all. He turned to the young man. "Do you know them?" he said.

Now his companion was sitting in the armchair and was trying to copy the gestures and the attitude of his neighbor. He shook his head in horror. "So you really don't know them?" he asked again. But he could elicit no sign of assent. He tried to picture how the lower floors were arranged, if they were easily accessible, if they kept a large staff busy, and many other things besides. All this was not easy to imagine.

Thomas was drawn out of his thoughts by the very quiet sounds of the bells. First he heard one in the distance, and it was as if it had never before struck a human ear. He heard a second one, which was no less calm. For the first time he felt at peace; perhaps he would have no rest, but his journey would have an end. One after the other, the bells were heard to sound, and their sound spread through the air in such a way that the air too was a bell softly ringing. Soon there were too many at once; the call came from every floor; it made one wonder just how high the house could rise and why no one was answering. After a few moments, there were footsteps echoing in the hallway. Someone opened a door. There was the beginning of a conversation, and Thomas bent his ear, but without being able to catch anything, for the walls were very thick. Other doors were opened or closed. The boards creaked under the footsteps. The noise of a service elevator shook the wall, causing it to rumble as if it were going to give way. Thomas looked with surprise at the part of the room where the noise was coming through, which the shaking lamps lit up in an irregular pattern. He looked along the wall for something new, and then his gaze fell again on the portrait. It made him feel impatient. Was there, then, nothing else to look at here? Besides, it was not even a portrait. It was a narrow opening covered by a slab of mica that let a little daylight seep through.

Without losing a moment, he rose to go to the window. He had to make the young man get up too. The latter, clinging to the armchair in which he was comfortably seated, pointed excitedly at the chain; one of its links had slipped under the leg of the table and held them both back. Thomas had to push the table back with violence; the cup turned over on the saucer, and its edge was badly chipped. Then he dragged his companion to the bed and kneeled down on the mattress to make him climb up too. It was not easy. The young man sank into despair and began to bellow outright.

"Why are you feeling sorry for yourself?" shouted Thomas. "Are you afraid of something?"

What was there to be afraid of? He glanced up at the skylight, which was now right next to him, and without a care for the savage resistance of his companion, he climbed up onto the second ledge. His right leg and right arm were left hanging in the other direction. But despite this uncomfortable position, he did not feel the burdensome attachments; he felt only the taut movement that allowed him to advance as if he were free from all constraints. The prisoner finally followed him. He heard the bed creaking under the tremendous weight and had the impression that the springs were snapping and standing on end with a loud crashing sound. For a few seconds it made a deafening noise. The mattress was vigorously protesting. This horrible racket was a far cry from the silent repose Thomas had found in the bed.

"What are you up to now?" he shouted.

He turned around immediately and saw the damage. Almost all of the springs had cut through the stuffing, as if suddenly the mattress were one that had been worn out by long use and ready to cave in at the first touch. The iron hoops shone in the light. Certain pieces of steel, brilliant and polished, had passed through the sheets like knives, others followed the outline of the mattress cover and were still hidden in the stuffing. Thomas looked with consternation at the remains of this ingenious machinery that, for him, had provided such a good rest. He noticed in the gaping hole of the bed an apparatus with pieces that seemed to spin endlessly over and through one another. Without disturbing the silence — indeed, it seemed that the silence was all the greater — a movement began to shake the entire bed in a rhythm that at first seemed gentle and soothing but that eventually became insatiable. Thomas felt the vibrations and experienced a sort of nausea that obliged him to rock back and forth from right to left in a rapid motion. The prisoner had turned to look in his direction. The unfortunate man must have been suffering terribly; the springs had pierced his sides, and he was lying atop knife blades and razors.

"But I really don't wish you any harm," Thomas said to him, but at the same time, with his finger pointed to the skylight, he made a sign to him to rise.

This skylight was easier to reach than he had thought. He held out his hand to the captive, and with his fingers entwined in these other enormous fingers, he helped him to stand up. He was astonished at his size. How big he was! One would have thought there were two men combined into one, so massive was his body. He moved toward the wall, and while only a small portion of the light from the window reached Thomas, this large man was easily able to look through the mica. What did he see? There was no way to ask him. The light was pleasant, but it wasn't the light of day, as one might have thought; it was the gleam of a gently burning fire that seemed to reach this point only accidentally. The window itself was there only by chance. It had been placed there out of a builder's whim or else according to a design that had since been abandoned. Viewed from up close, it appeared even smaller than it had from farther away. It was possible to look through it only when one's eyes managed to catch the right angle through the slot. Thomas pulled himself up onto the shoulders of his companion. Blood had flowed from his wounds, but now it had dried. Now they were so tightly bound that they formed a single being, and Thomas had the impression that they could never again be separated.

Through the skylight he could clearly see part of another room; its walls were covered with a glossy white paint, and the paving stones on the floor were white as well. The room was situated well below where Thomas was. It was buried deeply underneath the house, so deeply that all the other floors seemed to have been built in order to press it even farther down. It was not a cellar. On the contrary, it had been magnificently accommodated, as if it were meant to shine forth in broad daylight. Thomas immediately recognized the kitchens. A great fire burned in the hearth. On the wall were hung pots and pans, which did not seem to be in very good condition and at which a rather aged and sickly man stared intently. It could be that since he was an invalid and could no longer perform any other tasks, they had entrusted him with guarding these utensils, but he put all his pride into fulfilling his function as no other could. And perhaps the task was actually very important. From time to time he took hold of an object, usually in a general state of ruin, looked it over, shook it, held it up to his nose, then hung it up again with all sorts of careful maneuvers. Obviously this man had a considerable duty to carry out. But those with less experience were incapable of understanding. Some kitchen boys, whose only point of pride was the blinding whiteness of their uniforms, stopped behind him and imitated his gestures with exaggerated seriousness. They took from their pockets some meager item and pretended to ponder it, passing their hands over their foreheads before putting it back into their pockets. Seconds later they threw him to the ground and hurried away. Thomas did not understand everything he saw and would have needed some explanation. But the pleasure he took in observing was all the greater.

Despite the distance between him and these prideful people, he felt less out of his element; he was attracted by a brilliant and tempting hope; his eyes had opened wide onto something that was better suited to his vision than all the other things of the earth. Someone was rolling through the middle of the room a cart carrying huge steaming plates that could be opened and closed at will by lifting a hinged cover. The steam was very thick. The cook who stood by this mobile kitchen was twisting valves and spigots, and the steam rose majestically in a golden plume. What was simmering in the pots was no doubt less precious than this steam—which rose slowly in billowing wreaths only to be sucked into a large pipe leading up to the higher floors—for a kitchen boy, shabbily dressed, emptied the contents of the dishes from time to time into crude containers. The cook was not dressed in a very nice uniform either; he wore enormous boots that seemed to be covered with unspeakable filth, but the solemnity of his bearing, the slow deliberateness of his gestures, and, above all, the brilliance of his face when he approached the ovens gave him an importance that was immediately recognizable. He did not cease to inspire a great deal of respect in Thomas. How nice it would be to stand at his side and to watch his work more closely! The activity to which he devoted himself appeared to be very monotonous and required few fine qualities. He stood upright, his arms crossed over his chest, his head slightly tilted in order to smell the vapor given off by the dishes, and when he turned aside for a moment, finding himself in the ordinary atmosphere, his face lost all expression; he looked neither happy nor unhappy; he was only an aging man who had difficulties breathing and moving.

Thomas closed his eyes. "Would it not be better," he said to himself, "if I tried to go home." He felt his appetite growing and was afraid that they would forget to serve him for good. "When are we going to eat?" he said very quietly, bending down toward his companion.

He did not wait for an answer and turned back to the kitchen. The spectacle did not hold the same interest as the first time. Around a table stood men dressed in large white aprons washing dishes. In the center of the table was a hole filled with water. They threw all sorts of containers into it at random and pulled them out just as quickly; each one worked with care, but the water was so filthy that, despite the rapid pace of their gestures, the implements always soaked too long in the waste and were covered with greasy spots that could no longer be wiped away. These implements interested Thomas because they did not resemble the ones used in his own country. Everything was more highly perfected. The bowls had an indentation for the lips, and a mask, attached to the rim of the porcelain, allowed one to breath the hot steam while the liquid poured into the mouth. The mask was skillfully painted, and to look at it, one could only think that the presence of a fellow dinner guest was perhaps unnecessary.

Some of the pots and pans—there were all shapes and sizes of them—shone brightly in the gleam of the fire. None was the same as any of the others, and yet they seemed to be the parts of an important machine that could only vaguely be imagined as a whole. It made one think of an intricate ensemble of metal with cogs, gears, and chains. It could no longer simply be a question of cooking. At this instant, steps sounded in the hallway, and the door opened. There was no time to jump down. The two men fell like a block, and Thomas found himself on the floor half crushed by the enormous body of his companion. He suffered from bruises, but he suffered even more from being caught like this. How could he have behaved so childishly? It was frightful. The young man was astonishingly light on his feet as he stood up, and Thomas too was quickly upright. Before him was one of the maîtres d'hôtel holding in each hand a coffeepot and gazing at him with a rather grave expression. Thomas cast him a harsh look in return; there was no room for any but the most serious things. As soon as they were seated—and now the young man obediently followed all his movements—the maître d'hôtel approached and filled the cup. The brew was very hot; the odor it gave off seemed to seep into the entire room. Thomas could not hold back a smile, so great was his pleasure in this sweet smell.

"Is this drink prepared in the underground floors?" he asked.

But he soon stopped smiling, for his only thought now was to bring the cup to his lips. The liquid scalded him. It was not the heat that attacked his throat and entrails. It was the acrid odor, something intense and corrosive. He drank it all in a single draught without even leaving any residue in the bottom of the cup. Although he had a vague notion of the crudeness of his behavior, he was unconcerned for the moment with any idea of restraint.

"Can I drink a second cup?" he asked hurriedly.

There was no answer, and yet an answer was what he wanted. Even before he could look up to stare at the maître d'hôtel, his cup was full; the steam was rising in thick plumes, and there was nothing left but to drink once again.

"Another cup?" asked the maître d'hôtel when Thomas had finished.

He had no sense of what was impertinent in this question. This time the brew seemed to him rather insipid and lukewarm. His lips absorbed only the flavor of a liquid that has been exposed too long to the air and has gone stale. The maître d'hôtel stood opposite him in a slight bow. He was not as lively as he was when he had come before. He was like a man who has fulfilled his duty and devoted all his strength to it. Thomas had the impression that now he could easily enter into a conversation with him. He hesitated. What questions could he ask? What explanations could he hope for? Was not everything quite clear from a certain point of view? He turned to look at his companion, who in turn stared at him with frightened eyes. Such sad looks. It was as if he were contemplating his very self in his solitude and abandonment. He noticed that the door had remained partly open and that a thin shadow was cast across the floor. Was there someone standing hidden in the hallway? Outside the room there was silence. Everyone had returned to their rooms, and they were not permitted to walk about. He stared straight ahead. It was less the shadow that interested him—at times it blended in with the shadows of the hallway—than the lightly colored boards of the door. They were almost white, and a few lines in a uniform, but very fine, handwriting had been traced across them. He knew that the night before his eyes had already been struck by this brief notice; then he ceaselessly returned to it, though it was barely visible; but now the light allowed him to see more clearly the general movement of the writing. It was very small and slanted; only a few words stood out clearly, and he could read them without difficulty: they were the words *invited* and *regulations;* the rest was illegible, as if nothing except these words had any importance.

Thomas was of another opinion. As the maître d'hôtel stood leaning over the table, perhaps awaiting an order that could only come from someone of the house, it seemed as if he had no more interest in anything happening in the room. This was no doubt true; what was there that could interest him here? But Thomas also felt his sinister gaze—a gaze that revealed nothing, that simply rested on the things before it—weighing on him and preventing him from continuing to the end of his reading, although this same gaze suggested that he should read everything, without leaving out a single word. This was the moment to address him.

"Say, what is that written on the door?" he asked.

The maître d'hôtel straightened up briskly and regained some of the relaxed demeanor he had had before. He rushed to the door and pretended to decipher the lines, as if—what hypocrisy!—he had not always known them by heart. Then he turned around, repeating loudly in a guttural and unpleasant voice what he had first read to himself. It was a reminder: *You are invited, in accordance with the regulations, not to forget the staff.* Was it possible? Thomas did not want to go so far as to accuse the reader of altering the text, but by emphasizing certain words—and to hear him, one would think that only the last terms mattered—the maître d'hôtel could have given a completely different meaning to the text. Wasn't *regulations* the most important word? And wasn't the word *invited* given special emphasis, either in order to underline the optional nature of the observation, or else to reinforce the well-meaning advice and to make of it something more than an obligation? Not to forget the staff, that went without saying; besides, the staff itself made sure that it would not be forgotten.

The maître d'hôtel, having finished his reading, remained standing next to the door, looking at his client in a humble but scornful way, for his humility seemed only to be a reflection of the very modest person he had before him. Thomas withstood this gaze. He was struck by the expression that spread over the face of the old man. Had the latter noticed something

34

abnormal in the house? He continued to stare in a futile and petty way, but his face had become serious; it was not possible to look at it without trembling, and it was tempting to think that the suspicion it brought to bear on the house fell right back onto it. Suddenly, there was a stampede in the stairway, then in the hallway. Everything seemed to be responding to a call that Thomas now believed he had heard as well. Did this call concern him? Someone pushed open the door and the head of the first maître d'hôtel appeared in the doorway. He addressed a brief and friendly greeting to Thomas, then signaled to his comrade, and both of them disappeared in an extraordinary hurry. Of course they had not taken the trouble to shut the door. Such was their negligence. Thomas noticed in the hallway a girl who, with a piece of cloth on the end of a stick, was hard at work trying to cut through the dust. She came in as soon as she noticed that someone had seen her.

"Tell me, where are they going?" asked Thomas without thinking.

"To the summons," answered the girl, as she began to push the dust cloth across the room.

"Really? To the summons?" he said. "And what is involved in the summons?"

"They read out instructions," she said, "and listen to orders."

"And you, mademoiselle," said Thomas, with an air of insinuation, "don't you need to listen to orders?" The girl began to laugh, as if this question were best treated distantly and with a light heart.

"The orders do not come all the way down to me," she replied, pointing to the upper part of the house.

Thomas felt he could trust her. "And who," he asked, "gives the orders?"

"What a strange question!" said the girl, who seemed to be occupied solely with her work. "If they did not give the orders themselves, how could they carry them out? Well now," she added, stopping in front of the two box springs, "what a bed you've got there!" She looked with apparent consternation at the bloody sheets and the disgorged mattress. "That," she said, "was a real battle." She set aside her broom and bucket, and with a few handy gestures, she pulled off the covers and put everything back in order. Thomas watched her with pleasure. She was not like the others; wherever she went, she took away the dust and wiped out the traces of uncleanliness. Obviously her worked remained superficial. There was still all sorts of garbage in the corners, and the bed had only been covered over. But the room was all the same a much more pleasant place to stay.

"You are lively and young," Thomas said to her. "I am certain that you have many fine qualities. The house must be open to you. Could you not, during your free time, show me around?"

She laughed again. What was nice about her was that she understood immediately what he was saying.

"So you don't know the house?" she cried. "Then why did you come in? Did you not examine it carefully from the outside?" She arranged the cups and saucers on the table, but when Thomas grabbed her apron and pulled her toward him, she caught a glimpse of the prisoner and, seeing his wounds, let out a cry. "Oh you poor precious creature," she said. "What a state he's in!" Drawing near to him, she saw that the blood had dried, and a thick scab had formed on his back. "Has he even eaten anything?" She looked questioningly at Thomas, who shook his head no. Naturally, she managed to arrange everything in a few brief moments. In the hallway she found a pot, and sliding the cup next to the young man, she filled it with a thick and appetizing brew.

"Have a drink now," she said.

The young man's hand was too thick; all he could do was spill the liquid, and the girl, rising up on the tips of her toes, had to help him drink; despite her efforts to grow taller, she hardly reached the prisoner's mouth, and the latter, thrashing around blindly like a voracious animal, knocked over the cup and managed to take only a few drops. Nevertheless, he was satisfied.

At first, Thomas surveyed this spectacle with curiosity, but then he turned away; he was impatient to resume his conversation with the girl and above all to leave the room, for he was afraid that someone might come at any moment. The prisoner showed his satisfaction like a baby. He stared in turns at Thomas, the girl, the various objects in the room so that there would be witnesses to his happiness and so that this happiness would not be borne alone. His face was radiant. One no longer noticed his crude features, that air of bestiality that covered his face with another thick and vulgar face. And what mischief in his eyes!

"Do you know him then?" asked Thomas.

"He's asking if we know each other," said the girl to the prisoner. This remark sent them into spasms of joy. They both laughed endlessly, but the prisoner laughed rather in imitation of the girl and was the first to stop.

"Pardon me," she said. "There's nothing to laugh about. I'm seeing him for the first time just today."

36

She gathered up her broom, her bucket, and her bottle and carried them into the hallway. She had thrown the cup and saucer into the corner. The room was done. Thomas would have had a lot to say to her. Although he was disappointed by this last incident, he looked at the girl, and several questions he never would have thought of had she not been there were left in suspense. Overhead he heard a deafening noise of footsteps, mixed with the outbursts of high-pitched voices. They sounded like women's voices.

"Is it the meeting of the maîtres d'hôtel?" he asked.

The girl merely shrugged her shoulders in an ill humor, without making it clear if it was the question she disliked or if she judged these meetings ridiculous. She made a brief little sign and was about to shut the door.

"I'll go with you," shouted Thomas, and he stood up so abruptly that he knocked over the table.

In the hallway, the darkness was impenetrable. Gradually his eyes became accustomed not so much to the night, which remained perfectly dark, as to their own weakness. It was dark only to the extent that these eyes believed themselves capable of rising to any task. Thomas managed to recognize the girl, who was standing next to him in a small recess. How feeble and sickly she seemed to him! He leaned over in her direction. "Where shall we begin the visit?" he said to her.

She took his hand as if to guide him, but they remained standing in a moment of hesitation he could hardly bear; wouldn't someone find them there? Why were they wasting time? Was someone supposed to come to their aid? Feeling her little tormented and feverish hand still resting in his, he began to walk with her, leading her away without any resistance, and dragging the prisoner along too. After a few steps they were stopped by a door that marked the end of the hallway. He looked for the lock. He passed his fingers over all the rough spots on the wood and followed all the grooves, but he found nothing. He turned around, resolved this time to call on the girl and to ask her for an explanation not only of this last incident but also of her attitude since they had left the room. He groped toward her and heard her laughing beside her companion, whose arm she had taken. He addressed her roughly: "Shouldn't you be working?"

But she was not offended by this; she only pressed herself more gently against the prisoner and said, half turned toward him as if to question him: "Will we never have done with work?"

But then she quickly moved back to Thomas.

37

"Just leave this door alone," she said. "It can't be opened unless you are coming from the street. It is only for people who are passing through, for they too have their business to attend to."

Thomas wanted to have the layout of the house explained to him, but when the girl told him that the house had five floors with six rooms on each, plus some garrets for the domestics—garrets that in reality no one used because the staff preferred to share the empty rooms—he stopped listening, for he had the impression that she was speaking from hearsay or that she was not telling the truth.

The only thing to do, then, was to go back in the opposite direction. They began to hear noises again from the upper floors. It seemed at times that the house was like a sleeping person who was trying to wake up and who, after twitching around a little, fell back to sleep. The darkness was also lifting. The day seemed to rise throughout the house. As if her worries of a moment ago had vanished, the girl chattered aimlessly about all sorts of things, and one of her great pleasures was to speak to the prisoner in a senseless childish language. The prisoner himself seemed not to enjoy the conversation very much, and when they passed in front of their old room, he made an abrupt movement to go in.

"Hold on, Dom," she said. "Straight ahead, keep straight ahead."

Thomas noticed that she knew the young man's name.

"We gave each other names," she said," while you were searching so intently for the lock on the door; he calls me Barbe and I call him Dom."

Perhaps this was the moment to ask what her real name was, but Thomas said nothing. He had other worries. Where was this path really leading them? He now recognized all its detours, and his memory of it was so clear that he had difficulty believing that he would find anything new at the end of it. He knew that if he continued to follow it, he would come up against the door of the little painting salon and that soon he would have come back to his point of departure. Was that what awaited him now? He went slowly back, dragging behind him his two companions, who, receiving this aftershock of his disappointment, seemed incapable of guiding him. It was indeed the same pathway. He looked at several doors—they all opened on the right-hand side—with no desire to enter any of them. The best place was still his own room, and from the moment he had decided not to return there unless he were forced, all he could do was wander the hallway until he collapsed with fatigue. But he did not get very far. The girl called to him:

38

"Thomas," she said, "I have a message for you. Will you wait for me in your room while I finish my work, or would you prefer to accompany me?"

"I'll accompany you," said Thomas, enchanted with the invitation.

The girl took up her broom and bucket, and they walked back the same way once again, while she wiped down the walls and gently scrubbed the floors to erase the traces left by their steps. Thomas felt more free and at the same time less separated from her when she worked. He asked her for some explanations.

"How did you learn my name?"

She smiled with a slightly frustrated look.

"I saw the painting," she said. "I go every morning to the reception hall, and the attendant, who is a childhood friend of mine, secretly shows me the portraits of the new arrivals. It's strictly forbidden," she added naïvely, "and he'll be severely punished if they find out what he is doing. But there is so much disorder here that no one will find out. Besides, not all of the paintings are worth looking at. But yours was very well done."

Thomas was struck by the cunning expression on her face, and he thought that she was probably no more scrupulous about telling the truth than about following the regulations. And she had spoken to him of the message only for the sake of form.

"Why didn't you tell me about it sooner?" he said to her.

"Well, I had no time to speak to you about it," she said.

The work was quickly finished. Dom carried the bucket, and the girl sank the cloth into it before washing the entrances to the rooms. Thomas seemed to be there only to watch over them. When everything was clean and bright—the wooden floor and the tiling had a shine as though light could be reflected off it—Barbe shouted in a piercing voice: "Now, to work!" and she opened all the doors in a rush without pausing to catch her breath.

"Well, come with me," she said to Thomas, who hesitated to follow her.

He saw the rooms one after the other. At first glance they all seemed to be based on the same model. Most of them had only worn out and miserable furnishings: a chair, a mattress simply placed on the floor, a table covered with glasses and flasks, that was all. They had certainly given the most comfortable room to Thomas. From outside it was almost impossible to see anything. The only light was from the stub of a candle that was hidden by its own smoke. The air one breathed constricted one's throat; it was like air that has not circulated for a long time, and a strange medicinal smell cut through it, as though to bring out its impurities even more intensely. Although he felt ill at ease before these poorly kept rooms, Thomas gave in to his curiosity and took a few steps behind the girl. Was no one there? He questioned Barbe with his eyes, and she showed him a man sleeping in the bed, his head almost entirely buried in the covers. It was an old man. He wore a beard, and his mouth lolled open. The girl looked at him from afar and said: "It's not life that he's lacking."

Thomas wondered what she meant, for the very opposite seemed to him to be the case. There was even something disturbing in the fact that for him there was no longer any question of living and that nevertheless it was hard to see how, in the feeble state he had fallen into, he could sink any further in order to die. The air was unbreathable, but the candle occasionally threw off a small flame, and the smoke swirled all around, casting small bits of reddish light here and there. The girl went to the corner where she lifted a curtain that hid a portrait. She looked at it, and Thomas looked at it too as he leaned over her shoulder. Rather than a painting, it was the enlargement of a photograph that had been altered several times. It showed a young man running toward a girl as she waved a scarf in the distance. That is what Thomas saw, at least. The face of the girl had been crudely marked out with a pencil, whereas the young man appeared in relief, and the painter saw fit to decorate the photograph by placing in his hands an enormous bouquet of red hydrangeas.

"He's changed," said Thomas.

Barbe nodded her head, but it was impossible to tell whether it was out of regret or whether, on the contrary, she regretted that he was still the same.

"Not so much," she said finally.

Thomas turned to look at the old man.

"Are you the one who takes care of him?" he asked the girl.

At first she signaled yes with her eyes, but then, without taking it back, she thought it well to add: "He doesn't need any care."

That was possible, but Thomas was not convinced. "And yet," he said, pointing to the half-empty flasks covering the table, "here is some medicine."

"That was in the beginning," said Barbe. "I had not yet completed my apprenticeship, and I was very impressionable."

She walked Thomas over to the bed.

"I even put together a bedshirt for him, like the ones given to sick people here. He spoke of it every day until I agreed to sew one for him using an old dress of mine. How crazy I was! But at the last minute I realized what I was doing, and despite his complaints, I only let him see it and hold it every once in a while."

She showed it to Thomas. It was a ridiculously small nightshirt; it must have been all white at first, before black bands had been added to make circles around it. In any case, he would not have been able to wear it. Thomas was in no way interested in this little rag; it was the sick man that attracted him. Although the man had his head turned toward Thomas and stared at him with eyes that still showed some life, he did not give the impression of having noticed him; or if he was looking at him, it was in the way a person does who looks at someone he has already forgotten so that he can pursue his own thoughts.

"Why," said Thomas, "do you take in sick people here? Could you not send them home? Do you not have enough work to do with the ordinary clients?"

Barbe shrugged her shoulders.

"There," she said, "you're touching on a question that is close to my heart. We are never finished with the sick. On certain days I am so weary that I collapse with fatigue into a corner and wish for one thing only, that the house would collapse too. And yet it's not that the sick people here are very demanding. From the moment they fall ill, they have nothing else to ask for, and we leave them to do as they please. But, you see, you never know what turns they may take."

"What do you fear might happen?" asked Thomas.

"It's the doctors," said the girl. "The doctors generally have other things to do besides take care of these trifles, but if luck has it that a sick person is summoned—this always happens unexpectedly—and that he does not have his observation paper with him, this would be a true misfortune. In any case," she remarked, "I would not be the one at fault. I have taken my precautions. Whenever someone is registered as sick, I sew onto his shirt that paper from which he must never be separated. He has it on hand day and night. He looks at it, touches it. What more can be desired? And besides," she added with a sly look, "it's the same for people who are not sick."

She pointed at the crumpled sheet of paper pinned to the old man's rough nightshirt. The paper was white, of course. Thomas did not want to let his time be taken over completely by the girl; he was interested in what she said, and she explained everything clearly, but he also intended to figure things out for himself. He sat down on the chair and forced Dom to squat down beside him.

"But we're finished now," said Barbe.

Just then, the old man, who was lying on his left side, attempted in a frenzy of effort to turn over onto his right side so as not to lose sight of them. Hardly had he managed, under heavy breathing and coughing, to move his body a little, when he sank his face again into the pillows, now in a worse position than the one he had wanted to leave.

"Is it not up to you to help him?" Thomas said to the girl.

Barbe pulled his face up, gave him a few little slaps on his cheeks, and said a few words in her childish language. That was all. The old man, however, somewhat comforted, managed to pull his hand from beneath the covers and feebly waved it, perhaps in order to show it to everyone, perhaps simply to say, "I'm here." It was a fine, long, white hand, an artist's hand, from which a finger was missing. But this defect was hardly noticeable, for what was admirable was the elegance, the youthfulness, and, at bottom, the reality of this hand as a whole, so that the details were not important.

"What does he want with his hand there," asked Thomas.

Barbe shrugged her shoulders.

"Isn't it obvious?" she said. "His finger that was cut off—up to now that's the only malady he's been able to find."

Thomas looked again at this beautiful hand, which affirmed not sickness and fatality but a vigor and life maintained despite every misfortune. Then he stood up, wanting to put an end to the childish games that, as soon as he was no longer watching them, occupied the girl and Dom at every moment. The girl had taken a pencil from her pocket, the everlasting pencil she had to use for writing down her reports, and was amusing herself by licking the end of it and marking a black line along the contours of the tattoo. Although such contact must have made him suffer—his flesh was still sore and exposed—the young man held his head out stupidly and was not satisfied until the lead had re-traced the thousand details of the design. The girl had turned red, and her eyes were burning. Here it was indeed a question of sickness.

Thomas remained standing for a moment, unable to decide whether to leave. The presence of the old man did him good. He asked if he could wait in the room until the girl finished her work. The question was addressed to Barbe but also to the old man.

"You're so moody," answered Barbe with a sigh, and she left, but not before caressing the young man's face once again.

The light—a candle smothered in wax—began to fade. It was useless anyway, for there was nothing left to see in the room. The old man had huddled up under the covers as soon as the girl had left, and speaking to him or looking at him had become a senseless task. Thomas left the room and gently closed the door. In the room on the right, the young servant girl was singing or, rather, murmuring a song; he turned to the left, and slowly, as if he needed to reflect while walking, he set out down the hallway alone. He passed his old room again; the door was closed, but he heard the sound of voices. They were probably discussing his disappearance. After a few steps—it seemed that his brief rest had given him a great deal of strength—he reached the end of the hallway and stood before the door he had already examined. Now he saw it more distinctly. The boards had recently been cut, and the sap that formed on them gave off a strong odor; it was as if the tree, even after being uprooted, continued to grow and live. And yet the wood was as smooth as if it had been polished from long use. One could pass a hand over it without encountering the slightest indentation. Finally persuaded that he would find neither lock nor latch, he ponderously kicked against the door. To his great surprise, he received a response immediately.

"Who are you?" shouted an imperious voice.

"I am the new tenant," said Thomas.

The door opened immediately.

"You have taken a wrong turn," said a man standing before the door at the bottom of a stairway, a thick hood covering his head.

Thomas was seized with fear. Was it not the guardian? He responded nevertheless: "No, this is the right way." But he could not help asking: "Are you the porter?"

The man raised his hood not to show himself but to let in a little light.

"I am another guardian," he replied curtly.

So it was a mistake. But the resemblance remained. Now that he was looking at the face turned toward him, it was only with difficulty that he could distinguish the two men: he had the same eyes, the same emaciated cheeks, an equally feeble and decrepit body; but there was lacking in this one something that was attractive in the porter, which may have made him more fearsome but which also allowed for more contact. The stairs were half hidden by the man who stood right before the door and who seemed to have no intention of moving aside. If the little steps had not been different, one might have confused the two entrances. In the first case the steps went down, now they were going up, but in both cases they seemed to emerge from emptiness, as white and clean as if no one had ever ventured up or down them. As he looked at this new vestibule, Thomas's first thought was that the young servant girl had tricked him, for it was not guarded by someone from outside, and after crossing the threshold, it did not lead to the street; and yet, although this stairway sank into the depths of the building—so much so that it seemed to have been thrown like a bridge over an uncrossable space in order to join it to the house—there was a little light passing through the floorboards, as though the day, the real day, were still not far away. Thomas reflected as he studied the guardian. He had never intended to embark alone on a visit through the building. What would he have gained by such a visit? He simply wanted to find out for himself the way to go and not to be constrained to follow others blindly. Nevertheless, he turned to his companion and told him to move forward.

"Where do you want to go?" shouted the guardian impatiently.

He was not sure it was a question; the tone was that of a still uncertain threat, the execution of which depended on the will of Thomas.

"Well, where are we going?" Thomas asked the young man, but it was rather to that unknown part of the house that he addressed himself, to the stairway climbing before him like a steep narrow street and leading to a large balcony, from which, however, it was impossible to see anything except perhaps the painful and ridiculous effort of those trying to reach it.

This balcony looked like a surveillance post.

"Perhaps," Thomas said, lifting his head, "the only place you ever stay is up there."

"No," replied the guardian, "but it doesn't matter." And he repeated his question: "Where do you want to go? Here is the way that leads to the highest levels; there is the stair that goes down to the underground floors."

So there was another stairway? Thomas leaned over the guardian's arm; the latter had extended his hand, less to prevent him from advancing (for

44

the empty space was a sufficient barrier) than to protect him against the risk of falling. A second stairway, which seemed only to mirror the first, sank into the darkness and disappeared in the direction of the lower floors. It was accessible by two descending steps that were covered with a carpet. While Thomas was leaning in the direction of these other spaces, several people appeared on the balcony, where they stood leaning their elbows on the iron rail. They looked around distractedly without paying any attention to what was happening below. In any case, they did not respond to the greeting of the new tenant. They were carefully dressed men with freshly shaved faces, and their whole appearance exuded a kind of healthiness. One of them was rather corpulent; he gingerly smoked a cigar and seemed to regret letting the smoke drift away. This spectacle did not last—Thomas, at least, had the sense that it lasted only for a flash; he was so absorbed in it that he could see nothing else.

"Who are these gentlemen?" he asked the guardian, who slowly lowered his eyes without answering, either because he would consent only to address questions about the service, or else because he was too distant to hear his words. The window was opened again, and other men came to take a breath on the balcony. This window let out a sort of vapor that must have been caused by the high temperature of the room. All the rooms here were overheated. Thomas boldly repeated his question, and this time it was not only addressed to the guardian, for the other men could hear it too. Of course he received no answer, but, after all, it was not the answer that was important, for he had it right in front of him; what mattered was the possibility of establishing communication between himself and the people up above. But this communication had already been established. He pulled Dom behind him and placed his foot on the first step of the stair but stopped to give the guardian time to intervene. He expected to be brutally seized and perhaps thrown into the void. But the guardian, without turning around, went to close the door to the hallway, a very solid door equipped with an enormous lock, and again took up his guard duty, lowering his hood over his eyes. So Thomas had only to ascend. He climbed slowly, stopping to pause every two or three paces and avoiding any upward glance so as not to compound the boldness of his gesture with impudence as well. He stood up straight only when he had arrived: the tenants were leaving one after the other and passed so close to him that he could have touched them. So they had waited for him; they had watched him as he came up. What a surprise! The window was half closed. Reflections of an intense light shone on the glass, but the darkness that covered the surface of the panes was all the greater for that. All that could be distinguished were the shadows of the people who passed and who for the most part went away immediately, as if the outside no longer existed for them.

After a few moments, Thomas, having partly regained his freedom of mind, pushed open the window and entered the room. It was very spacious. It must have taken up the entire width of the house, and at the other end was probably one of the windows that opened onto the street. On either side, two rows of people who were trying to approach the center completely blocked the way and formed a semicircle. The number of tenants who had slipped into these two processions seemed very large. It was impossible to count them because they were all dressed the same and all seemed to look alike. Some had been unable to find a place in the crowd; they ran from one person to the next and stopped only to whisper a word into someone's ear. There was a deafening racket. No one spoke with a loud voice; everyone even made an effort to whisper, but the least breath was transformed into a thundering noise and grew into an uproar that rumbled from one corner of the room to the other.

Although he was dazed by the noise, Thomas was rather reassured by the immensity of the assembly. He could easily believe that his presence would be lost in the general throng. Yet it was not a throng. On the contrary, everything was regulated according to a meticulous order. Even the ones who had no definite place and wandered far from the groups were obeying a plan.

"Silence," shouted someone at the window.

Was this addressed to Thomas? The entire room received the watchword; the conversations rapidly became incomprehensible; although the noise was still very great, it was impossible to understand anything. Someone approached and murmured: "What do you want?"

Thomas had to step back to understand more clearly what was being said to him.

"To play," he replied.

The man examined him in silence. The result of the examination was probably unfavorable, for the man shook his head and walked away, as if, after penetrating the meaning of this response, he were incapable of keeping it to himself; Thomas ran after him. He did not know how to call to

46

him; he grabbed his arm and shouted in a stentorian voice: "I have been given a message to deliver. I am only passing through the room."

Although it had a whole crowd to contend with, his voice forced several people to turn around; they stared him down. Someone uttered a loud "Shush!" In any case, the intervention had an effect: his interlocutor, thinking only of getting away from him, echoed his first response: "To play?" he said. "Naturally. And why shouldn't you play?"

And without adding another word, he tried to lose himself in one of the processions. Thomas wondered if he would be able to cross the room despite the obstacles. It was an enormous room, and none of the people who were standing in the lines seemed to be moving forward. Supposing that this immobility was a kind of illusion explained only by the large size of the crowd, the best one could hope for was a difficult, and in any case imperceptible, advance. But this hope itself was diminished by the fact that in order to belong to one of the processions, it was first necessary to have an invitation from someone already in it, an invitation that depended on who-knows-what goodwill and on the general rules of the meeting. The tenants who ran back and forth along the rows were in principle never admitted; Thomas at least had not seen a single instance of this. Deep within themselves they may have had reasons for hope, but nothing of the kind showed on the outside. Yet, however far they were from the goal, they were not the most unfortunate, for they could at least make their entreaties heard, and they held on to the satisfaction of pouring out for other ears the words they must have whispered a thousand times in their own hearts. There were indeed some who were worse off, who did not know where to go, who said nothing, who walked on without a goal—the true goal having been forever barred to them—seemed to be even more estranged from what they were seeking. Thomas, however, looked upon them with envy. They were the only ones on whom his eyes could come to rest. Some of them had sat down on seats that had been put at their disposal. Their faces reflected their exhaustion. Their eyes were closed, and they opened their mouths, as if they were allowed only to imitate sleep. Others were standing behind slanted writing tables that came up to their shoulders. Fatigue must have prevented them from moving, but they were not, for all that, reduced to sitting down. There were also some who continued to walk with mechanical steps, edging along the carpets, going to the window, and, at times, taking the arm of a companion.

Thomas thought to himself that his situation was even worse. Nevertheless, a slight shiver passed over him when in the center of the room a man rose—he must have climbed onto a chair—and demanded silence. Silence soon reigned. The large chandelier was extinguished; the room fell into a suffocating darkness. For a few moments, Thomas leaned on Dom's arm; then something caught his attention. He heard a deep, harsh, unusual noise, the noise of a slowly turning wheel that seemed to be constantly held back by the hand that set it spinning but that succeeded nevertheless in escaping from it in order to complete its revolution. The wheel finally stopped.

"There's been a mistake," several voices shouted. "We want to file a complaint."

The chandelier was re-lit. Thomas, his eyes bedazzled, saw that everything in the room had changed. The processions had disbanded; the crowd pressed toward the writing desks; those who were seated along the wall seemed to be in command of everyone. Thomas was especially surprised to find next to him the man who had already spoken to him. He looked timidly at Thomas. At first he had avoided him; now it appeared that he was seeking him out. He leaned over to Dom and murmured with a smile: "Chance has passed me by."

Then he remained there, motionless, waiting for something, perhaps a confirmation from his interlocutor. Although Thomas had not been explicitly included in the secret, he could not hold back from asking: "What chance? What passed you by?"

The player addressed his response to Dom.

"Do not use the word 'chance.' Say 'it' or 'she' or whatever you want; it's a word that is painful for me to hear in someone else's mouth."

His smile softened the unpleasant nature of his remarks, but his brow was furrowed; he gnawed his lips; he could not hide his nervousness; perhaps he was sick.

"Of course," said Thomas, "one cannot always win."

A dispute began around one of the tables. A man, old and tired, leaning on a cane, had reached the board that served as a writing table. It was a true miracle. Now he did not want to move away, and even though he had received a white piece of paper, he clung to the desk, groaning and shouting. The others took him by the shoulders and feet and deposited him in a corner.

48

"What's happening?" said Thomas, looking at one of the men seated near the wall. "What's happening?" he repeated with irritation.

The man he was staring at in such an impertinent way rose with a bound —what an energetic man!—knocked against the player whom he threatened with a stick, and took Thomas aside.

"Have some consideration," he said, "for those around you. We are not accustomed to so much noise."

Was someone paying attention to what he was doing? Thomas looked around him in a conspicuous manner and saw a few people who, interested by the incident, were approaching.

"Very well," he said, "I have no desire to linger. I only want to cross the room."

The man assented, but said: "Are you not making an error? In the beginning one is almost always mistaken; you believe you have only one desire, to go away, to go away as quickly as possible. But the truth is quite different."

Thomas listened attentively to these words; they were said with kindness, and there was nothing offensive about them, but they remained ironic. He responded that he did not know how he would see things later, but that for the moment, he was quite sure of what he wanted.

"I don't want to contradict you," the man said with a sigh. "What good would that do? Only the events can do that; it is not my role. On the contrary, I am here only to remove from the room all those who refuse to leave."

So this was one of the employees responsible for keeping order. He must have enjoyed a certain authority in the house.

"Then what should I do?" Thomas asked him.

The man made a movement with his hand as if to say: "And what are you doing now? What more do you want to do? Why all these worries?" Nevertheless, he seemed to be involved in these preoccupations; he took Dom by the arm, and the three of them tried to cut a path through the crowd, which was no longer so dense. In places it seemed very sparse; in other places people had not yet been able to regain their freedom of movement; it was as if they were glued to each other and would not separate, even though there was open space all around them. Thomas noticed with impatience that his guide almost always pushed him through these groups, which resulted in an extraordinary confusion, a veritable mêlée that made every-

49

one lose his place and in which it was necessary to overcome the passivity of people who were almost asleep and who understood only very slowly the orders they were given. Thomas quickly grew tired—and how much farther he still had to go! The guide apologized, invoking the obligations of his assignment.

"But soon," he added, "everything will be better."

Was this true? Was it simply a word of encouragement? The farther they advanced, the more obstructed was their path, and the greater was the incomprehension of the people in the way. It was incredible. People stood in tight embraces; it seemed as if they had tried to push each other away one last time, but that in leaning against each other, they suddenly lost all their strength and remained now in an inescapable state of repose. The man himself finally became discouraged. He had shouted several times: "Make way for the staff!" and clapped his hands, but received no response. He held a whistle to his mouth and brought from it a very sweet sound, but in vain.

"Do you see," he said, looking at Thomas with an air of satisfaction, "how they facilitate my task."

Dom took action. Whether because there was a natural sympathy between him and these people or because he was so rough that he did not back down from their threats and violence, he got the attention of some of the ones who resisted and even brought them back to a semblance of life. "Are we next?" they shouted, or: "We're ready," although immediately after the three men had passed, they again appeared exhausted and benumbed.

Despite this help, Thomas encountered nothing but difficulties in making his way. The heat became more and more oppressive. The clothes he wore were made of a thick, crude woolen cloth, which he only realized upon seeing the fine brilliant material of the other outfits. He asked if they still had to walk a great deal more. He received no response, but his two companions stopped, and the room was once again filled with darkness.

"Here we are," said the man.

Was it possible? There was certainly a misunderstanding. The spot where they now stood was the darkest part of the room; they could not see two steps ahead. Thomas tripped against the edge of a large basin. Whispers rose from someplace nearby; from another part of the space there came a thick mist, which the feeble rays of a lamp hanging from the ceiling could not penetrate. He leaned forward and looked into a deep cavity where there was a wheel spinning slowly and silently on an iron pivot. This is where they played the game. The wheel seemed to be half buried in this pit. All kinds of garbage and old papers had been thrown into it, probably out of a general spirit of disorder.

Thomas crouched down to see more clearly how the machine functioned. It had been installed deep down in the hole. The apparatus was separated from the floor by a few yards, but it seemed that one's gaze had to cross a veritable abyss to reach it.

"No doubt the machine does not please you?" said the man, bending down to him.

"And why not?" said Thomas, refusing to turn around. Looking through the slats in the wheel, he had just noticed a large marble ball rapidly spinning in the opposite direction, at times following the rim, at other times one of the spokes, and bouncing over the knots and bumps in the wood.

When he saw this ball, he guessed that what he had before him was a game of chance. The machine had every appearance of it. Apart from its rudimentary character and the crudeness of its mechanisms, it was indistinguishable from the machines he had once admired in the cities. The wheel soon stopped spinning. The ball continued a few more times around, but its momentum had diminished, and Thomas was hard pressed to interest himself in it until the end. Before it stopped rolling, he looked up. What a terrible disappointment! The man who had led him here was gone, and a few steps away, seated at a table, was one of the tenants who had surprised him on the balcony. Thomas addressed a mute appeal to Dom, but Dom was distracted by a mirror hanging from the chandelier above the pit; an image of the wheel was reflected in it. The light was shining near the newcomer; it lit the table and all the papers that were scattered on it, leaving everything else in the shade. A document caught his attention. It was a large transparent sheet on which a plan of the house had been crudely drawn. The employee moved his finger along a line traced in red ink that passed through a vestibule and a hallway, stopped at a bedroom, and ended by disappearing into a maze of various lines. Its path led nowhere. The plan itself must have been interrupted. The other parts of the house that were untouched by the red line were covered with a light gray shadow.

The employee, after considering his work for a long time—work that did not seem to satisfy him—slowly sat up and met the gaze of Thomas. He signaled to him to approach, without considering the pit that separated them. Then he crossed his hands on his chest and half closed his eyes. In all likelihood he was continuing his reflections, digging tirelessly into the problem, attempting to clarify the question, the grave question of how the newcomer had arrived in this place. Finally, pushing away the table, he stood up. Hardly had he even begun to move away when ten people leaped at the papers, snatched them up at random, each one taking them as quickly as possible to the writing desks set up along the walls. Thomas arrived only after a detour. Naturally, the table was empty; there was not even anyone there to look after the inkwell and the pencil. This was not surprising, but at the same time this solitude and tranquility—while everywhere else people were suffocating, fighting for a little air, dying on the spot—was unbearable. He felt greedy for this space that was refused to him, and he dragged Dom into the middle of the crowd that besieged the desks.

"So you are still in this room," his former guide said to him. He had sat down again on a chair.

Thomas turned his head; he did not have to tolerate this useless arrogance. He felt the need to make a connection with someone in this immense crowd, someone who could help him take advantage of his experience and who would not hide the truth from him. This would no doubt have been easy if he could have stayed with the companions that chance threw in his way, but he had to fight to avoid being thrown outside, and he himself pushed away those who, sticking next to him, threatened to take his place. A small lean man grabbed onto his arm, not for support but to make him feel by this contact that he had the same right as Thomas to space and air. Thomas said to him: "What are you looking for?"

"And what are *you* looking for?" his neighbor replied.

"I'm still a stranger here," said Thomas.

"Oh," said the man, pulling away from Thomas, "you're not from here." But before throwing himself into another part of the crowd, he took the trouble to turn around and say: "We will talk again when you are no longer a stranger."

Thomas was not discouraged; he only felt a more intense desire for a response to his question. This desire must have shown on his face, for another man stared at him vehemently—as if such curiosity had disturbed him and distracted his attention from the true duty at hand—and he shouted: "What do you want?"

What he wanted was no one's business but his. He shouted in turn: "To go to the desk."

Someone who was already standing close to the writing table laughed at this, but everyone around him began to nod their heads.

"You know very well," one of them said to Thomas's interlocutor, "that conversations are forbidden."

This was odd, for indeed everyone was whispering, and at times veritable shouts would rise from the crowd.

"Tell me what isn't forbidden," the man responded. "The games are also forbidden."

At this moment someone began to knock on the top of the desk; this noise seemed to come from very far away, although there were only a few rows between Thomas and the desk.

"So now is the time to keep quiet," said someone near Thomas.

"What's happening?" asked Thomas.

One would have thought that this question had been expected and that for all these people it reminded them of the reasons for their wait and their struggle. Everyone looked passionately toward the desk. Thomas stood on the tips of his toes and saw a man with a weak constitution who was examining several pieces of paper through a magnifying glass. Someone said: "This is one of his good days."

"I see," said Thomas in a skeptical tone. He saw nothing inviting in the physiognomy of the employee; he noticed only his scowling and sickly appearance, his punctilious manners, and, from time to time, his gaze that looked wearily over the crowd. As Thomas observed him, he heard him call a name. Was it not his name? At first he was sure he had been asked to approach, and he raised his arm as a sign of obedience; but everyone else raised their arms, either because they did not want to give him the benefit of his initiative, or else because everyone was given over to the same illusion. The employee also raised his hands, to ridicule the petitioners. In a rage, he commanded everyone to approach—since everyone wanted to come—and knocked violently on the desk.

"Oh, this is one of his good days," said Thomas.

"Yes, it is," the man next to him answered gravely.

So everyone attempted to move forward again, but it was pointless, for those in the first row, after so much effort to reach this place, naturally refused to move away. Thomas began to lose patience. "Is it worth waiting for?" he wondered; he probably would have withdrawn if the man next to him, almost holding him in his arms, had not begun to stare at him in a mysterious manner, murmuring: "Why are you staying here?"

Thomas nodded in agreement, as if to say: "Yes, that is precisely the question that interests me," but he was too mistrustful to speak.

"Almost all of the winners," added his neighbor, "have already left. The others will probably be designated at the last minute, but the employee only picks out people whose faces he knows. So you have no chance."

Thomas listened distractedly. This man was not yet the one who would tell him the truth. "So it's the employee," he said, "who designates the winners?"

"No," said the man, "the names of the winners are written on the documents."

"So," said Thomas, "the choice does not belong to the employee."

"Of course not," he said. "The employee merely identifies the winners; he obeys what is written; but as for the rest, he is free."

"That explains everything," said Thomas finally, bringing the conversation to an end.

In reality, as he well knew, nothing was explained, and even if his neighbor's explanations had been better, he could not have put any faith in them, so obvious was the attempt to lead him astray. Still, the man believed he had seriously shaken him.

"Not winning means nothing," he said in an encouraging tone. "It is only a momentary failure; all the chances still remain. What must be avoided is losing. Perhaps it is wrong of me to speak to you about it," he added, lowering his voice.

"It doesn't matter," Thomas answered, "since I'm not here to play. I came to look for the plan of my apartment."

"Very well," said his interlocutor. "In that case, you'll be sent away the next time around."

Thomas found it difficult to understand what was being said to him. He had to struggle against this man who, under the pretext of sharing inside knowledge, was pushing him farther and farther away; voices were droning all around, and from time to time he heard the sardonic voice of the employee shouting: "Come forward!" Yet he did not remain silent, for he was afraid of being forgotten.

"You seem to be giving yourself a lot of trouble," he said.

54

"It's true," said his neighbor; then the latter seemed caught off guard, and after reflecting on the character of the remark, he added, as if these words were as dangerous for Thomas as for himself: "Everyone is absorbed in his own affairs."

At this moment there arose a great commotion that made the disorder intolerable; it was provoked, apparently, by the expulsion of the people in the first row. Dom was carried away so violently that the chain almost snapped. Thomas felt the tugging pressure throughout his entire body. A deafening noise clattered in his ears. He tried to turn around to see where it was coming from, but he was enveloped on every side by the howling of some sort of alarm signal. The noise grew continually more intense; it became so sharp that he thought he was being especially designated by its call. What should he do; what was being said to him; what was the meaning of this warning? Although his eardrums were bursting, it seemed to him that the noise remained too vague and that it was coming from too far away.

"Louder!" he shouted among the shouts of the others, "louder!"

Surprisingly, he received an immediate response, and the deep, serious voice that gave it to him, coming from very distant regions, easily made its way to him.

"You have been called," someone shouted in his ear. "The employee has pronounced your name. What are you waiting for?"

It was as if the thick wall that held him prisoner had collapsed; suddenly, he saw clearly; space had opened. A few quick strides and he was standing before the desk. The situation was not at all what he had imagined. The writing table, beneath which he stood, rose steeply before him, and he was forced to raise his head to see the employee, who, for his part, had to lean forward whenever he wanted to speak to his client. It was a magnificent desk made of black wood; it seemed to have come directly from the workshop, and yet when he looked closer, Thomas saw crude inscriptions that had probably been carved with a knife by the petitioners. One of them served as the caption for an ill-formed drawing meant to represent the employee. Someone had drawn a man standing on a platform and holding in his hand a large white sheet of paper. By straining his attention, Thomas managed to read what was beneath it: "I am just." He was so absorbed in these childish scribblings that the employee had to knock on the top of the desk to get his attention. He found it difficult to focus his eyes on him. His face was not particularly malicious, rather it was bleak and barren; as soon as one turned away, it was forgotten. Likewise, Thomas understood his words only with difficulty. Was it because he was distracted? He thought of the crowd that had just disappeared so quickly. One would have thought that the meeting was over. The people who passed in the distance did not cast a single glance in his direction, as if everything that was happening now had lost all importance. What was the meaning of this interrogation? He stood up as straight as he could, and without bothering about what was being said to him, he asked how he was supposed to interpret all these questions. The employee pushed away the papers that were piled up next to him — there was an enormous mass of them — and taking the magnifying glass from his pocket, he looked by turns at Thomas and at Dom, as if he were examining an indecipherable manuscript.

"I do not know your face," he said.

Was he going to send them away? Thomas quickly revealed his request regarding the plan of the house.

"Ah! The famous plan," said the man, without, however, doing anything to look for it. He did not seem to be in any hurry to carry out the interrogation. Besides, was it an interrogation? His gaze rested distractedly on Thomas, guided, so it seemed, by the hope that he would never have to see him again, but at the same time he kept him close, as if his presence could serve to keep his attention away from more painful thoughts. He said in a confidential manner, in a tone full of admiration but also of regret — a regret at being unable, because of his bad eyesight, to take everything in with one look: "What a beautiful room!"

Seeing that Thomas only lowered his head, he thought it necessary to add, so that his praise would not appear to conceal any blame with respect to the other rooms: "The house is beautiful too."

Thomas remained quiet.

"I am an old employee," said the man. "All requests for information and instruction are addressed to me. If ever you are in need of explanations, come to me. Here we gladly give all the desired clarifications concerning the customs of the house."

"You are not easily approachable," remarked Thomas, without committing himself.

The employee laughed loudly. "You are mistaken," he said. "You need only try me out, if you should judge it to be useful. Whatever you may ask me about," he added, gently caressing the papers piled next to him, "I will make sure that you are well informed; all possible cases have been foreseen; we have an answer for everything."

Thomas did not want a ready-made answer, and he did not believe that his questions had been foreseen. So, turning toward the rest of the room, which was now three-quarters empty, he said: "There are, as far as I can tell, many people who need information, and there are very few who receive any."

"Mere appearance," said the man, holding out his hand toward Thomas. But he thought for a moment and added: "Almost everyone believes they have something to ask; they are bursting with questions; they want to clarify everything. We are here to respond; we even take our courtesy to the point of asking questions in their place. Do you think they take advantage of it? They don't; once they are here," he said, pointing his thumb at the desk, "they no longer want to listen, and they look at us as if we were about to tear their eyes out."

"What a waste of time," observed Thomas. He had been staring at the skeletal hand that was stretched toward him. Then he abruptly turned around and examined the room. "This is a gaming room," he said. He was making a statement, but it was a question as well.

"That is indeed the name by which it is usually designated," said the employee.

"That's not its real name then?" said Thomas.

"Well, yes, it is," said the employee. "What else do you want to know? Do you also want to learn about our little secrets? When we are among ourselves, my colleagues and I, we call it the grand hall, for there is no other room that is so grand to us, or so beautiful. But that is an incomplete opinion, for all the rooms of the house are remarkable. But this is the one we know best, for we spend our lives in it."

"Still, it's a gaming room," said Thomas.

"And what else could it be?" said the employee. "The apparatus is not enough for you? It is neither sufficiently new nor sufficiently well maintained? No doubt," he added timidly, "you would like to have other machines installed and other gaming tables? This would be a useless wish; reforms are not tolerated."

"You are wrong to worry," answered Thomas. "I do not intend to ask for changes. But I am surprised all the same that the project of introducing a few improvements here—and the improvements would not be superfluous—seems to you such an unpleasant thing to imagine."

The employee sadly shook his head. "You are ignorant of a great many things," he said. "You have been in the house no more than a few moments; how could you take part in discussions in which only the most experienced among us really have something to say?"

"Then tell me nothing," answered Thomas.

"Obviously," said the employee with a sigh, as if he had received such responses from time immemorial, "you know only too well that I will speak; and even if I refused to speak, I could not prevent myself from telling you how things stand. Tell me what else I could possibly be thinking about. What could I discuss with the people who come here if not that? Is there any other subject of conversation?"

He looked at Thomas with annoyance and anger; one would have thought that Thomas himself had no right to any other preoccupations. "If you will permit me," said Thomas, "I would like to ask you a question; but it is very indiscreet." The employee said nothing. "Well that's what I thought," said Thomas. "I won't ask it then."

"That," said the employee, "is how everyone is when they come to this desk. They want nothing other than silence, and then they interpret it as they wish. I authorize you to speak."

"How long," said Thomas, "have you been in the service of the house?"

"Very well," said the employee, leaning back suddenly as if to gather his strength. "If I answer you, do you promise not to place any importance on my answer in your future relations with me? An easy promise, for you will probably never have the opportunity to see me again."

"That's a surprising request," said Thomas. "How could I promise you to forget words that will no doubt have a great impression on me, judging by the apparently justified precautions you wish to take?"

"What I can tell you," declared the employee with weariness, "has no importance for you, but it has a great deal of importance for me. I could not tolerate it if my words were handed over to a stranger who would then take the liberty of making whatever use of them he pleased, especially when it comes to a question of service."

"Are you obliged to answer me?"

"Yes," said the employee, "but I am not obliged to tolerate your insults. Keep in mind that I am the oldest employee in the house."

"Now that is something," said Thomas, "that I wasn't supposed to know."

"Did I not tell you so?" shouted the employee, suddenly rising. "Did I not tell you so by presenting myself at this desk, while the public session is over, whereas the other employees, however well trained and capable they may be, could not stand the fatigue and do not even have any voice left to make themselves heard, while I stand here before you—you who stare so intently at my face, as if you wished to hide some secret from me? It would truly be the height of audacity to try to make me responsible for your ignorance. No, I am hiding nothing from you."

Thomas looked at the employee in silence.

"Why are you looking at me?" said the employee. "Do you want to make me regret my indulgence? Have you made up your mind to disdain the explanations I am disposed to offer you, despite the favor they represent and the excess work it involves for me? The only thing for you to do is to listen."

"Fine," said Thomas. "What's the story then?"

The employee gave him an irritated look, but he said with resignation: "It is a very simple story. In times past, the room you are in now was not a gaming room; it was reserved entirely for our services; people came only to receive information, to look at the employees assigned to the information services, to breathe the air—that was enough for most of the petitioners. But one day we received the order to install a machine for games of chance and to transform our writing desks into gaming tables. Who gave the order? There was no way for us to know. Had the order really been given at all? To what concerns did it respond? Of course, each one of us immediately thought of an explanation. At the time when we changed the setup and the purpose of the room, our services had been abandoned for a long time, the room remained empty, only a few people came with their floor mats to take advantage of the warmth and to sleep. The reform thus served to bring as many people into the room as there had been before, and in this regard it was good; but in another sense it was bad, because now no one cared about receiving information or had any desire to clarify his position with respect to the authorities. Did they commit an error in ordering this transformation? Or were they perhaps in the right? One can discuss these questions endlessly. For it is quite true that the room had lost its renown and that the path leading to it had been erased. We spent entire days without seeing anyone at all; we remained motionless and silent, numb from the heat and the discouragement; nothing ever happened. Nothing.

And if by chance someone entered here, perhaps with the intention of consulting us—who knows? such a case may have occurred—we did not have
the strength to speak to him; all we could do was to turn slowly toward
him, and our looks expressed so much indifference—whereas deep down
we were burning with enthusiasm and devotion—that he went away without revealing the meaning of his visit here and only added his voice to the
rumors that depicted us as dead or stricken with some grave illness. Obviously, from this point of view, a certain progress cannot be denied. Life
has returned; the room attracts even those who know nothing about it,
like you; we recovered the habit of speaking and can tolerate seeing others'
faces again, although we are far from being capable of the resistance that
distinguished us in former times, so that at the end of each meeting even
the youngest of our members are almost in a faint. We only came to realize all this little by little; at first we noticed nothing but the misfortune that
had struck us, and even now we do not know whether all these advantages are not simply the sign of a disaster whose effects are only reaching
us by degrees. For in this past that we evoke in order to compare it to the
present, if the room had fallen into disuse, to such a point that in the rest of
the house no one knew if we still existed, at least it had kept its reason for
being; it had remained intact; it was the information room; and we could
even say—and this is indeed what we said among ourselves at the time—
that if no one ever came anymore, then it was because no one ever needed
to come, because the room fulfilled its function so well that its mere existence was enough for the house still to have its share of light and for the
tenants to live in a way that befitted them, instead of groping in darkness
and ignorance, as would have happened as a result of their abandonment.
All this was represented by this room, the grand hall, and that is what it
lost. As for us, is our situation, which is apparently much improved, not
in reality a hundred times worse? If we give the impression of being alive,
and if we have recovered the privilege of speaking and seeing, is it not because at bottom we have sacrificed our true life and have renounced other
much more important privileges? When we are overwhelmed by fatigue,
is it because of our work or rather, on the contrary, because we have the
crushing feeling that the whole day has passed without our having fulfilled
our task, because we have failed in our duty and because—even worse—
we have devoted all our strength to making it impossible to fulfill it. It is
this feeling that, after a few hours, reduces the less robust among us to a

state of utter weakness; and they are not the ones to be most pitied; because of my vigor and my age, I am condemned to turn this affair over on every side, to scrutinize its every detail, always to invent new explanations without finding in this painful malaise a single moment of peace."

The employee had been standing, but now he slowly sat down, as if the words had been spoken by someone else, and he had been waiting respectfully for the end of the speech before sitting down. Thomas turned to look at the room; it was empty and filled with darkness, though a thin slice of light still shone on the mirror that reflected the machine. He said: "So after all, it's only a gaming room?"

"What do you mean by that?" said the employee, raising his head with an air of caution.

"I am very grateful to you for the explanations you have given me," said Thomas. "How could I not appreciate such a mark of favor? However, despite the interest I have taken in it, I cannot hide the fact that I am disappointed. My disillusion is complete."

"And why is that?" asked the employee proudly.

"Well," said Thomas, "is it not perfectly clear? I came here to be informed on the ways of the house, its regulations, the formalities it binds one to. Could I have chosen a better place? You are admirably competent; you are familiar with all the customs, and you take your task to heart. One could not dream of anything better. Unfortunately, it is a dream. For it all belongs to the past. I do not want to insist on the causes of the decline that has gradually deprived you of your status and brought you from the glorious position as a member of the bureau of information to the function of an attendant guard in a gaming establishment. You have given a magnificent account and even the dullest mind would have the means to understand it. As for me, you have poured out great streams of light. It is unfortunate that I did not understand how much you suffered from the actual state of things and that I did not understand more clearly how in coming here I had gone astray. I have therefore committed an error. There is nothing for me to do but take my leave."

"That is a misinterpretation," said the employee abruptly.

"Where is the misinterpretation?" asked Thomas. "I see only a misunderstanding, the one that led me here full of hope, thinking I would find a flourishing organization run by a large number of enlightened employees, whereas all I see here is a room for public spectacles from which every vestige of the past has vanished."

"That is a misinterpretation," repeated the employee, shaking his head, "a regrettable misinterpretation. Your eyes are not yet accustomed to looking at what's before you."

He stared into the darkness and fell silent.

"Do you seriously believe that?" said Thomas.

"Very seriously," said the employee.

"What have I not been mindful enough to see?" asked Thomas.

"The room," answered the employee quietly. "It would appear that everything is as you have indicated. The room has changed, and there is nothing more in it that corresponds to the original purpose it served in times past. It is no longer the same room, and we are no longer the same men. Therefore, in a sense, you are right; you are perhaps even more right than you think, because, in truth, you are a thousand miles from that room, and you will never be there. But, from another point of view, the real situation is completely different. They wanted to transform the room, and not only transform it but destroy it from top to bottom—a childish idea. They did everything they could: scrape the walls bare, cover the wooden floors with carpet, raise our desks in this ridiculous way, and, especially, install in a pit this sinister machine that shakes the foundations and pollutes the atmosphere; but what has come of all this effort? The transformation did modify the outward appearance of the room for those who had never seen what it truly is, and they have continued to see nothing. But the others? What do they see? What has changed for them? They open their eyes and see that everything is as it was before. How could I explain that to you? Take our work, for example. The papers I hold in my hand seem to bear no relation to my old occupation; given the disorder that reigns here, they are usually worthless; it even happens sometimes that I rip them to pieces simply to prove to myself their insignificance. What's more—and this would be enough to make them contemptible—they come from the machine; it is the machine that prepares the decision, we have only to apply it. The machine seems therefore to control everything. And yet is it really so? No, it is not; our affairs proceed quite differently. For the machine itself, this accursed apparatus, has been put into the service of our bureau, and it has become its principle working tool. On any day whatever, at any moment whatever, someone may push the wheel and send it spinning. We are not the ones who provoke this gesture; we sit here quietly, like so many underlings, and do not see anything. But when we hear the sound of the axle scraping against its casing, we know that the machine is working for us. At the same time, a secretary takes from the mass of documents spread on his table all the papers he keeps for us. Do these papers correspond to any indication given by the apparatus? Is it not more likely that they are prepared and written up before any indication is given? This is something we have no way of knowing. The secretary, for his part, thinks only of getting out from under his task. He gives his papers to a domestic, and the domestic, although he pretends never to make a mistake, passes them around to suit his whims. Seen from the outside, the documents are irreproachable. They are written out legibly, and for each name there is a corresponding number. But as soon as we cast the slightest glance at them, we see what they are, grim piles of paper that will be meaningless until we have deciphered them. Just look at them," said the employee, pointing to a large white sheet on which some names were written.

Thomas could examine them only from a distance; the employee did not allow him to come closer.

"The writing has no elegance," he continued, as he looked at the paper himself. "After reading it, one comes to realize the immensity of the work that remains to be done."

"What work?" asked Thomas.

"I have nothing to hide from you," said the employee, "but all the same I cannot explain our methods to you. Besides, they would reveal nothing. What happens is perfectly clear. The machine works in such a way as to avoid any cause for complaints. But of course it cannot express the verdict itself. It is in need of competent, authorized men who interpret the sentence, or, as we say, who transcribe it. It is therefore necessary for the public to turn to us, and each one files before our desks in the hope that our gaze will enlighten him. Occasionally, we call to one of the petitioners and ask him to approach. Does this mean that he has been chosen? No. And yet it signifies much more than that, for we add new information to his file; we complete the description of his face; we make his identification easier; all this in order to enlarge the dossier that is handed over to the employee who is responsible for reading the list of winners."

"And this is not one of your responsibilities?" asked Thomas.

"It is an insignificant task," answered the employee. "Whoever has walked through the room, and whoever has presented himself before us, knows more than any crude reading will ever teach him."

Thomas moved a few steps away to look around the room. Was it true that his eyes did not allow him to see everything? To him, the room appeared large and beautiful; it would probably be pleasant to walk all the way through it. The impression it gave was not a bad one. It was rather the employees who were disappointing to him.

"Now," he said when he came back, "it is time for me to withdraw."

"So you are leaving," said the employee timidly. He came down from his high desk, and after struggling with his legs, which had grown numb from such a long period of motionlessness, he found himself next to his visitor. He was short and scrawny. Thomas had to bend down so as not to tower over him.

"No doubt you do not believe what I have told you." The employee spoke in a low voice. Thomas did not answer; he was in a hurry to leave, to go at least to the far end of the room. But the darkness prevented him from going away without help.

"You should not judge my words too quickly," said the employee. "I have not explained everything, and I can begin my story again. Do not worry about tiring me; certain people have only understood after the seventh narration."

"I thank you," said Thomas, "your explanations have enlightened me." He began to walk with slow steps. The room was almost entirely filled with darkness. From time to time a patch of light seemed to shine somewhere far away, but the shadows were no less dark for all that. Where were they now? Had they come again to the middle of the room? Were they far from the machine? Thomas saw the dim reflection of a metal cabinet that then disappeared into the shadows. So as not to discourage the employee, he asked him: "Do the windows open onto the street?"

"There are no windows," said the employee.

"Where are we going?" said Thomas. He did not need an answer; the darkness rendered it superfluous. He took a few more steps, and then, after touching the wall and noticing its gentle curvature, he called to his companion. He responded in a trembling voice, as if walking had taken away the last of his strength.

"What else do you want to explain to me?" asked Thomas.

"Aren't you leaving?" said the employee.

"Yes, I am," said Thomas. "Besides, I have no right to stay."

"Well then, go!" said the employee.

64

Struck by this abrupt change of tone, Thomas turned around and took the man's arm. He wanted to hold him back, but they began to make their way again. Nevertheless, he felt the need to hear his voice once more. He almost shouted: "Who are you?" and violently shook his arm. He heard the clanking chains that bound him to Dom. It was Dom he had next to him. The man had already left.

He thought he could explain the mistake, but it mortified him. He had completely forgotten that the chains had not been taken off. It seemed to him that he was emerging from a long insomnia in which no one could communicate with him and in which he himself was unable to express his thoughts. So the employee had left? He had been unable to keep him near? Perhaps he would have been able in the end to understand his language and to listen to him. Now it was too late. After a few slow and weary steps, they reached the far end of the room and found a large window that let in a feeble light. But they tried in vain to see anything at all. What was outside? Was it nighttime? Was the street there? When they opened the window, they were struck in the face by the icy air from outside. How calm it was here, how far away everything was! They moved forward again, and despite the unchanging darkness, Thomas recognized the balcony. He was not disappointed. No doubt he had taken the wrong path, but the night transformed everything. The balcony appeared larger to him, and more isolated. It was like a vast terrace where one could walk in every direction without encountering any obstacles and where nevertheless one did not have the feeling of getting lost. One was already lost. Thomas lay down along the railing, pulled his coat over himself, and Dom's enormous body pressed with a shiver against his own.

Suddenly he was being shaken: "They're waiting for you," someone shouted to him.

He sat up wearily and said in a solemn voice: "Why have I been disturbed?"

Was the night already over? He lay down again in search of sleep, but he was shaken a second time. It was an authoritative appeal; whoever was there had no doubt that he would be obeyed. Thomas waited for him to explain why someone had been sent to look for him. He was still huddled under his coat, but he listened carefully and did nothing to make one think he was asleep. Nevertheless, the messenger remained silent, and after a few moments he went away. During part of the night, he walked around with quiet, regular steps. From time to time he was no longer to be heard; it seemed that he had completely disappeared; but a moment later his steps resounded again, and it was as if nothing could interrupt them. Thomas pondered this incident. Finally he curled up under his coat and closed his eyes.

He was drawn from his torpor by the opening of a window. He abruptly stood up. The noise was coming from the upper floors. But his gaze was not drawn upward; right next to the balcony another window was illuminated, and—a strange sight—a man held in his outstretched hand a pitcher he was swinging back and forth, as if he were trying to cool some boiling liquid by exposing it to the freezing air. Thomas yelled to him: "It's very cold out here. May I come in for a moment?"

The man stared at him intently. "Come in if you want," he said. This response was meaningless. Where could he go in? Thomas made a gesture to indicate his predicament.

"How did you get here?" said the man. Thomas did not answer. The moment for asking such a question had passed. The man spoke again: "Who are you?" He spoke with a curt voice that showed no hint of indulgence. "Since when have you been staying in the house?"

So many questions! Yet Thomas did not have the sense that he was really being interrogated. The man did not wait for any answers, as if to emphasize that the answers didn't matter; only the questions were important.

Just then someone began to beat carpets on the floor above; they were certainly doing some large scale cleaning; water flowed over the window panes; brooms knocked against walls; dust rags were snapped into the wind. At this hour? It was incredible. What was going on? One might have thought that the morning had already come and that the large vestibule never received any sunlight. Thomas looked up, but in vain; he saw nothing, but although he could not penetrate the shadows, he stood there listening to the echoes of this calm, regular life, feeling that in this existence full of tranquility lay the hopes for which he had abandoned everything and which justified its perils. He said in a hushed voice: "I am expected on the uppermost floor. Could you not tell me the way?"

"Absolutely," said the man. "But first you are expected here." His tone was threatening, and it was difficult to take his assent seriously. There was nothing to say in response to his objection either. Thomas passed over it in silence.

66

"Is it possible," he asked, "for me to reach the second floor without passing through the grand hall?" Receiving no response, he added: "This probably is the second floor," and turned to his interlocutor. He noticed with surprise that a ray of light was emanating from the pitcher. What he could see of the man's face was manly and beautiful. His eyes appeared to sink deeply under thick eyebrows. A short beard covered his chin. After examining his face, Thomas thought it necessary to say: "Forgive me, I did not think that I had really been summoned."

"Come on then," the man said curtly. A strange invitation, for it was he who closed the window and went away.

Thomas now thought of nothing other than leaving the balcony and making his way to the bedroom above. It was first necessary to gain the support of the person who was working up there. He approached the far end of the railing and stared into the darkness, and the darkness was as thick as ever. He shouted. A sly sounding voice responded. A light was suddenly lit, and a young girl appeared in the window. It was Barbe. She did not seem at all resentful of his abandonment of her; he left, she forgot him; he returned, she welcomed him; this is what made his relations with her pleasant but useless. With no consideration for the present time and place, which might have caused her to be a little more reserved, she cried out with joy, and her gaiety became truly unbearable when she saw Thomas's companion. "And where is my darling?" she cried. "Where is Dom?"

Thomas was almost glad when he saw the window on the balcony open and the man coming toward him. He was large and strong. His presence was imposing. But Barbe was not impressed. "Goodbye," she said, waving her hands, "goodbye to my little pet." She cried out again when the man crossed the threshold: "What a handsome fellow!"

Thomas blushed at hearing her speak so, but the man paid no heed to this childishness. He led the way for Thomas, who almost had to run after him. It was all the more difficult in that Dom, still half asleep and only now catching on to the maidservant's sweet talk, kept turning around and wanted to go back. They quickly passed through the large room, now lit by small candles placed at regular intervals, and could hardly recognize the arrangement of the desks and the placement of the carpets. The whole room had been turned upside down since they had left. Someone had certainly come with the intention of cleaning the room, but as often happened in the house, the work had been interrupted, and all one could see were overturned chairs and papers scattered everywhere, not to mention the curtains that were spread out on the floor. At the other end of the room a large and beautiful doorway—probably the counterpart to the window— was open. Heavy sculptures decorated both of its door panels. The golden hinges shone. It was the most majestic part of the room.

"Go in," said the man.

Had they arrived? Thomas bumped violently against a wall and knocked over a small rack loaded with brooms, brushes, and cleaning rags. It was only a narrow hallway, probably serving as a garbage room. As he tried to put the implements back in order—surrounded by the dust he himself had raised—the man opened a door at the other end of the corridor, and, in a gentler tone, he asked him to wait for a few moments. Thomas did not notice at first the strangeness of the request. He was too taken up with his annoyance at the existence of such a small room whose filth and horrid smell inspired the most vigorous revulsion. "A real dump," said Thomas to himself. At that point he thought there was no need to wait, and he knocked on the little door.

"Come in, come in!" someone shouted to him.

His first thought upon entering the room was that he had stepped into a café. There were tables placed along the walls, and several people were sitting with drinking glasses or large white bowls. The middle of the room was empty. On the right, at an angle, there was a platform that could be used by a small orchestra. A young man approached Thomas and asked him to sit down at a table where two men were waiting for him. He was greeted with indifference. The people nearby were whispering with a forced and weary animation, holding their heads down, their foreheads leaning almost onto the table. Their cheeks were radiant, but this appearance of life did not give an impression of good health, and the fever that agitated them showed their desire to say everything, to see everything, before they were plunged by fatigue back into their usual passivity. The young man who had accompanied Thomas, a domestic no doubt, poured some thick coffee with a refreshing odor into a large cup. Thomas drank greedily, unconcerned with the others; he had never drunk anything so delicious and was suddenly overcome with a great thirst that he could not seem to quench. The domestic remained standing next to the table for a moment, no doubt so that he might pour a second cup for him if he so desired; Thomas had only to make a sign, and the magnificent brew flowed for him again.

"It's time to get to work," said one of his neighbors at this point, partly in order to impart information and partly to silence the conversations.

The word *work* penetrated Thomas's mind only very slowly. Before he had understood its meaning, the others had grasped it, and the way in which each one repeated the phrase, or an analogous one, out loud or in a murmur, prevented him from considering the significance of this word very carefully. Then someone knocked on the little door, hidden under a drape, through which he had entered. These sharp knocks resonated in the room in an extraordinary manner, to the point that he considered it surprising that these people, so curious, so avid, so intent on offering endless commentaries about everything, greeted such an intervention so indifferently.

"Someone knocked," he could not help saying to the man next to him. The latter gazed at him with brilliant eyes.

"Yes," he said, "it's a joke played by the domestics who work in the small room outside. It's best not to pay any attention."

He had spoken with an air of importance and continued to stare at Thomas. It seemed that he had waited for this opportunity to take a good look at Thomas, to study him in silence, as he was doing, without it being possible to know what his purpose was. In his immediate irritation, and so as to take no part in this impertinence, Thomas turned to the domestic and held out to him the empty cup. But the domestic did not understand that he meant for him to take it and to go away. On the contrary, he came closer and stood so close in fact that, to escape from his zealousness, Thomas had to push back his armchair, only to find himself almost pressing against his neighbor. The latter, having satisfied his curiosity, smiled amiably and arranged the seat's cushions, which he moved skillfully into place. Then he said in a low voice, looking at Thomas again: "When can we talk?"

The domestic, suddenly very interested, leaned over the table, and Thomas could only make a gesture indicating how difficult any private conversation would be.

"It doesn't matter," said the young man. "All the domestics here are indiscreet. So you be careful," he said, turning to the servant, who, far from taking offense at this remark, began to laugh without changing his position.

Thomas abruptly pushed him away and turned his chair in the other direction.

"Now we can talk," said his neighbor. "My name is Jerome, my companion is named Joseph. You are new here?" he asked. In reality it was not a question; it was rather a reminder of the situation in which Thomas found himself and which alone made the conversation possible. So Thomas did not answer.

"As a result," he continued, "you are ignorant of many things here, and you have a tendency to pass harsh judgments on what you see. All the beginners are like that. How could they make their way into this dark and poorly kept house without receiving a very bad impression? They see nothing but reasons for complaining. And what reasons! Do they even know what room they live in? Hardly have they gotten settled, when they are forced to move. We have a habit of saying that the tenants are eternal vagabonds who do not even know their way. That's somewhat exaggerated, but at bottom it is true. Aside from a few very privileged people whose whims we must respect, no one can rightly swear that he will sleep twice in the same bed, and it's nothing but a constant coming and going of people who, sometimes walking in their sleep, pass down the halls half dressed in their disheveled nightclothes."

"I have not had to suffer from such inconveniences," said Thomas. "I have not yet been assigned a residence."

"Just as I was saying," the young man began again. "It's incredible. How can one tolerate such things? Not that your situation is the worst there is, far from it. Obviously it's unpleasant not to have a room and to have to rely on chance. At first, you take a certain liking to it, such freedom has its charms, and you believe it's always possible to return to the room you left behind. But these illusions quickly vanish. When you have understood what worries you expose yourself to if you do not know your residence beforehand, when you see yourself driven from door to door, when even the empty rooms are closed to you, then you no longer enjoy the uncertainty of the beginning, and freedom seems a disgrace from which you seek in vain to be redeemed. Already in the morning you think of nothing but the evening's shelter; you think of nothing but the night, and it is common that, in their obsession with this twilight that each hour brings closer, the tenants no longer even pay any attention to the day and live in perpetual night. Such an existence wears down even the most sturdy among

70

us. The searches that at first absorbed every minute are now abandoned. What good are these exhausting journeys on foot when the discovery of an empty apartment comes to nothing? So you pass your days mulling over ridiculous hopes; some even memorize the plan of the house—or rather what they believe to be the plan, for of course the true layout of the rooms remains unknown to them, and they content themselves with the most miserable scrap on which a few lines have been drawn at random. Most do not even have the strength to think about the future; they stay where they are without moving or thinking, absorbed in memories of their past successes in which they now live as though in an ideal home. Sooner or later they fall, and when this happens they must indeed be given a place, which is done in secret so as not to damage the good name of the house.

"That's a sad picture," said Thomas. "And this is the situation I'm supposed to be happy about? Where are the advantages?"

"It's hard to imagine them," said the young man. "And yet they are real. How can I explain this to you? As far as I can judge from my modest insights, they consist in a sort of freedom with respect to the staff. If you are deprived of a room, the staff is not obliged to serve you; you do not officially belong to the house; you cannot therefore claim the attentions that are due only to real tenants. But of course everything happens in reality in a much less rigid way, and the domestics sometimes take it upon themselves to give you a hand."

"Pardon me," said Thomas, "but I still don't see the advantages."

"Just wait," said the young man. "We're coming to that. But first you must tell me something. Have you already had dealings with the staff?"

"I think so," said Thomas. "I would respond in an even more positive way if your question did not give me cause for doubt. Does he not belong to the service staff?" he asked, pointing to the domestic who, leaning comfortably on his elbows against the back of the armchair, was following the conversation.

"No doubt," said the young man, smiling with an air of superiority. "Of course. Hey there, do you hear what this gentleman is asking," he added, turning to the servant. "Do you really belong to the service staff?"

The domestic thought this was an excellent joke and went into fits of convulsive laughter accompanied by all sorts of gesticulations. The young man did not share this raucous joy, and he gave him a look that was both sad and severe.

"He is only too much a part of it—of the staff, I mean," he said. "You need only look at his face: indiscreet, lazy, proud, they're all like that here. What's more, he is the most insignificant of all; he is the most negligible of the negligible. That's why one can hardly tell that he is attached to the service of the house; he is but a distant reflection of the true domestics. He has, therefore, only relatively small defects. One can tolerate him if need be, and in any case he is forgotten when he is no longer there. Unfortunately it is a completely different story when it comes to those who are responsible for the house. A truly detestable crowd they are. These fellows are almost always invisible; it is useless to call them or to think of meeting up with them; since we know that they live in the basement, some tenants, angry at having to wait for them in vain, sometimes go down to look for them in their lair. What happens then? What do they see? They come back up racked with such disgust that they are incapable of answering our questions, so that we give up asking any more about it. Later they explain that they found huge unoccupied rooms stuffed to overflowing with every kind of waste and garbage. And this is quite possible when you know their habits. But others counter that domestics have never lived in the underground rooms and that they spread this rumor only to get rid of clients."

"Now that does not surprise me at all," said Thomas. "Until now I have had very little to do with the staff, and strictly speaking perhaps I have had nothing to do with them at all. But what I have seen is enough. With this in mind, I must ask you a question. Tell me why the tenants tolerate such disorder?"

"It isn't a question of having to tolerate it," said the young man, with a sigh. "It is not even certain that we suffer from it. What do we have to reproach them with? The bad upkeep of the house, the rooms that are never cleaned or that are only half cleaned, the meals served to us at any hour of the day without any announcement beforehand? All these are really only small matters, and we learn to look the other way when it comes to many things. No," he added, "it cannot be said that we put up with too much; if we suffer, it is because we do not put up with enough."

"It is not my place to offer an opinion," said Thomas. "As you said, I'm a newcomer. You have certainly reflected on the situation before I ever had a chance to. Yet I cannot approve your method. Look at the rooms. You acknowledge that they are generally neglected or badly kept, and indeed I'm expressing myself with moderation; in reality, they're downright pigsties;

it would be difficult to find dirtier rooms; the air is unbreathable; staying in one for only a few hours is torture. Do you not agree?" Thomas asked the young man, who listened without showing any approval.

"I know," he responded, "I know it only too well; I have a particularly delicate nature, and for me it's a veritable torture."

"Well," said Thomas, raising his voice, "why don't you file a complaint? Why don't you make a report? Why don't you bring together the other tenants who certainly must think as you do and who would be happy to have improvements? Could it be," he added, almost shouting, "that they take no account of complaints? Could it be that, far from taking account of them, they would bring them back down on the heads of those who have the courage to say out loud what they think? I would not be surprised."

"Quiet," said the young man, looking terrified and distressed. "Please, don't shout. If you let yourself get carried away, you'll never be able to hear me out. Things are not exactly what you think. File a complaint? Who hasn't filed a complaint? That is only too easy, and it is not what gets the attention of those gentlemen. On the contrary, whenever they are over-whelmed with official complaints, they seem happy about the fact. Apparently, at these times they have been heard singing in their meetings. There is no better way to please them. Aside from this result, what are the effects of these complaints that seem to you to be such a good method? The only effects I see are disastrous. If you are unfortunate enough to trans-mit your request through official channels, you are lost. For during the time it is being examined—and God knows if anyone considers it with any care—your room is subject to a prohibition. Under the pretext that an investigation is being carried out, you do not have the right to inhabit it; and if you disregard the prohibition, you'll go through hell. Not only does your room no longer benefit from these little chance cleanings that in ordinary times can always be expected at the whim of a domestic, but each day servants secretly bring heaps of new trash, disgusting garbage with an unbearable smell. Why do they do this? They are only acting out of zeal-ousness and can in no way be blamed. They are domestics who have taken your cause to heart, who absolutely want it to triumph, and who, in order to attract more attention to the scandal, try to make it even more obvi-ous. They can only be encouraged. Despite the disgust and the depression it causes, we beg them to redouble their efforts. What else is there to do? If they were not thanked and encouraged in their work, they would become your worst enemies, and the cause would be compromised. In any event, you are ruined. Supposing you have had enough energy to bear the troubles that resulted from your complaint, and admitting—as incredible as this would be—that you have not given in to the requests of your neighbors who, seeing that you are waging a battle against the house, burden you with all their disputes, you still have no chance of surviving the investigation to which your complaint would normally lead. What happens then? What kind of operation is involved? To my knowledge, no one has ever arrived at the moment of undergoing this ordeal. Those who have overcome the other obstacles, however calm and sturdy they may be, have fallen apart in the anguish of waiting, in the meticulous preparations for this day, in all the various inconveniences that accompany the preliminary work. From the day you learn—most often by chance—that these gentlemen have decided to come for themselves to make an inspection, you never leave your room; you do not sit down; you stand in the middle of the space with the door wide open, despite the drafts and the cold, so that you can hear them approaching from a distance. Moreover, it is customary not to wear shoes and to go almost entirely without clothes. Obviously these precautions are exaggerated, but they correspond to the idea we have of the members of the staff, according to which they again provide first-rate service when they are in the presence of the very sick. Is this one of those mad dreams originating in the gossip that never ceases to run through the house—or is it the truth? Everyone gives in to such thoughts, and those whom care has not devoured are carried off by sickness and fatigue."

"So that's how it is with the domestics," said Thomas after a moment. "So these are the abuses one finds here. I am truly at an advantage, it seems, in having no fixed residence, despite the difficulties you have pointed out, if this situation spares me too frequent relations with such menials as these. I could not stay far enough away from them. Thank God I have so far eluded their advances, but now not a word, not a single request for service; you won't see me running around after them."

"You're wrong," said the young man, with sudden violence. "You are utterly mistaken. What do you have to complain about? You have had numerous contacts with the staff; I know very well—for I know everything concerning you. You have exchanged words with several of them; you have received advice from them; they have guided you. Invaluable acts of kindness, unheard-of favors. And you want to start fleeing from them,

74

to break with them? It's insane. You'll be lost forever with such mad ideas in your head."

"Really?" said Thomas. "I find it difficult to understand what you're saying."

"Pardon me," said the young man. "I lost control of myself. But indeed you gave me good reasons for losing my head. When I heard you scorn and, so to speak, trample underfoot something that in the life of a man is a unique chance, and that represents in any case the extraordinary privilege of your situation, it was impossible for me to maintain my composure. What a tragic error! What ignorance! But now I will try to remain calm until the end. But you must answer this question honestly: How many times have you spoken with a domestic?"

"How would I know?" said Thomas. "I am probably very ignorant, as you said, and you can expect anything from the ignorant. Therefore I find no embarrassment in saying that I have not always been aware of my relations with the staff."

"That is as it should be," replied the young man, wiping his face with his hand. "What was I thinking? Such are the illusions bred by rash and reckless hopes. Listen to me," he began again. "Despite what I may have revealed to you, you assert that you know nothing of our relations with the domestics, of the misfortunes to which they condemn us, of the grievances we raise from the bottom of our hearts, and that, whatever I might teach you, you still know nothing about any of it. Experience will be your only teacher. Besides, how could I speak to you about it? The essential thing is precisely that there is nothing to say about it, nothing happens, there is nothing. I have told you that the staff is invisible most of the time. What a foolish thing to say; I gave in to a prideful temptation and am now ashamed of it. The staff invisible? Invisible most of the time? We never see them, ever, not even from a distance; we do not even know what the word *see* could mean when it comes to them, nor if there is a word to express their absence, nor even if the thought of this absence is not a supreme and pitiful resource to make us hope for their coming. The state of negligence in which they keep us is, from a certain point of view, unimaginable. We could therefore complain about how indifferent they are to our interests, since many of us have seen our health ruined or have paid with our lives for mistakes made by the service. Yet we would be prepared to forgive everything if from time to time they gave us some satisfaction, and what satisfaction! One day, a tenant found his pitcher filled with hot water. Well naturally there was nothing more urgent for him than to run to his neighbors and tell them the news. The whole house heard about it. For a few hours we were in a fever of excitement, sketching out projects, demanding explanations, dreaming about this domestic who had disregarded years, centuries of negligence and had suddenly remembered his duty. No trace of jealousy clouded our joy. It seemed that each one of us had received a drop of that tepid water, and its warmth passed through us all. Needless to say, it ended badly. It was an error, a misunderstanding. A friend of the tenant had wanted to surprise him, and although he was horrified at the consequences of his gesture, he resigned himself to confessing that he was the cause of it all. But what hours those were, what days! He was the only one among us who did not join in our delirium, and the more our happiness grew, the more somber he became. Despite the blindness that prevented us from seeing that there was no reason to rejoice, we were offended by his distress, which, he told us later, came less from the confusion he had brought upon us than from the impossibility of sharing our conviction. As proof of the general madness, he even tried to persuade himself that everything had happened as we thought, and for a few moments he almost believed that he had been the instrument of the staff whose designs he had unconsciously realized. Fortunately—but was it so fortunate?—he had a positive sort of nature, admitting only what he saw, and reason won out in the end. How could I describe to you our discouragement when he informed us of our error? We refused to hear what he said and would have preferred to go deaf rather than to allow these terrible words to penetrate our understanding. What was our first thought? We imagined that, in a truly perverse spirit, he wanted to deprive the staff of the praise we were heaping upon them after so many years of complaints and curses, that he was trying to belittle them by denying any generous impulses on their part, that his plan was to force us back into the despair of a life that no ray of light could reach from above. There were those among us who thought that he should die. What other punishment did he deserve if he were really guilty of such a crime? However, while the most outraged among us demanded a punishment, others began to have doubts. They interrogated the accused. They made him reenact his deed in their presence. We gathered in his friend's room to watch him pour the water he had taken from the basement. It was a melancholy room, only recently decorated with flowers and imbued with perfumes, but from which the adorable presence that had inhabited it was imperceptibly withdrawing. Alas! We had to acknowledge our illusion. There was nothing but to return to the common room where the others were waiting and where we sat together without saying a word, with lumps in our throats, overwhelmed as much by our too eager hopes as by our disappointment. There were many, it is true, who refused to believe us, and certain doubts continued to shroud this painful affair. The tenant who had been its protagonist searched everywhere for allies, witnesses, new arguments to advance; we heard him screaming in his room, where he closed himself up day and night in the hopes that another act of kindness would be bestowed upon him. He became unbearable to the other tenants, who were already forgetting the circumstances of the event—happily, forgetting comes quickly—and although he had not lost his reason, he had to be placed in the special infirmary.

"This story," the young man began again, looking at Thomas, "will seem extravagant to you. Indeed it was, and for many reasons, but it became even more so in what happened later. It had aroused a profound emotion, and although in itself it was almost ridiculous, particularly because of the misinterpretation it had sparked, it revealed at the very least how far we had been driven into fever and weakness by the state of abandon in which they had left us. Despite the orders given by some of the oldest tenants, whose age and experience we respected, to speak no more of this affair, there were some who continued to brood over it. They could not give up the thought that there was something strange about it and that it corresponded to designs whose meaning deserved to be examined in depth. They met every day, and whether in the course of solitary reflections or in discussions that often ended in blows, they sought to determine the conclusions that could be drawn from such an event. Report after report was written—we write a great deal here—and these reports were collected into books that were preserved and studied in order to absorb their contents. What were the conclusions of all this research? There were a great many, no doubt; that is still one of the defects of the house, I mean our lack of mutual understanding and the diversity of interpretations. But one project was adopted almost unanimously. Since, after all, nothing more than the charitable initiative of a friend was needed to restore our appetite for living and to fill all our hearts with hope, we wondered what would happen if we were inspired by this example and what changes would result in life if some of us offered to supplement the staff and to carry out the services we awaited in vain from the real domestics. So that no one would misjudge the origin of this activity, we decided to make the project public and to announce it to all the tenants. But at the same time we were careful not to give the names of the benevolent servants. It was a satisfaction granted to those who took on a task that was in some ways less than honorable. It was also a means of protecting them against the tyranny of certain extremely demanding tenants. Finally, since everyone could sooner or later be called to join the corps of enthusiasts, it was natural that all the tenants were suspected of being domestics since all of us would eventually receive the order to become one. We decided, then, to follow these conventions. The first day was one of great and awesome solemnity. Several tenants were assembled in one of the most beautiful halls; of course not everyone was there, for certain very old and sickly tenants are never seen in public, and others live apart and appear so infrequently that they have long since been forgotten; the arrangement of the house lends itself to a withdrawn existence, so that it is impossible to know even approximately the number of inhabitants and what their names are. We looked at one another feverishly. One would have thought that something unheard of was about to happen. Some were trembling. Had they not lent their approval to a sacrilegious action, to a sort of shameful parody for which they could be punished? We had to comfort them with drinks. Then we read an oath stating that each tenant promised not to attribute to the staff the services from which he benefited and never to reveal the names of those providing them should he ever learn them. We swore. We put out the lights and withdrew back into the night, and it really was night, for what was to become of an undertaking so audacious and so contrary to the habitual ways? The first results were rather positive. With the exception of a few who lost their senses and who had to be reduced to silence, most everyone was on their best behavior, and we witnessed a great effort of solidarity, concord, and mutual aid that established a new atmosphere in the house. Nevertheless, although nearly everyone enjoyed a pleasure and comfort they had never known before, no one was happy. Something was missing. Boredom cast its shadow over people's faces. We did not know why the days remained empty, or why, on rising in the morning, we thought with such melancholy of the long hours we would have to live through before the consolation of sleep. At the same time, we began to observe some strange phenomena, or that seemed

78

strange at least to our idle, disengaged minds. First there was a relaxation of enthusiasm and of discipline. This was, you might say, very normal. Enthusiasm gave way to halfheartedness; charity and patience gave way to ill will. From this there resulted some irregularities and anomalies in the service that were reminiscent of the methods of the staff itself and particularly of those methods it practiced, according to the oldest among us, in the old days before they had abandoned their activity. What had happened? It's not difficult to imagine. Certain people believed, in good faith, that the domestics, their pride wounded by the new attitude of the tenants, which was to them a reproach and a blame, had resolved to take up their service again and, at least to a certain degree, to fulfill their obligations. Certain odd occurrences were remarked. Some claimed to have seen, through those little windows cut into the walls of some rooms, great strong men lighting ovens in the basement and preparing meals that, it must be said, we never tasted. But, in principle, the lower floors were abandoned and access to them was very difficult. Others affirmed that the sick had received exceptional care and that it was enough to pay them a visit to see on their faces the gleam of a satisfaction that could not have come from any ordinary intervention. Since the sick said nothing, all we could do was attribute our own fancies to them, but the rumors spread no less for that. On top of that, the precaution we had taken to keep the service anonymous was a source of ambiguity and superstition. Whereas in the beginning it was impossible not to recognize the men who were involved, soon, as a greater and greater number participated in the project, it was no longer possible to know whether in fact some real domestics had not insinuated themselves among their replacements and—whether it was to keep watch over them or to ruin their efforts—were collaborating with them. As this was not at all unlikely, we could not help but believe it. We believed it all the more in that certain volunteers, driven by an ambiguous desire, did all they could to imitate the morals of those for whom they were, in a sense, the representatives and the spokesmen among us. They became, like the others, corrupt, mendacious, and tyrannical. They neglected their service not out of lassitude, which might have been excusable, but willfully, with that special taste for disorder and evil that the domestics seemed to possess to an unusual degree. Some gave proof in this corruption of an ingeniousness and an audaciousness that seemed to make them truly the equals of those they were imitating. Was it their function that had corrupted them,

79

was the influence of the menials having real effects on them, or had the servants in fact returned? All of these are possible. In any case, the situation became again what it had been. When we wanted to stop the experiment, which now was causing more and more damage—spreading sickness and confusion everywhere, creating more ruin than it had repaired—we could not reestablish any order. We no longer knew with sufficient accuracy the names of those who, under the pretext of giving assistance, were destroying the house; all we had were clues and guesses; those whom we enjoined to abandon their roles feigned surprise and seemed not to understand, and perhaps in truth they did not understand; perhaps they themselves had forgotten everything and, troubled by the image of these domestics whose places they had taken, had confused themselves with them entirely, in an identity we could not destroy and that no longer allowed us to distinguish them from their models. In any event, it was too late. We could only put forth hypotheses concerning the causes of these metamorphoses. It was no longer even possible to examine them all, for the mind grew tired trying to imagine them, and, as time passed, the real circumstances eluded memory. Our memory was overcome by vertigo whenever we looked to the past—which was yet so close—whenever we tried to relive earlier days, and whenever we compared to the faces of the friends we had known so well the vicious and insidious countenances of the domestics in whom we could hardly recognize them. These transformations were the subject of interminable reflections. At times it seemed that changes occurred with no preparation. We may have cast a friendly glance at someone only a few moments ago; now we were afraid to look at him again for fear that he might have taken on that sinister appearance, that detestable air of majesty that—so we imagined—served as a mask for the servants when they mixed with the tenants. So we would avoid him. We were seized with fear upon perceiving him even from a great distance, an absurd fear that disturbed our gazes and our minds. Sometimes this fear was so great that one would no longer have the strength to move away. One would look with insurmountable terror as he approached, a man whom one had loved and on whose face, in an illusion born from fright, there slowly emerged a strange and mad resemblance. Was this a human being? Why did he have two pairs of eyes? Why had his mouth disappeared? For it was yet another of our superstitions to attribute to the domestics a bodily physique different from ours; we believed in particular that they had no mouth, which explained their incomprehensible muteness. We even believed that the ones who had been domestics for the longest time were entirely deprived of senses, that they had no ears and could not see or smell, and some spoke of repulsive creatures whose heads had dried up or came to resemble that of a serpent. This was all quite mad; we finally realized it when, at the height of our delirium, no longer able to flee from the monstrous being coming our way, we rushed toward him, threw ourselves at his feet, kissed him in convulsions, and finally regaining a little calm in exhaustion, we perceived that most of the changes were imaginary and that the once cherished face was only contorted by fatigue, hunger, and servility. Naturally such moments of recognition did not succeed in bringing us to our senses. What did it prove? That some of those to whom we ascribed the role of domestics were only tenants like us and were as frightened and confused as we were? We knew that; we knew it all too well. For our utter inability to distinguish, by signs that were truly convincing, between the servants and the people they were supposed to serve led us gradually to another belief that created even more disorder. We believed that the domestics did not exist, that they had never existed, and that our imaginations alone had given birth to the story of this accursed caste whom we made responsible for our ills. This was a sort of revelation that, while liberating us, almost led to the ruin of the house itself, this house that had remained unshakable amidst our follies, that seemed to disdain them and to cast them back into nothingness. When the thought that we had been fooled in this way took hold of our minds—there is always some great collective movement being stirred up here—we were blinded by a terrible anger and threw ourselves into frightful excesses. If we had maintained a little reason, our indignation would only have turned us against ourselves and against those who had given themselves over to this lamentable comedy. But it was not so. Rather, there were some among the sick whom we hated—we hate them all but those in particular with their calm and satisfied air, with the happiness they seemed to have found, these drove us mad—certain of these were beaten and tortured; we wanted to tear from them their secret; we desired that they too be shown the truth and that, stripped of the consoling thoughts that were lacking to us, they would cease to be a gateway of contagion and moral uncleanliness. We tormented them in vain and could not make them understand what this gang of furious men was trying to reveal to them with blows and shouts, and soon we passed on to even more formidable projects. The thought in all our minds—but why? what drove us to this tragic extravagance? it's a mystery—was that we must transform the house from top to bottom. Some said that we had been victims of the defective arrangement of the building, that we had allowed ourselves to be affected by these dark rooms, by these hallways that lead nowhere, that there should no longer be any separate floors, that we would make new windows and knock down walls, and countless other crazy ideas. It was insane, for the house did not belong to us, and up until then we had found it admirably laid out; we were at a loss for words to appreciate its harmony; we sang its praises from morning till night. But all these judgments were forgotten. In an instant we were seized with a fury of destruction that drove us to annihilate what we loved the most. And yet when we saw certain maniacs hurling themselves against the doors to break them down, grabbing hold of chairs to demolish the walls, or even attacking them by kicking and scratching, we had the courage to stop them. Standing before this distressing spectacle, how could we not have realized our error? And yet, on the contrary, it only led us to conceive a more grandiose project, one that was apparently more reasonable but that, by pretending to apply logical rules to an incoherent undertaking, contained more madness even than the vain and absurd revolt of our companions. In order to avoid the disorders caused by individual initiatives, we wanted to draw up a plan of the entire house, a plan that would reveal the errors we needed to correct and that would allow us to take on our task to the fullest extent. Was this really the thought that guided us? It's possible, so lost were we to all moderation and good sense. But as soon as we began to discuss our project, we also saw the desire that dwelt in our hearts, and our faces turned red with shame. "What's this!" one of us said. "Do we not have the right to know the house? Why would we be forbidden to visit any part of it? Are we not tenants of the entire building?" Thus seeing that each one of us had been stopped by the same remorse, we hardly had the strength to say yes to our companion. In truth, how could we admit that he was right? Did we not know that in one of its most important clauses our tenant's contract authorized us only to occupy a single room, to use the common spaces in an appropriate manner, and, in cases of necessity, to stay over in the rooms of tenants who live on the same floor? It had never occurred to us to dispute this clause, for habit had rendered it unassailable, and we took it as our duty never to visit any floor other than our own. We were allowed to come and go only on the level at which our residence had located us. It was forbidden to go upstairs or downstairs. In practice, however, certain exceptions became customary. Since the use of the large meeting rooms was granted to us, and since almost all of these rooms are on the ground floor, everyone had access to this level. Likewise, on the first floor, where most of the inhabitable rooms are located, the bizarre layout of the building—which had no doubt gone through several different periods of construction—the large number of stairways, the absence of any separation between this level and the ground floor had forced the majority of tenants to disregard a prohibition they had no way of observing. Was it always possible to know whether one lived on the first floor or on the mezzanine? Did one not have to walk from one place to another over floors that were slightly inclined and that the hallways, the famous hallways, prevented one from seeing clearly? All these reasons had mitigated the contract to the point of making us unaware of the inconveniences it imposed on us. It was enough in any case to be roughly familiar with the plan of the building—there could of course be no question of entering into details—to understand that the more reasonable tenants must have had no idea of the curiosities that were forbidden to us. First, there was the basement. The basement had very limited means of access. The only way to reach it was by a stairway half rotted by dampness, and since the way down fell sharply into the void, we had no desire to risk a fall in order to visit a place that repelled us more than it attracted us. Indeed, the basement had, and still has, a bad reputation. Whether because of the kitchens that had been set up there, or because the people who inhabited this somber and isolated part of the building were all quite unpleasant, we came to believe that whoever lived there did not belong to the house: they were too close to the street; it was only possible for them to live and die far away from us. Besides, we were not explicitly barred from the basement floors, and the existence of the kitchens, though they had long been abandoned, granted us the freedom to go there, a right that some of us took advantage of, as I told you, under conditions that did not increase our desire to imitate them. But the higher floors were a different question altogether. The prohibition applied to them especially, and at bottom applied only to them. We were banished from them forever. A strange restriction, no doubt, but at bottom it did not seem strange to us. These two floors, like the attic rooms above them, are so completely separated from the rest of the building, their means of access are so far away from ours—

they are connected to the neighboring house and can be entered only by its stairway—that it no more occurred to us to set up residence there or even to visit them than it occurred to us that we had rights to every building on the street since we lived in one of its houses. This thought put our minds at rest, or at least it had done so for the older tenants, who had respected the contracts all their lives. But for us, it was as if we had already felt how tenuous the reasons for our obedience had become, and we could only add to such a restriction other more formidable prohibitions. We did not dispute the agreement we had signed. On the contrary, we were filled with dread to think that we had been given the opportunity to break it. For if it was true that there were no ordinary passages between the two parts of the house, it was also true that there was a stairway common to both which might be put back into service at any moment. Nothing, not even a posted sign, warned the tenants that they would be punished if they went beyond the ideal line, which passed constantly through their minds. Sometimes we would stop in front of this stairway simply to look. But was even this much allowed? Did we have the right to raise our eyes? Whatever point vision could reach, imagination had already passed beyond it, and our imaginations did not cease their efforts to climb higher and higher. For a long time what calmed our desires was the fact that we were unsure whether some of us might actually live in these heights. It was difficult to believe, but not impossible. What did the contract say? That each person must live where his home is, an elementary moral principle, and that door-to-door relations, so to speak, were permitted under duress, which was easily explained by concerns to establish a neighborly rapport and to encourage mutual aid. Access to meeting halls remained unrestricted. In that case it was possible to believe that certain tenants who took part in the common gatherings— you see how numerous we are; how could we all know one another?–were among these privileged people, and it was only a matter of finding out who they were and questioning them. Of course, there were a few who tried to pass themselves off as those we called the unknowns. But they were quickly unmasked. At the same time, and even though such measures were repugnant to us, we kept up a discreet surveillance of the stairway to see if anyone ever came down. No one ever did. But did that really prove anything? Our surveillance was not complete; we were too scared; as soon as we heard a noise, wherever it might be, we disappeared, though it was precisely at such a moment that surveillance would have been necessary. In short, we had to limit ourselves to the stories that went around concerning the mystery of the upper floors and that, we weren't sure why, seemed unbelievable to everyone. It may be that there were too many of these explanations. It would have been impossible to count them all. Each of us had his own way of interpreting things that even he didn't believe in, though he would have defended it as fiercely as if he were defending his life. I will only tell you about a few of them. Some said that these floors had been abandoned after an epidemic that could be attributed to the filthiness of the place. Others said that they were inhabited by terribly sick people and that the contagion condemned them to isolation. These were very widespread notions. But there were many others. People said that the upper apartments were infinitely more beautiful and more finely furnished than ours and that the prohibition against visiting them was based on the desire not to attract too many tenants and not to inspire jealousy in the ones who could not live in them. People said that these apartments were reserved for scholars and men of knowledge who needed calm and silence for their studies. They also said that the restriction was only a ruse of the staff, who lived there peacefully and comfortably without anyone ever daring to request their services. And they said that the apartments did not exist, that these floors did not exist, that there was only a façade masking a void, since the house was never completed and would not be until much later when, after years and years of ignorance, the tenants finally understood the truth. We saw ourselves as the vessels of this truth. An extraordinary and ridiculous arrogance. But it was easy for certain ambitious men to enflame the people by announcing that their hour had come, that the veil had to be torn away by a generation that had already run roughshod over so many secrets. These speeches were delivered timidly at first but were soon taken up by everyone in concert, and they resounded through the halls with such violence that the walls trembled, and the entire house seemed to arise from its muteness into a language we did not understand. The more fearful souls tried in vain to draw our attention to these confused words that seemed to fall from the sky. Sometimes, in the far ends of the corridors, to which the echo slowly carried its sounds, we ourselves were surprised to hear our conversations repeated in indistinct rumblings that expressed their true, their repulsive nothingness. Were these even our words? And if they really were the words we had used as the instruments of our derangement, was it not permitted us to recognize them not as we believed we had spoken them but as the house had heard them in its grave and mournful solitude? Although we were disturbed by a prophecy that rose from our hearts, this disturbance, far from holding us back, inspired us with new rages and new plans for vengeance, as if we had been assaulted by an enemy who had pursued us into the depths of our very selves. In a spirit of method and order that was like the victorious counterpart to our inner confusion, we made use, according to their abilities, of all the tenants—at least the most courageous and daring among those we knew—and soon enough we had teams of masons, carpenters, and workers of every kind who were full of a zeal that burned to be seen. This preliminary work was not finished in a day. We threw ourselves into it with scrupulous attention; we continually started over in order to impose an ever more perfect discipline; there was no end to the exertions we thought necessary to avoid the errors that might have been fatal for us. It is possible that already we were anxious to find pretexts for delaying the completed work itself, for it was a terrifying prospect, but we were not aware of this. We only sought in our miserable way to diminish the grandeur and the impossibility of our task through reflection and foresight and through a preparation that was so complete that no difficulty was capable of putting it in danger. All this work in itself was very beautiful; never before, or so it seemed, had knowledge and ingeniousness been taken so far. When it was torn apart and burned after the collapse of our pride, some of those who had helped make it, despite the shame and terror that had come over them, saw the work realized in a revelation whose beauty they could not conjure away and that fell back upon them like the derisory image of their hopes. And yet the large mass of those who did not understand the reasons for this long effort and who saw in the delays— perhaps rightly—the expression of a supreme timidity ended up showing their impatience and threatening the discipline that we had taken so many pains to establish and that we still did not quite consider strict enough or altogether perfected. A revolt began to stir. Certain mediocre men, precisely those whose insufficient merits destined us to banal tasks and who were, so to speak, not of a piece with our troop, liberated themselves. One day we found them gathered together, and they told us that the wait had gone on long enough and that they were prepared at that very moment to go up to the higher floors to take the first necessary steps. "Madmen!" cried our leaders. "What folly has taken hold of you? Do you wish then to reduce all our efforts to nothing and to destroy yourselves in the process? Anyone who leaves this room will be punished, and this punishment will exclude him henceforth from all communal work." But these threats and exhortations—while they made them afraid of losing the hope that spurred them on so ferociously—only managed to increase their anger, and they set out to execute their hateful plan. Then, already beaten, we began to implore them, trying to convince them of their error and their foolishness; we too were beside ourselves and were reduced to invoking the prohibition in the contract; we described to them the terrible dangers that tradition associated with these unknown places. Ridiculous memories. We had done all we could to destroy these legends and to render these superstitions innocuous. They answered us with mockery, and our behavior, so full of weakness and incoherence, shook our partisans and unsettled even ourselves. Soon the threshold was crossed. For a moment we wanted to follow them and to hold them back from any excesses, but whether it was fear that mounted within us, or whether our concern for our work outstripped every other thought, we decided to abandon them, and the door closed behind them. Alas, what we had foreseen was far surpassed in horror and malediction by what actually happened. First, the tumult of their departure was followed by an extraordinary silence. We had not left the room, and we forced ourselves to continue working as usual—as though our work still had any sense. But already our minds condemned what our hands were doing. At the first noise we heard, we all stopped, silent and pale, casting glances toward the place from which the noise seemed to call to us. It's a strange fact, but the noise seemed to come from below, from the basement or from a place even more hidden away. One would have thought that somewhere in the foundations of the house there rose a voice that, without anger but with a terrible and righteous gravity, proclaimed our misfortune to all. But we hardly had the time to look around to see what each of us was thinking. From above there came cracking sounds, noises that were sometimes muffled, sometimes sharp, a grinding together of beams and planks. Well, what was this? Were they going to bring it down on our heads? And yet above us there were only the rooms of the first floor, a place that seemed untouched by any mystery. What was this unexpected danger? With what tragic and unpredictable effects would we all pay for our blindness and for the madness of a few? A new silence fell over our uncertain thoughts. We did not have the courage to speak to one another; we remained motionless, as if a gesture, a shout would have been enough to bring down upon us the fate that our obedience was still holding in place. At times, overcome with fear, we imagined hearing the crashing noise of a collapse, and our eyes saw the walls shaking and the drapery trembling. Absurd terrors that were only the first signs of a reality that was infinitely more terrible. We were abruptly shaken from our imaginary fright by a shock that rumbled through the entire house. Then we heard inhuman cries that could only be coming from a horrifying anguish. The light went out. Even more grave and powerful tremors reverberated in the upper spaces. We began to hear calls, but in truth they were so separated from us, and so distant, that they seemed not to be calling for us but saying farewell. And yet these cries awakened us, and we rushed to the door. Hardly had we opened it when a veritable quake shook the edifice, and in the middle of a deafening tumult, part of the ceiling of the large hall collapsed, burying our friends, our leaders, and the best part of our work. Today such moments seem incredible. Those of us who were not wounded were even more to be pitied than the dying. While those in their death throes, struck down at the high point of their dreams, believed they saw shining through the shadows the work for whose sake they had succumbed, the rest of us saw only the punishment, a punishment that was all the more unbearable in that we did not know how it had fallen upon us and could only attribute it to obscure powers, to invisible masters, to the law that had punished us because we had trespassed it. And yet what we believed to be the height of our misfortune was only the beginning. Soon we saw some of our unhappy companions returning. They were ragged and bloody. They collapsed at our feet; but others came in turn, trembling more than if they had witnessed their own death, and childish tears coursed down their cheeks at the sight of us. These, however, were peaceful men, inhabitants of the first floor who had always refused to take part in our enterprise and who lived very retired lives. Why had they too been drawn into this madness at the last minute? For a long time we were unable to learn anything about it. We were all dead and alive, lying inanimately in the night. From time to time a few of the poor wretches returned, but if reason, in taking leave of them, had left the least trace on their countenance, we were unable to see it. It was only gradually that we returned to life, if one can call life the curse with which we were stricken. A man lying next to me was invaded by a wave of words. What he said to me was almost incomprehensible, but did I myself still possess the strength to understand? Have I ever regained it? The words were as foreign to me as if they had been cast out at random by a formless mouth. I heard nothing; I saw nothing; the words echoed in me with a painful sonority and put me in touch with a truth I tried to push away. And yet it is this story that has remained for me the only real explanation of this great drama. Later, I collected other calmer accounts, and I have been able to connect some of the facts. What is this version worth? Does it have more value than the inexpressible confession of that unfortunate man of the night? How could I ever know? Who will ever distinguish the light among these shadows? What had happened was in a sense the result of a very simple confusion. When they left our room, blinded by their own temerity, struggling in vain against the terrors we had reawakened in them, prisoners, perhaps, of the law that inspired their derangement, the troop of rebels rushed toward the stairway leading to the first floor, as if in that instant they had crossed the line of demarcation beyond which they had no right to go. It seemed already to these men that they were in the forbidden zone, surrounded by threats and driven by fear into the very place they dreaded most. A strange illusion, a profound mirage. The entire house was forbidden to them. They could not [accept] that what they had before them were ideal barriers that they had to break down but that they could not overcome.[1] With each step they committed the fault of violating the rules, although they were still completely free, and this fault seemed to them so weighty and so terrible that they felt they were lost and required the greatest excesses to redeem themselves from the feeling of their crimes. With an ax they broke down the first closed door they came to. They hacked at the stairway, attempting through an instinctive prudence to cut themselves off from the path they believed it was scandalous to follow. But they pressed ever onward. They arrived on the first floor without recognizing it, and in their fury, they believed they had reached the accursed spaces. Their madness knew no bounds. They wanted to annihilate everything, disperse everything, kill everything, and kill themselves too, so that as the house collapsed, they and their faults would be buried in the rubble. Such murderous rage, such destruction — memory alone cannot contain its traces. Coming across the unfortunate tenants who were panic stricken from this avalanche, they saw in them

1. This sentence is ungrammatical as it stands in the original and requires a verb here; accordingly, a word has been added as a likely possibility. –Tr.

the strangers whose vengeance would soon strike out against them; they let loose the blows that would forestall this condemnation; they knocked against the walls and attacked the floorboards. Everything ended in a sinister collapse. But there were a few who must have climbed even higher. They actually reached the upper floors. What did they see, what did they do? The only thing they have ever said, again and again, is that it was the same. Naturally, the same. How could these forbidden places have been any different for them compared to the places they had just left, since even the latter were already forbidden to them? Beginning already with the first floor, what they saw, with their eyes and their minds, was the tearing apart of appearances that had made life possible up to then. They perceived what we did not see, because we had remained faithful to the rule. Hardly had they set out on the old familiar ways when they found themselves already, and in fact, in this separate world where they had no right to be, having reached in a single step the heights from which they could now only fall. This is what is expressed in their terror and their madness. In the unreason that struck them, they behaved like reasonable beings whose eyes, now opened onto nameless things, commanded them to perform unnamable acts that they could not carry out and that they replaced with acts that were merely desperate. Their loss itself was the only thing that could console them for what they were losing. How it was that all these thoughts arose in our minds, how it was that in our overwhelming distress we pulled together the scraps of truth made audible to us only in the language of the dead, that is what would be incomprehensible if the curse that befell us had not conveyed us little by little into the heart of evil. For the true curse began only after the disaster itself. I am not speaking of the physical pain, which we managed to ease, nor of the material upheaval, which later on, thanks to the trained teams that remained with us, we were able to repair, more or less. But one day, while we were dragging around like sick people, we saw all the rebels—all those whose wounds had not hastened their end—rise up together all at once. Even the ones we believed to be struck dead regained their strength and joined their companions. It was a mysterious sight. Would they attempt new acts of madness? Had disorder brought them together once again? No, no. Silently, with a quiet discipline, they formed a sort of troop, the ordered and yet derisory counterpart to the little army they had been at the time of the rebellion. They set out for the basement. The worm-eaten stairway that used to lead there still existed. They worked their way down it. Fearing that I had guessed their thoughts, I ran after them, took one by the arm, held on to his clothes. What would they do? Where were they going? For the first time I contemplated their faces. Sad, impossible looks. There was no need to stare at them for very long to understand what they had in mind. Their faces were unrecognizable. Although their features had remained the same, they already resembled one another and no longer bore any resemblance to us. A sort of beauty ravaged them. Their eyes, which seemed tired from the light of the place, gave off a kind of spark that made me ashamed. Their cheeks took on strange hues that attracted and repelled. They seemed to bathe in life and joy, and yet there was a desperation in their smallest gestures. I threw myself at their feet and called to the other tenants, and we all begged them to give up their plans. Some of them heard our prayers and broke down in tears. We said nothing more; their pain itself overwhelmed us, for it only proved to us that we could not hold them back. We would have had to encircle them with chains, as we sometimes did later, trying to stop them from setting out again, but everything seemed useless. Their hearts were no longer able to bind them to us. So they left; they left the house. Such a step was unheard-of. What did they hope to find outside, what did they want? Peace? A new life? But no such things could be given them. So then who was driving them far from our dwelling, who was transforming them so much that it had become unbearable for them to stay? Perhaps an illusion, perhaps remorse? When I asked them to explain their decision, they responded with childish babbling. Some of them said that they could no longer live surrounded by four walls, that they needed open spaces and sunshine. Others spoke for the first time of their families and friends to whom they wanted to bring news. Such ideas were ridiculous. What was this sun, what was this climate they were now going in search of, when already long ago they could bear the memory of it no more? Could they even have relatives and friends anywhere other than in the house? Such madness! And what happened next confirmed this. Seeing that their resolutions were unshakable, we tried to gain time in the hope that they would not remain so. Since they were numerous and the half-rotten stairway threatened to collapse whenever a single person stepped foot on it, we managed to convince them that a new one had to be built. All our hope lay in this return to life in common. We mingled with them; we never ceased by our very presence to press them to abandon their plan. The construction proceeded slowly. They were as docile as they were disciplined. They worked with a sad eagerness that seemed to come not from their impatience but rather from the very habits of diligence that we ourselves had imparted to them and that today only served to hasten their exile. These were heavy, oppressive days. Not only were we unhappy because of these companions we were losing, we were also tormented by the thought that this departure, more than any collapse, would be the end of the house and that it would drastically alter our lot. These fears took shape in our minds. We began again to look anxiously at these creatures who were sacrificing us to their misfortune. Our contact with them, already a cause for repugnance, filled us with disgust. Was it because of the judgments they had made against us, or because of the bizarre transformation they had undergone, whose effects I was the first to feel? It seemed to us that something evil was being exhaled through their mouths. Their smell was no longer like ours at all, and when they touched us, their hands made us shiver. We had to keep ourselves at a distance. We avoided speaking to them. The words they themselves spoke seemed to us so clamorous and so strangely chosen that they left us numb and sometimes remained completely incomprehensible. It soon became impossible for us to maintain ordinary relations with them. We addressed each other with gestures and signs, and even then we did not always understand them. We came to the point of wanting them to disappear as quickly as possible. Was not their stay here now regarded with disapproval? Of course it was; they were leaving because they no longer had the right to stay, and if they did not like the house, that's because it was entirely forbidden to them. The house was pushing them out. The prohibition had slowly come down from the closed spaces in which it originated, and now it was making its way to them, forcing them into a position where no defense was possible because no hope was possible. How insane we were to hold them back! Should we not have driven them out instead? We completed the construction in a few hours and prepared everything for their departure. How long it took us to relieve ourselves of their presence! But now, on the verge of finding that freedom they had desired, they felt nothing but the shame, the distress, and the fear that it represented to them. We had to send them down to the basement and barricade our doors. We shouted and screamed, trying to frighten them. We heard them moaning, and these moans excited our hatred all the more. "Go!" we said to them. "Go to the sun you love so much; console yourselves with your friends who will never be ours. The house is forever closed to you." Since they did not understand what we were saying, our voices, which sounded like the voice of the dwelling, attracted them more than it pushed them away. They came around to the balcony with tears in their eyes; they wandered like shadows around the enclosure they could not enter. It became necessary to use force. One evening, we heard them no more. They must have completed the external stairways that we had not wanted to help them build, since the cold outside air prevented us from going that far. So they left, or rather they were no longer present for us. Some believe that they could not have left the house, that in any event, whatever their faults may have been, they were still tenants and could not have broken the contract. These people claim that they set themselves up in the basement rooms, or perhaps in new basement rooms that they dug deeply into the ground and where they live, outside the house, to be sure, and yet all the closer to its foundations, cut off from the comfort it brought them but not liberated from its commandments and its rules. Others believe that they are still weeping at the door in an effort to soften us or, since we are not there, to soften the wall that stops them, they who were not stopped by the wall of the law. Perhaps they are indeed very close to us, invisible and incapable of making themselves heard. But how could they be close to us? Wherever they are, even if it is right where you are, they are infinitely far away, and we have no more of a right to think of them than we have the means to see or speak to them. Some of them, it is said, have set up in the street, and by making signs they try to draw us into the curse under which they live. An infernal dream. Such thoughts lead to damnation."

There was another knock on the small door.

"Is it the domestics again?" asked Thomas.

"Yes," said the young man, "but this time it's to call us back to our work. Damned domestics!"

"So there is still a staff here?" asked Thomas.

"Naturally," said the young man. "How could a house do without a staff? Do you hear me!" he shouted at the servant. "Could I really do without your services?"

The servant, who had fallen asleep with his head on the back of the chair, woke with a start; he certainly had not heard, and thinking that someone had called him to order, he hastily wiped the table.

"No," said the young man, gravely answering his own question, "we could not do without it; so we have a large number of domestics."

"Always invisible, of course," said Thomas.

"Invisible?" replied the young man, with a look of sadness. "Invisible? You may be a newcomer, but you have nonetheless had the opportunity to make a few observations. So you will know what I am talking about. Well, do you know of a building where one encounters the staff more often than here? At every step there's a servant, behind every door a maid. If someone begins to speak up to ask for something, the domestic is already there. I would even say that it's unbearable. They are everywhere; you never see anyone else; they are the only ones you ever speak to; 'Discreet service,' it says in the brochure. What a joke! The service is utterly oppressive."

"So everything has changed," said Thomas, "since the incident you just recounted to me."

The young man looked at him wearily.

"Everything has changed, if you wish," he said. "But in my opinion nothing has really changed. How could there be a real change here? The rules do not permit it; the house is untouchable. It's the young tenants who see only appearances and who believe that the world has been turned upside down as soon as the furniture's been rearranged. The older tenants know that in the end everything is as it was before."

"So what you told me has no real importance," observed Thomas.

"That's for you to judge," said the young man. "It's a question of interpretation. Allow me to remark, however, that practically nothing that happens here is without importance; all the more reason, then, for the events I have related to you to be given their proper value."

"I don't see," said Thomas, "how they are important for me."

"And to tell the truth," said the young man, "I don't see why they would interest you. The house does not need the interest of those who inhabit it. It receives them when they come; it forgets them when they go."

"So it is possible to leave the building," said Thomas.

"It's not a prison," said the young man disdainfully. "You are free; you are entirely free, and your freedom, I'm afraid, will only be too great."

"I can see," said Thomas, as he stood up, "that there are many things I do not know. Let me therefore take advantage of my ignorance; it will leave me even more free."

"Stay," said the young man, who stood up in his turn. "In the name of all I have said to you, I demand that you stay."

Thomas gave him a questioning look.

94

"We have not yet begun our work," added the young man, "and this work concerns you."

Thomas sat back down. The room was loud. At every table a tenant was leaning over speaking to his friends in a low voice, but the echo made the words resound so much that they fell back onto everyone else with an oppressive force. The acoustics of the room were such that certain words stood out while others were muffled, which gave the impression that the same conversation was being repeated at every table and that everything they were saying was being said at the same time by the entire room.

"What is this work?" said Thomas. The young man looked at Joseph, who had been listening attentively, as though he were hearing of these events for the first time. Thomas wondered if the conversation were not meant for Joseph, who after all was much more capable than he was of understanding its true meaning.

"I hesitate to respond to your question," said the young man. "My friend is so sensitive, and the subject is so deeply serious, that he may not be able to bear my words. Therefore I will be brief. But first promise me that you will never forget where you are. What I have taught you is not without importance, whatever your opinion of it may be, and in a certain sense it is impossible to live here without having these facts engraved in one's memory or without the possibility of repeating them at each moment, even if their true meaning escapes you. But on the other hand it would be foolish to believe that I have told you the whole truth. In the ocean of our life, you have seen only one drop of water; it is only a miniscule slice of the events that occur incessantly; I would have to pass my entire existence with you to retrace the main lines, and then, as I have said, we quickly forget; how could we hold on to the memory of everything that happens to us? That would be insane."

He fell silent, as if he had suddenly plunged into that dangerous immensity in which he risked being lost, but he soon returned to himself. At that moment someone called to Thomas from another table. He recognized two people from the grand hall; although their faces were rather unpleasant, he greeted them and leaned toward them to hear better what they were shouting to him. He had the impression that they were out of place in the café. He was struck by the poor quality of their clothing, and their attitude was far from what would have been proper. These two men carried themselves like peasants; they were robust and overbearing; and at every opportunity they addressed people they knew, people for whom these signs of attention were terribly aggravating. Conversations from one table to another seemed to be forbidden, which was perfectly reasonable since the bad acoustics would have created an unbearable racket. Despite his desire to respect the customs, Thomas was glad to speak to his new neighbors. He only wanted to say a couple of words to them.

"Who are you exactly?" he said in a quiet voice, but the echo immediately took hold of his question, and it was as if he had shouted it with all his might.

Everyone turned to look at him; it was very unpleasant, but now it was too late—he could no longer take back his words. A response came, and it was no less jarring. "Your former guide," said the older of the two. Was it really he? Indeed, from his imperious demeanor Thomas should have recognized the man who had led him through the crowd; now there was not the least trace of irony on his face, but his manner was all the more unpleasant. The other was the player who had spoken to him when he had first entered the room.

"Do you know them?" asked Thomas, turning to Jerome. "I saw them both in the grand hall."

He waited for an answer, but the young man went no further than to say with a certain coldness that he never went to the gaming room.

"Never," said Thomas, with a look of surprise. "Do you mean that you don't like the games?"

"I adore the games," said the young man. "It is certainly not because I have no taste for it that I have left that room behind."

"Perhaps it's the noise that drives you away," said Thomas.

"Indeed, the noise is unbearable. We have asked more than once that measures be taken to make the room less resonant; our requests have not been granted. It seems that the players cannot do without the noise, that it helps them overcome the emotions to which they would succumb entirely without some distraction."

"How superstitious these people are!" said Thomas. "For you that is no doubt yet another reason to stay away?"

Before answering, the young man looked around the room, letting his eyes wander from one person to another in search of some solid point they could rest on. He looked slowly and solemnly, as if everything threatened to disappear and as if he were afraid of no longer finding this scene still there after giving his response.

"One must always tell the truth," he declared. "You are questioning me because you were shocked by the customs that have been established in the house, and you wish to hear from my mouth the truth that you believe you have already come to know. I cannot hold it against you; it's quite natural that our conversation has not yet penetrated your mind and that most of the facts I have shared with you seem without interest. How could it be otherwise? Are you not a stranger to this place? Are you not so distant that at times I can hardly believe you are present and must say to myself: 'He is there,' so that I can continue my story? It would be very unusual and even illegal for you to be interested in my conversation, but it is not necessary for you to be interested in it; there is hardly any need for you to listen to it at all; it is enough that I say what is useful for you to be able to profit from it. And yet, since through certain circumstances you may become mixed up in our relations with the domestics, I have a duty to enlighten you. Of course, I am not speaking of our real relations, these pass at an infinite distance above your head; you may try your best to look upward, but you will not even glimpse what we have in mind when we describe them. The important thing for you, what you cannot in any way afford to neglect, are the practical relations with the staff. You may be called on at any moment to give your opinion, and you must not let your ignorance — this ignorance for which you congratulate yourself so heartily — lead you to commit any errors. What, therefore, should you know about the domestics? They have their good qualities, that is undeniable; they are devoted and capable, and they are so proud that the slightest reproach makes them ill. It is all the more touching, then, to see them neglect their work when concerns of a higher order demand this negligence. No one suffers more than they do from the disorder, and yet everything here, as you yourself have noticed, is pure incoherence and waste. For them this is a terrible distress. It is almost tempting to close one's eyes to the imperfections of the service, because while the tenants find it extremely inconvenient, for the domestics it is a perpetual torment. How can we punish them for something that in their eyes is already such a terrible punishment? Nevertheless, this point of view is not enough to justify their behavior. Are they not domestics above all else? Is it not their duty, their primary duty, to fulfill to the letter the obligations of the service — without thinking of anything else and without wishing to rise above their functions? Is it up to them to interpret the desires of the tenants? Do they not already commit an error when they reflect and meditate on the orders they have been given and when they try to discern whether these orders correspond to the true well-being of their clients? But—so they answer—we are not only in the service of the tenants, we are also in the service of the house. No doubt; but even that is not always admitted. The tenants make up an integral part of the building, and from the moment they have entered and begin to live here, from the moment they respect the laws, one cannot neglect them without at the same time neglecting the house. Otherwise, if they did not have the real and effective feeling of participating in the entire building, how would they know they are really there, how could they not let themselves be carried away by the desperate thought that they are still outside? One might even say—though this is a risky proposition—that the tenants are more important than the house itself, or at least that they are the house, that the house has no reality except through them, that if there were no tenants, there would not even be a building, and that if they all went away, this would be enough for the rooms, the walls, and even the foundations to disappear completely. These are bold and daring thoughts, and they are largely false; it is the same with them as it is with those explanations often passed on to newcomers when they are told: The house is the staff; the house is the rules. As though one could stuff such vast and undefinable truths into a definition! What it is useful to remember about these debates is that no one can bring the house over to their side or use it as an argument in a dispute. Whenever one introduces it, it blasts everything apart. The domestics themselves say this in their own defense when someone accuses them of not keeping up the building and of damaging its reputation. 'The house is not well kept?' they ask. 'How can that be possible? We are not powerful men; we are merely modest servants, and you well know that even with all the power in the world we would not succeed in lessening the value of the building, no more in any case than we could increase it. No, the house is always at every moment in the state that perfectly suits it. It is essentially out of reach. We serve it as it demands to be served.' There is some truth in this line of thought, and yet the servants are wrong. For they too belong to the house; they are its main gears; they are thus to a certain extent everything it is, and if, through their irregularities or their negligence, they cannot really harm it or shake its foundations, they are responsible for the bad thoughts that distort the judgment of the tenants. Good God, no, they cannot reach it. Who ever could? But if it remains untouchable and indifferent, if it does not feel the effects of their faults, they are nonetheless at fault in relation to it, and all the more so in that it does not move and does not risk crumbling down on them and so only judges them with its impassive and utter contempt. It has therefore seemed necessary, because of the harm they may do, to exercise control over the domestics and to submit them to a strict jurisdiction. This is what we call 'attracting them to us.' But then, in the name of what can they be judged? A first difficulty is that they do not think of themselves as responsible to us. On the one hand, they see the tenants as nothing but a parasitic caste who—because they do not live as intimately with the furnishings, the implements and utensils, the obscure corners of the house—have not been initiated into its secrets and can even be considered as still belonging to the outside; such people would in any case have no grounds for judging those who are superior to them. On the other hand, they claim that their activity is determined by rules known only to them, and they add that if one day a judgment were necessary, this judgment would emanate spontaneously from these rules or, if need be, would be pronounced by way of a tribunal established by them. The confusion of powers is obvious. And yet, it is indeed true that in some ways we find their presence disarming, for among their obligations—and this proves the importance of their role—they have been given, as one of their most sacred duties, guardianship of the rules. They cannot release the register that contains them without committing an unheard-of error. They cannot admit therefore that a few pages ought to be entrusted to us, even if our judgment should end up purifying them and relieving the remorse that consumes them. They prefer to be tormented by their errors than to be cleansed of them by a new crime; and who can blame them? Besides, we could never be tempted to lay our hands on these rules and enforce them, for we do not know what they are. No," he continued, looking at Thomas with a provocative air, "we do not know what they are. Of course we do not know the ones that concern us. There is no need even to say that. Otherwise, would we respect them, would we have for them that veneration without which the rules are scorned even as they are observed? What would the law be if our only duty toward it were to conform our behavior to it? As though one were able not to follow the law, as though one could cause it to break down. An absurd, ridiculous thought. May it not come to cloud our minds."

He stopped to take a deep breath and to expel the bad air that such words had drawn into him; then he continued with greater calm: "How then do the employees behave, these employees who not only have guardianship over our rules but who are not even ignorant of the precepts pertaining to themselves? It is a situation that makes one tremble. If one dared to speak lightly, one might say that it is from such an anomaly as this that all our misfortunes, and theirs, proceed. It is unheard-of that men would have the ability every day to look at the book and to read in it what they ought to do, what they ought not do, why they ought to do it, and what texts they are violating if they do not. Is this possible? The employees themselves deny it. They claim that the book itself has never been opened, that they keep it before them without ever looking in it, that in any case if they had ever looked through its pages, they could never have deciphered it. We believe them; we are glad to believe them. Understand the text of the law? And why not write the law itself, falsify it or modify it? Those who say that the law does not exist commit an infinitely less serious crime than those who play around with such thoughts as these. It is always possible to declare that there are no rules, and this is probably true; the more one thinks that the rules are distant, that they escape our experience and our language, that they are inaccessible, the less one risks overstepping them. And this is equally true of every person who is in charge of the rules. Do you understand," he added, looking once more at Thomas, "why we say that the staff is invisible?"

Thomas avoided giving any response; he only nodded his head gravely. But the young man took no notice of this reticence.

"Should we then renounce judging the domestics?" he asked everyone there. "Will we be exposed to their caprice and to their depraved imaginations? And this because the domestics have in their possession the material documents and the texts on which every judgment is based and perhaps even the judgments themselves, and because, on top of that, they refuse to heed our summons? We can do without all that. Naturally, in a certain sense, we will never really be able to judge an employee, even the most insignificant among them. But we do not wish to do so. We are even happy not to have the means. Carrying out such a task would require that we indulge in a simulacrum of justice, and the very thought is repugnant to us. Dispense justice to a domestic? What an idea! We can detest them on the whole as much as we want; we can pursue them out of anger for all the harm they do, or out of envy for all the benefits they enjoy; we are nonetheless all too aware of how much we owe them not to leave them in peace in matters of justice. Where would that take us? Most of the time, as you have seen, the employees seem to be outright criminals. Of course they have all sorts of little defects that make them very unpleasant; they meddle in everything; they have no idea what work is; they love to play jokes—and what jokes! They're also thieves and gluttons; in that regard, I'm surprised that the servant didn't drink your coffee, it's almost the rule; all these defects certainly make of them something other than model servants, but since they also have all those good little qualities that correct such imperfections, we pay no attention to them, and in the long run we forget their trifling errors."

"What good qualities are those?" said Thomas sharply.

"They are qualities of considerable value," answered the young man, with an angry look, either because he was annoyed that Thomas had interrupted him, or because he considered this too insignificant to apply his mind to it. "I'll give you one example: they are terribly indiscreet, but in their indiscretion, they know how to forget, so that if we grumble at them because they are always looking over our shoulder, we are also grateful to them for seeming not to be there at all and for never saying what they think, and in the end we feel happy about this almost invisible presence that comforts us, that warms us and helps us, at the price of disturbances that are overall quite minimal."

"But," said Thomas, "there is nothing pleasant in the jokes they play."

"No doubt about that," said the young man. "They are generally exasperating, and I can understand why the loud knocking at the door made you angry a moment ago."

"Was that for my sake?" asked Thomas.

"Naturally," said the young man, with a smile. "Whom else would it be for? But, you see, you yourself had knocked in a way that was so solemn, so important, as if your entry ought to be taken for some sensational event, that they might well make a little fun of you. Besides, it's always like that. Their jokes are ridiculous, but we often behave in such ridiculous ways; we attach importance to too many things; how could one not be tempted to laugh at it?"

"Do you approve of everything they do?" asked Thomas.

"Of course not," said the young man. "What a strange creature you are! I am often reproached for being too harsh with them. My God," he added, with a kind of horror, "if you are already so worked up over such trifles, what will your reaction be to the other misdeeds they sometimes commit? Shall I tell you what they are?"

"That's up to you to decide," Thomas answered, "but perhaps you think that I'm more ignorant than I am; perhaps I know a little something about it already."

"What childishness!" said the young man, with impatience. "How could you know about it? Do we ourselves know everything? Have you heard about what goes on in the bedrooms, or what happens up above with the sick?"

"I know nothing, that's understood," said Thomas. "But I do know that —to put it bluntly—the domestics can be accused of murder."

"That's a manner of speaking," replied the young man. "Are you referring to the measures they take to get rid of certain tenants by making their stay particularly uncomfortable, by transforming their beds into little infernal machines? That isn't so serious; it's rather a bad joke. One need only take a few precautions. To avoid these difficulties we have given up going to bed, and in many rooms the beds have been removed at the request of the tenants. This is no doubt precisely what the domestics wanted, since they hate making the beds; generally, in the midst of their work, they are overcome with dizziness and are forced to lie down on the mattress where an excruciating sleepiness overcomes them, for they claim that they never sleep. None of this is very serious. If we had nothing else to reproach them with, we would never even give them a second thought. But there are countless other things they do that are much more reprehensible. And to tell the truth it is not, properly speaking, a question of actions, although some of them are truly nasty; it is rather a way of being, a general conduct that we sense is driven by dishonorable motives. When they enter our rooms— elsewhere they are not so bold—they merely stare at us with sly, suspicious looks, as though they know what we're thinking, and what looks! Or rather, no, that's not it; they don't look at us; they're incapable of looking at us; they circle around us with eyes that look at nothing in particular, that watch over us and inspect us there where we are not to be found. What are they looking for? What do they think they see? To all appearances their inquiries are legitimate; they take care not to leave us alone with thoughts that, out of negligence or timidity, we would hesitate to express; they want to anticipate our desires; they put themselves as much as possible in our

102

place. This is an explicit part of their obligations. But, as you will have guessed, it is not their duties that they have in mind. They couldn't care less about preventing us from doing evil. On the contrary, with their looks of vague suspicion, they are thinking only of how to convince us of the evil we have done or of how to impart to us the idea of having done it. Nothing, alas, could be easier. Not only do they have tremendous authority—and despite the general contempt they have been unable to avoid, they enjoy a situation of the first order—they also know everything about us. They have gigantic catalogues in which the slightest details of our existence are recorded, everything there is to know about our tastes, our habits, our relations, and even—the very thought sends a shiver—our past before coming into the house. This is their favorite work. Gathering information under the pretext of dispensing it, interrogating us with a servile air about what we are lacking in order to know what we desire, catching us in intimate moments because the service has to be impeccable—in all this, believe me, they spare no trouble. Perhaps they know more, perhaps less than we think. It hardly matters. We are overwhelmed by such a belief. We cannot stop ourselves from believing that they are aware of our most vague and fleeting impressions. They know us better than we know ourselves: that is our unshakable conviction. So they have an easy time of it. How could we resist the feeling of malaise and anguish that they evoke for us whenever they come to visit? The suspicion in their eyes reflects the fault in our souls. We know that the evil is here. It is somewhere near us; it is within us. Oh misery, how to deliver ourselves from the thoughts that then oppress us and impose such inexpressible torments? For all of our misfortune comes from our feeling of innocence, an accursed innocence that vainly contradicts the suspicion chasing after us. If we had really committed a fault, then we could rest easy; in agreement with this suspicious domestic, we would smile at him in recognition of his insight, and everything would be over. But this consolation is not available to us. We know only too well that our hearts are pure. We can rummage through our lives all we want, inspect every corner of our conscience, all we find are honest actions and virtuous thoughts. So where is the fault? For it does exist; we feel it with no less force than we feel our purity. It is within this world in which we feel so happy. It suddenly stinks up the air. We can no longer breathe. We say to ourselves that we must find it and uncover it. We go to our friends and ask them questions; we beg them to find us guilty. Wasted efforts. They do not know where the fault is to be found either. All that remains for us is to become criminals, and that is no doubt the ultimate goal of the domestics. It is true that some tenants claim that this is not so. They believe, on the contrary, that the staff has such an elevated idea of purity, such an inflexible conception of the morality of the house that where we see only clarity and whiteness, they are offended and literally blinded by the stain that has been made; their eyes are drawn to it; their sight grows dim from it—hence their troubled and insidious looks. This is a likely interpretation. But at bottom it does not contradict another thought, the thought of those who see the domestics as vicious monsters with a sickly curiosity, ready to do anything to witness new events and to transcribe them into their records. At any rate, whether it is out of concern for morality or a sadistic curiosity, they have but one desire, to drive the evil they have perceived, or implanted, toward a resounding action that will suppress the danger of this evil. Here we are, then, back at one of their primary duties. How is it possible to judge it? Some claim that the rules forbid sly thoughts, unformulated complaints, plans for revenge that one keeps to oneself, which are all sources of malaise and disorder in a public establishment. Does such a text really exist? This is unverifiable. In any case, it has always been difficult to enforce. Can one distinguish between the thoughts that are allowed and the ones that are forbidden? What are the true limits of a bad mood? In the midst of such a mood, does not everything in one's mind suffer from its influence? The domestics, aware of such difficulties, used them as a pretext for extending to all thought the prohibition that should only have applied to dubious reveries concerning the house. Thus, in principle, it is forbidden us to think or—but this comes to the same thing—to keep our thoughts to ourselves. We must speak and act. As soon as an idea passes through our heads, we are obliged to communicate it to a neighbor or to carry out immediately the plans we have thought up on our own. Now do you understand the reasons for the interminable discussions in which we turn over every aspect of these often insignificant facts? Can you make sense of the incoherent, puerile, or downright insane actions we undertake on so many occasions? It's the law, or the law of the staff at least. Notice that such a rule serves their curiosity quite well. They have no need to fear that deep down we are keeping some great secret or even some more or less vain reflection that it would torture them not to know. Notice too that this rule is far from being a burden to us. Aside from our conversations in groups, why would we think? To what object could our thoughts ever turn? If it were not for the rules, we would probably experience the emptiness of our souls as an imperfection that would make us suffer, but, as it is, we are glad for it and see it as a sign of good moral standing, from which we derive a certain joy. This rule, which, I repeat, is excessive and certainly a recent invention, has had the most unfortunate consequences. When the domestics decided to put it into force, they found themselves confronted with the embarrassing case of the sick. In principle, one text applies to all; no exceptions are allowed, for this would occasion an infinity of abuse; but in reality, everyone can find some excuse to behave however they wish, up to a certain point at least. But when it comes to the sick, the domestics were particularly insistent on applying the new rule to them; one might even suspect that they established the rule only for the sake of these people who are called half-tenants because now they only partly belong to the house. The sick are a torment for the staff; not that they complain or make demands but precisely because they never complain, and it is a noteworthy event when one of them goes so far as to express a desire. The staff finds this unacceptable. They cannot bear being kept at a distance. They are tortured by the silence of those who would have the most to say. They would at least like to catch them at their groaning. In vain. The sick, it is said, do not fall under the influence of the staff, and that is supposed to be the cause of their illness. But with the new text, the employees saw their chance to transform this situation. They began by enforcing the rule with people who were only slightly sick and who, no doubt, were not completely free from their control. They were ordered to speak and act in accordance with whatever thoughts they had. The experiment was dreadful. It was scandalous to see these creatures, fevered and paralyzed, exerting themselves ridiculously to rise from their beds and attempting to express the thousand idiotic notions that rattled their feeble minds. Naturally, these sick people saw their state growing worse, and they fell into the inalterable and incomprehensible—not to mention worrisome—state of repose in which the false commands of the law could no longer reach them. The domestics, however, refused to accept defeat. They decreed that the text was still applicable to everyone, and they explained that the case of certain sick persons only constituted an apparent exception, that these latter kept silent only because every thought had vanished from their minds—which, after all, is quite possible. But since as a practical matter they could no longer force obedience on any of the tenants officially admitted to the infirmary, they took their revenge by giving them the runaround. From that day forward it became very difficult to obtain any care and to enter into the special rooms; the formalities are interminable; one can hope for a doctor's visit and expertise only by providing grounds for believing there is something wrong; but how to prove that there is an illness without a doctor? By consulting with the domestics? Precisely, and there you have it. Then one is faced with unlimited postponement and the certainty of countless frustrations; for the domestics are convinced that illness is a particularly vicious form of indiscipline, and they consider it one of their duties to prevent its ravages by turning away from those whom it threatens. So they deliberately neglect the tenants who are most in need of their help. They do not allow them to be sick, and yet they treat them as if they really were. It's a hopeless situation. You can see the consequences for yourself," the young man added sadly. "Most, not to say all of them, are very seriously ill. They suffer without respite, and all they know of the staff is its meticulous, tiresome control that brings no real help."

"Well," said Thomas, "here are some grievances that lead you to make judgments."

The young man had turned to face his companion, and Thomas saw that he had taken his hands and was preventing him from standing up. He returned no less quickly to the conversation.

"We are coming to the end," he said. "But it is not the one you have in mind. Look," he continued, in good humor, "just reflect on the situation. The servants behave very badly, no doubt about that, and although they have excuses to justify everything they do, even in our eyes—despite the fact that they can legitimately be proud of all their actions that are inspired by a respect and love for their calling—they do not for all that deserve any less resentment from us. And why do they deserve it? Because of the difficulties they create for us, only a few of which you're aware of? That is one reason, but it is not the real reason; from the moment they act under the cover of the law, we have no more grounds for resenting them than we would have to resent the law. What protects them from judgment also spares them our anger. Such petty sentiments could never touch them anyway."

"I do not share your point of view," said Thomas.

"What are you dreaming up now?" said the young man. "Your head is stuffed with ideas from the outside. You always believe that everything is mysterious; I bet you are thinking about some judgment. Never mind this idea of judgment, just let it be. Never mind this idea of judgment, just let it be.[1] Look, we cannot judge the domestics; and, what's more, according to you, we're supposed to judge them because we have grievances and resentments against them? Really, what a piece of work you are." He looked at Thomas reproachfully.

"And yet," said Thomas, "you hate them."

"Granted," said the young man, "I regret having confided in you, for God knows how you may end up interpreting all this; but I cannot take back what I have said. Yes, we hate them; there, are you satisfied? Does this get you any further? Do you even know what we mean by hate, anger, ill humor? With your crude ideas—allow me to express myself this way; there is nothing hurtful in it to you—with your overflowing imagination, you must certainly be subject to confusions that hardly bring you any nearer to the truth. So I will stick to the facts. It may be that we hate the staff and that our desire to control it, to judge it, as you say, can be understood in terms of this feeling; for my part, I am convinced of this; and I will tell you my reasons in a moment. But I recognize that others have a different point of view, and although in my opinion it is cowardice—the simple fear of seeing things as they are—that leads them to these thoughts, they merit consideration nonetheless. What they say is easy to understand. Their main argument is that we cannot hate the domestics; we can complain about them; we can heap them with insults if we give in easily to anger; if necessary, we can punish them; but truly hating them is inconceivable, if only because, however clumsy and disagreeable they may be, they are still in our service and consequently deserve a minimum of gratitude. These tenants add that we could hardly hate the servants, given that we are incapable of hating anyone since all real feelings are now unknown to us. How are we to answer that? Is it possible to give a serious answer to a joke? We are rather tempted to say the opposite about ourselves. The habit of living in our own world without any external diversions and the meditations that we continually discuss among ourselves, as I am doing now, these have greatly developed our sensitivity, and the slightest incident echoes endlessly through our lives. Our relations with the staff are in this regard quite

1. The French text repeats this sentence verbatim. — Tr.

remarkable. In truth, there is nothing to prevent a perfect understanding between us. Whenever we think of them with calm, rejecting all interpretations driven by passion, we understand their behavior and approve of it. They find that deep within us there is complete adherence. But that is where the drama lies, for we are even less inclined to pardon them when we admit that they are right. We have for them a groundless hatred that seeks in vain for grievances, that rejects the ones it finds because they are not worthy of its violence, and that is content in the end to burn and smolder in this absence of a cause. The truth is that the domestics naturally inspire hatred. One does not realize this right away; it is often tenderness that one seems to feel for them; but one day it becomes impossible to escape from the obvious: the staff is despicable. What are the reasons for this? That is something we should not dwell on too much, for in reflecting on this we risk looking for extraordinary mysteries where there are probably only very simple causes to be found. It is natural that there would be something weighing down and obscuring the fate of the servants, who, if some of their qualities did not turn us against them, would end up receiving from us such excessive sentiments of friendship and respect that the whole order of the house would be disturbed. We would be reduced to worshipping the servants. Now, such excesses are absolutely forbidden. The domestics are so distant, and show such indifference in our presence, only because it is imperative for them to maintain the hierarchy; they take advantage of it, with their depraved character, to make us feel how high above us they soar; they humble themselves—as we plainly see—so as to place themselves on our level; but, whatever their intentions, the general equilibrium is preserved. We might therefore believe that this strange feeling, so unjustified in certain respects, is nonetheless indispensable to the harmony of our little community and that it is even dictated to us from high above. It is the gaze of the law upon us. We are its instrument, and it would be a grave fault if we tried to empty ourselves of the passion it imposes on us or to find grounds for it according to our point of view. Can one try to justify the law? As a result, we have only to feel as it wants us to feel, without giving ourselves over to empty disputes. This feeling of hatred—how could it be otherwise?—is very painful and heavy. It dries us out; it takes away our taste for everything. We hardly experience it, so insensitive does it seem to make us; we sense in our organs the surge of a vague warmth rising like a thin column of fire; our cheeks turn red; our eyes begin to shine; our mouths go dry; all we can do is keep silent. Since such a feeling is more disagreeable to us than it is pleasant, we tend to see it as a righteous sense of justice, though it no doubt has nothing to do with justice. But it is all the more unassailable, since it eliminates all deliberation and all judgment. We need only look at the man who is in the position of the culprit, we need only judge him, as you put it, and the interrogation, the examination of evidence, the verdict seem useless; or rather all this is implicitly hidden, and actually contained, in this simple look, burning and empty, through which we in turn enforce the law."

At that moment Joseph tugged at the young man's arm to make him be quiet. Perhaps he did not want Thomas to hear any more. For his part, Thomas was relieved to escape from the conversation. At first he had found in it a certain comfort and rest; he forced himself not to interrupt; he would have liked for everything to be explained to him. But now he thought only of how to get the young man to stop talking. Not only was it extremely tiring to try to follow the conversation — for at each instant it seemed to him that the most important words were escaping him — it also made him uneasy and weighed down his mind with details he would have preferred still not to know. He stood up.

"I was only passing through," he said. "I must go."

"That's not possible," answered the young man. "What are you thinking? We'll begin our work in a moment."

Thomas tried to make Dom stand up too, but he had fallen asleep and didn't understand what was being asked of him.

"Exactly," said Thomas. "I am a stranger to this work. It is not possible for me to take part in it."

"What are you saying?" said the young man slowly rising, as if he were mentally repeating the words he had just heard. "How could you stay out of this affair?"

He reflected for a moment in order to examine the objections that Thomas might make and added: "You're mixed up in it in any case."

"You are certainly in error," said Thomas. "I came in by mistake, and I have no right to participate in your discussions."

"I understand your hesitations," said the young man in a milder tone. "But I can ease your mind with just a few words. Although you are right to consider your presence here as a privilege — a privilege whose value you yourself are unable to appreciate — there is no one who is not to some extent in the same situation as you. So rest assured. Your presence will be tolerated."

"That is more than I can ask," said Thomas, and he tried to wake up his companion.

"Just a moment," said Jerome. "I don't want to go back over your strange statements; they concern only you. But it is my duty to point out to you that you have misunderstood the reasons for your presence in this room. You have forgotten that you did not come freely but in response to an order. Therefore you cannot leave until you have fulfilled your obligations."

"That is not quite correct," said Thomas. "The order did come from here, but the desire and the action came from me. I responded to the call only because the call seemed to me worthy of respect."

"The order came from much farther away," said the young man, "and it came from you as well. Did you not go into the gaming room?"

"Yes," said Thomas.

"Then you cannot escape your duty," said the young man. "We must judge these two men," he added, pointing to the two players. "You are one of the witnesses."

"Well that changes everything," said Thomas, as if he had been waiting for this conclusion. "What are you accusing them of?"

"We aren't accusing them," answered the young man. "They themselves have come to ask for our judgment."

"Then what fault," asked Thomas, "has brought them before you?"

"You and your strange questions," said the young man. "Why do you think we would keep ourselves informed about everyone's little secrets? If they are here, it's because they have been attracted by our room, and as soon as they entered, they were taken under our jurisdiction. What drove them here? We could only learn that by chance. Perhaps they cheated, as they claim; perhaps they had a disagreement with a member of the staff; perhaps they have passed through one of those crises that ends with a desire to leave the area where they live, the floor they are allowed to enter, and to go somewhere else; perhaps—and this is the most serious—they themselves do not know why they have come, and they entered on an empty pretext, pushing the first door they came to."

Thomas looked at the two men who were drinking slowly from their cups. "One of them," he said, "is an employee."

The young man also looked and said: "They are both members of the staff."

"You surprise me," answered Thomas. "In the large meeting room only one of them fulfilled any function. The other one seemed to be threatened by a punishment. He held no authority; he only submitted to it."

"An unimportant detail," said the young man, sitting back down. "It is not through such signs that one can distinguish a tenant from an employee."

"So there are distinctive signs?" asked Thomas, without taking his eyes off the two players.

"There are all kinds," answered the young man. "Some are rather crude, like the inscriptions on the arms of some of the servants. We might have some real trust in this sign if it were subject to official control, but unfortunately that is not the case. Other signs can be read from the details of their suits: the clothes worn by the employee may resemble a uniform, or they may be distinguished from the common types of outfit by their refined elegance. These are unreliable indications; others no longer have any value in themselves, but they attract more attention. In general, the employees, while keeping close watch over their manners so as to approximate them to ours, are ill at ease among the tenants; they say nothing, or else they talk too much; their voices have a jagged sharpness they cannot quite hide. They are either overly attentive or indifferent to the point of excess. So, as a likely consequence of this disoriented state, they demonstrate a physical awkwardness that is often taken as ill will."

"It is not very easy to make use of these indications," said Thomas doubtfully.

"Why would it be?" answered the young man. "They are even, if you wish, completely worthless. One can always find other details that deprive them of all their significance, just as it is easy to find other indications that make one reconsider yet again. But isn't this natural? Are there such marked differences between the servants and the tenants? Have I not told you how the staff was recruited from among the inhabitants of the house? No doubt, the domestics have always been tempted to set themselves up as a separate caste that, because of the originality of their occupations, they had a duty to defend against the influences of ordinary life. The caste exists, but it does not depend on the choice of particular persons, since everyone can, and actually does, participate in it; it is connected to a way of seeing that is imposed on each one of us. Why would we want to oppose the tenants to the domestics when the tenants are always domestics, more or less, and cannot be distinguished among themselves, even—and especially—by the most penetrating eye? We are at fault when we refuse to see in each being a man who will one day be called among the members of the staff."

"That means," said Thomas, "that you too may be a domestic."

"Perhaps," replied the young man, with a smile.

"It is not certain then," Thomas added, "that your way of seeing is that of an ordinary tenant."

"Judge it however you will," said the young man, "it corresponds to the truth."

"It may also be," Thomas continued, "that I—who am not even a tenant, do not even inhabit the house, and remain here as a stranger—it is possible that I must be wary of your words, not because they might inspire me with mistrust, but because I cannot trust my own strength."

"That is a useless concern," said the young man. "I have not forgotten who you are."

"I sense now," said Thomas, "that my presence here is out of place and that I am not equal to the role for which I was brought here. I am incapable of being a witness in an affair where I cannot distinguish the nature of the accused."

"All your remarks are superfluous," said the young man, who had listened with an impertinent indulgence. "Now it's too late to evade your duty since the proceedings have begun. I will limit myself, for the sake of facilitating the operation, to drawing your attention to two points. The first is that however minute your task may be, it proves that you have been distinguished and that consequently those who have observed you have recognized your capacity. The second point is that you are uselessly tormenting yourself over the relations between the tenants and the staff, given that when you took your first step into the house, you also took your first step on the very long, almost infinite, and yet already traced out path that will lead you to the status of a domestic. Now, keep your eyes on the two employees."

The invitation may have been ironic, for Thomas had not ceased staring at the players, casually at first, then more severely, in order to discover the crimes for which they felt it necessary to reproach themselves. Now he could think only of looking around the room and studying certain details, especially the paintings on the ceiling, which he looked up to contemplate at length. These paintings, which Thomas now perceived with surprise, were curious; they represented in a very precise manner the room itself, such as it might appear on the day of a gala ball. The clients—certain faces could be recognized on careful inspection—were dressed with great distinction; they had flowers in their buttonholes and shiny decorations dangled across their chests. In the middle, couples were dancing, and the spectacle would have been altogether graceful if the cavalrymen, probably in the middle of a dance figure, were not blocking the faces of their partners. Some of them, in an excess of enthusiasm, were covering their eyes, showing with this naïve gesture that the view they were forbidding to others was unbearable even to them. On the platform, instead of musicians, the painter had depicted three persons of great beauty, seated in richly decorated armchairs, gravely contemplating the scene.

The examination of the painting greatly moved the two players. They rose abruptly, and as if they had lost all sense of politeness, they demanded in loud voices why there was no dance show that day. The others around them, disconcerted, did not know how to answer. They rose in their turn and stuttered a few words whose meaning was not very clear but that must have meant: We're not in charge; we have nothing to do with it.

"Then who is in charge here?" shouted the two men in a tone of ecstatic reproach.

To calm them down, they were directed to a table chosen at random in the corner of the room. The younger of the two began to sing, and his voice, rising slowly above the murmurs of the crowd, let out a song of unexpected beauty. The words were probably in a foreign language; Thomas understood so little of what they said that he thought he was hearing a melody in which music took the place of words. It was a sweet and happy song whose sounds came in quick succession but did not all die away, for some continued on and, without blending with the new notes, remained untouched by the rest of the modulation. This singularity—which one was tempted to explain in terms of the acoustics of the room, but that Thomas attributed to the vocal memory of the singer—did not create a cacophony but finally transformed the melody entirely, a melody that was at first gracious and light but then took on a gravity and a poignant sadness. The columns of sound seemed to surround the singer and to separate him from the crowd, placing him at the center of a melancholy peristyle that he himself could not shake without endangering his life. It soon seemed to Thomas that the man's voice had gone silent and that, overwhelmed by the sonorous monument it had constructed, it could find only in silence the expression of joy to which it had devoted itself. The words then sprang from the confusion in which they had been lost. The song exalted the good fortune of a man who does not avoid his duty and who finds in a benevolent action the compensation for a difficult labor. A remarkable fact was that in listening attentively, one had the impression that the first part of the melody, which was perceived as a whole and, as it were, simultaneously, reproduced the words in the opposite direction, beginning from the end, and that only the second half presented them in their proper order. All these inventions were no less beautiful than they were odd, and the emotion one felt in discovering them far surpassed the feeling of a peaceful artistic enjoyment.

Thomas was therefore very surprised to hear some of the spectators burst out laughing in mockery of the unfortunate young man, as though he had been engaged in a ridiculous burlesque. He looked back at the audience, and seeing the open mouths and the gestures full of compunction, he saw that a large number of people in the room were singing and that Jerome himself, together with his companion, were letting out a long note on which they lingered indefinitely. He thought then that the spectators, to ridicule the singer, had taken up the melody and, instead of singing it in the order it required, sang various passages of it according to a new design with which they were familiar. The singer was therefore condemned to silence, and now all that was left was to hear the tragic essence of the song that had until then seemed to express the peaceful and noble happiness of life.

Shortly after that, everyone fell silent, and the last sounds, softly echoing, sought in vain to prolong this painful parody. One spectator rose; he stepped up to the two men and said in a firm voice: "Dancing is no longer allowed at present." This deferential response threw the first of the two players, the very one who had just been so cruelly humiliated, into great confusion, but the other one, without being shaken in the least, stood halfway up and asked what was the point of the musician's platform in such conditions as these.

"It still has its uses," said the spectator politely. "On this stage those who have grounds for complaint come to express their grievances. Also, bottles of cognac and casks of beer are kept beneath the planks."

"Very well, very well," answered the employee in his great raucous voice, and without further ado he invited the spectator to sit at his table.

114

He accepted, and now their only thought was of drinking and singing. Thomas drank several glasses of an excellent wine. Jerome was also drinking and began to speak to him again, as if there had been no disagreement between them. He told him that this meeting was very important, because it helped one understand how the staff could be monitored and controlled. The domestics, he said, who were so gluttonous and perverted, were always very sober in public. Eating or sleeping was for them a depraved act that they dared not perform in front of the tenants. This was indeed why one saw them so rarely. But at times, after a crisis whose significance it was very difficult to understand, discipline became relaxed, and they mingled with the other inhabitants of the house, taking part in their entertainments. This was notably the case when they made their way into this room. Was the atmosphere particularly depressing? Did it have an effect on the nervous systems of the domestics, or did they come here only when they already felt on the verge of succumbing to it? One thing that is certain is that they indulged wholeheartedly in all the little pleasures that previously they made it their business to do without. If their suggestions had been heeded, certain long forbidden customs would have been revived, and their bodies, by neglecting the precautions taken since time immemorial, would have lost at one stroke the advantages of this healthy regimen. Although they were not permitted to indulge all their whims—whether out of humanity or for the sake of decorum—the excesses into which they threw themselves were enough for them to feel a double effect that was both moral and physical. As a result of their lack of training, they were more sensitive than the tenants, and as soon as the intoxication had worn off, they experienced a sudden increase of bodily vigor, a revival of their appetites, an expansion of all their senses that for a long time made them generally unfit to carry out their functions. The distinctive signs still attaching them to their caste faded away, and they fell back into the pleasant but monotonous existence of the tenants. Added to this was the shame that tormented their souls—at least during the first hours—and forced them to struggle in vain with themselves against the temptations to which they had already yielded. The consequences were so harsh for them that the very sight of the other inhabitants was unbearable, and if they ever thought they were exposed to it, they probably would have perished. For this reason, they would be locked in isolated cells where they remained for some forty days and where they believed themselves to be sheltered from the world. This was an illusion, for the tenants took such pleasure in seeing them thus—a pleasure that by the way was very pure and undisturbed by any feeling of revenge—that they could not do without this spectacle, and during the imprisonment they took turns standing in front of the door where a small sliding window was perfectly situated to offer them the delights that made them so curious.

"Is any of this unclear to you?" the young man asked obligingly.

Everything was indeed all too clear; Thomas looked with disgust at the cup that still held a little wine, and he stood up, dragging Dom along with him.

The room had grown dim. But the curious fact was that now there were several people on the platform holding in their hands a pitcher that emitted rays of light. Drawn by this sweet light, Thomas walked over to the table occupied by the two employees; several guests were drinking with them, and they stared at him with that insatiable curiosity they had so often shown already.

"Let's go," said Thomas to the two men.

"This is our tenant," answered the older of the two, but neither one of them got up to go with him.

"Well, I'm leaving," said Thomas.

He had to push against the spectators who crowded around him and blocked his way; one of them grabbed his arm and wanted to accompany him. "A sorry bunch," he thought. The faces he saw seemed eaten away by sickness, and their fine features appeared to be a sign of debility. The two employees, seeing themselves suddenly abandoned at their table, preferred to join the little company gathered around Thomas, and in a triumphant procession they went toward the door amid laughter, shouts, and even singing.

This gaiety was turned into disorder by another turn of events. The guardians on the platform raised their pitchers, and light filled the room. The flames enclosed in stoneware pots gave off such an intense brightness that everyone hid their faces to avoid the assault; and there were some, already half drunk, who fell to the ground believing they had been struck and who cried out with all their strength, although there was no real cause for this. Thomas stopped only for an instant. He wanted to leave the room as quickly as possible. What a dreadful meeting! In his desire to remain free, he wondered if it would be better to leave the two employees behind.

But these two, seeing his hesitation and thinking it was a sign of discouragement, held on to his arm as though to counterbalance Dom; and the four of them walked with long, hurried strides to the door.

A guardian was waiting for them. It was the man who had called to him on the balcony. He had broken his pitcher; its shards were scattered on the floor where the flame was gently burning. "You must separate," he said in his authoritarian voice.

"Is it really necessary?" asked Thomas.

"I have to take these two away," said the guardian, without answering directly.

"Then I'll keep you company," said Thomas, and all of them left together.

They very quickly reached their destination. The guardian was extremely familiar with the way there. It was still the same hallways and vestibules, only larger and brighter; one might have thought that the house was searching for freedom and carelessness in these paths leading nowhere, even though they were also part of a rigorous plan. They stopped in front of a giant stairway whose steps slowly rose and widened on the way up, such that at the very top they seemed to blend into the enormous landing of the first floor.

"You may go no farther," said the guardian firmly, although now in a more conciliating tone. "Your safe-conduct as a tenant is no longer valid beyond this point."

"What safe-conduct?" asked Thomas. "I am in possession of no such document."

"It would indeed be surprising if you had such a thing," said the guardian. "It is mentioned in the file that bears your name, and this file cannot be removed from the archive."

"I was not aware of this," said Thomas. "But in any event the authorization does not concern me. For it is not as a tenant that I wish to go to the first floor, it is in the capacity of a witness that I am obliged to accompany you."

The guardian reflected and said: "You recognize your role as a witness?"

"Can I do otherwise?" asked Thomas.

The guardian sidestepped the question, and putting out the lamp, he said: "Follow me, then."

At the top of the stairway there were three doors. Thomas chose the most modest of the three, but at the call of the guardian, he entered the large door in the middle with him. It was the infirmary. The room was enormous; since there were not many sick people, it seemed empty at first. The beds, covered with white sheets and set up in a long row one after the other, did not appear to be made for sleep. The guardian pushed Thomas and his companions into a tiny room, which must have been used as a waiting room, made up of two thin walls and closed by a curtain.

"You are responsible," he said, "for these men. As long as they have not received another place to stay, you cannot leave the room."

Thomas thought it useless to respond; his intention was not to obey orders but to follow his own path. He was therefore quite vexed when the employees, throwing themselves at his feet, begged his pardon and beseeched him not to abandon them.

"If you do," they said, "we will never be free again. We'll be locked in the infirmary or, even worse, in the room of a very sick man. We will never return to life."

"What fantasies you have," said Thomas, trying to pull himself out of their grip. "No such misfortune threatens you, and if you really were exposed to such misery, I would have no way of protecting you from it. I have no support in the house."

"No support?" they cried. "We can see that you don't want to help us; the others have no doubt told you all sorts of things and taught you to despise us. And yet we hoped that you would not give up your freedom of judgment so easily."

Then they suddenly changed the subject and began to ask him with great passion about his country, his memories of it, his adventures on the road. Thomas was very surprised by these questions. This was the first time anyone had spoken to him about the place he came from, and already he saw it as so distantly lost in the past that he no longer had the strength to direct his mind to it. He pushed away the two men who were still hanging onto him and kept silent. They remained there motionless until the old man, getting back up, said to him: "But you are our witness. If you are free in relation to us, you are not free in relation to the wrong we are accused of. You cannot abandon us. Otherwise, you would have to stand as guarantor for us and take care of our affairs at every instant."

Thomas was not about to get caught up in more explanations; he saw how trapped he was by the difficulties that had been revealed to him, and this weakened his resolution without helping him to see the goal any more clearly; nevertheless, he could not get rid of his obligations as a witness so quickly.

"I don't believe you," he said. "If I leave you, I will never have to think of you again, and you will never hear any more of me. On the contrary, it's only by staying with you that I would be constantly reminded of your miserable little affairs, and I have no desire for that."

"Don't leave us," they cried out again in unison, imploring him to be merciful. The younger one seemed on the point of losing consciousness. The older one pressed against his guardian and embraced his legs, which he seemed to be begging to stay where they were.

"Leave me alone," said Thomas in disgust. What abject creatures! How could he get rid of them? "What do you want from me?" he shouted finally.

The old man immediately straightened up and said: "There is a great deal that you can do, for your testimony is what will determine the treatment to which we will be condemned. You have no idea what threat hangs over us. Life in the hospital is hell. For days on end we will remain in a dark room where we will be forced to read endlessly over lines that have been minutely transcribed from some book. After a few hours of this, your eyes begin to water and to swell, and your sight grows blurry. After a day, night falls over everything; your gaze seizes on a few flaming letters that begin to burn through it. This night grows deeper and deeper with each hour, and although your eyes are still open, the darkness covering them is so great that they are not only extinguished, they become aware of their blindness and feel as though struck with a curse. The torture usually lasts a week; when this interval has passed, the patient who has not ceased to stare at the text, which he no longer sees, begins to perceive within himself, with perfect clarity, the words he reads and understands, and he regains his sight. And so it goes for each one of the senses. The most painful ordeal is the purification of the sense of hearing. The room in which they keep us prisoner is sealed off from all sound. At first you enjoy this silence, this peace. The world has been cast out of the place you now occupy, and the repose there is sweet. You do not even know that you are alone. The first dreadful moment comes from a word that the patient speaks out loud; it is apparently always the same: a name, I know not which one, a name that he pronounces at first indifferently, then with curiosity, and finally with a love full of anguish; but the sense of hearing, already desiccated by the silence, merely takes it as a word lacking all sensibility and warmth.

It is a strange and cruel discovery. The patient begins a conversation with himself in which he invests all his tenderness, and it is repeated to him with ever greater indifference. He speaks passionately, but what he hears is colder and more foreign to his life than any random word spoken by another man. The more heated passion he puts into his words, the more what he says leaves him frozen. If he calls on what is dearest to him in all the world, he perceives it as separated from him forever. How to explain this terrible anomaly? When he thinks about it, and of course he can only think by speaking, he sees that the words he hears are like those of a dead man; he hears himself as if he were already deprived of consciousness; he is his own echo in a world where he is no more; he undergoes the torture of receiving from somewhere outside his existence the words that have been the soul and the speech of his entire life. This impression is invaded by delirium. The ear becomes enormous and takes the place of the body. Everyone who goes through this believes he has been changed into this hearing in which the most beautiful songs, the most beloved words, and life itself die away in an eternal suicide. Then they open your room; they speak your name. You hear it as it deserves to be heard. After that comes the purification of the hands."

"That's enough," said Thomas. "The story you're telling me is probably supposed to soften me up; in this case, you have missed your target, for it has only increased my disgust. But if it is in accordance with the truth, then that's even worse, since only tremendous crimes could have merited such terrible punishments."

"That's not true," said the old employee, roughly seizing hold of Thomas. "They are not punishing us, and we have not committed any crime. And you, are you guilty? No, but you will be submitted to a similar treatment if you do not agree to help us."

"Absurd threats," said Thomas. "Why would I be exposed to the same punishments as you, when everything between us—our past, our behavior, our situation—is different?"

"Because of the infirmary," said the employee timidly.

"The infirmary?" asked Thomas.

"Yes," said the employee, "don't you know? Almost the entire first floor has been transformed into a vast infirmary where the very ill are cared for. These patients, because of their weakness and the nature of their malady, are particularly afraid of contagion, to such a point that whenever the proper precautions are not taken for approaching them, they contract all sorts of new diseases. They are therefore obliged at first to sequester anyone who must enter these spaces. This is called the disinfection stage."

Thomas reflected; the employee's remark was a very unpleasant surprise. "I will not be entering the rooms of the sick," he answered finally.

"How could you do otherwise?" said the employee. "Have you not come here as a witness?"

"No doubt," said Thomas.

"Well," said the employee, "then you will be forced to enter their rooms, at least ours, since you are the one who will be in charge of watching over us."

"But you're not sick," said Thomas.

"We will be," said the employee, with a groan. "I already feel ill at ease in this room. As for you, I am already beginning not to recognize you. You are almost another man, taller, stronger, the very image of your companion. You look at me with eyes that seem never to have looked at me before, and you have such an impeccable appearance. Oh!" he cried suddenly, "I have been oddly mistaken. You are not who I thought you were; you're the executioner."

He crept into a corner of the room, staring at Thomas with fearful eyes. "What am I going to do with these two drunks?" he asked himself. Could he leave them there? Would he be allowed to leave the room, and if he did, would he not have to cross through the large sick room? He spoke to the young employee who was sprawled out on the ground in a nearly inanimate state.

"Put a stop to this childishness," he said. "Don't try to mislead me with your lies. You seem to be less steeped in vice—can you not speak to me honestly instead of trying to make me complicit in your crimes?"

The young man—at this moment he seemed a mere boy—raised his imploring eyes to Thomas, but he could not speak. The old man shouted from his corner: "Be careful, Simon. Don't trust anything he says to you. He came with us only to be our torturer, and he's in a hurry to begin his task." Then he threw himself on the young man asking him to repeat what Thomas had said. The young man tried in vain to move his lips, but all he could do was grab the throat of his companion and give it a feeble squeeze.

"You," said the old employee, turning to Thomas. "Here's the fine result of your efforts. He can't talk anymore. Won't you please have mercy on him? He is still so young, and weak; I, who am old and sturdy, have many more reasons to be pitied. What would become of me if you scrupulously fulfilled your function?"

"I am not the executioner," said Thomas. "I have not been officially assigned to give you a thrashing; but if you persist in your shameful behavior, I will need no one else's order to inflict on you an exemplary punishment. Why," he added, "do you think I'm the executioner?"

"We see it in your eyes," said the old employee, raising himself up with a cringe. "Your way of looking is like that of a person who has been given a mandate. You don't look at us; you look at what you have to do to us. You don't see our fault; you keep your eyes focused on your action. All executioners are like that. Some of them are deaf and mute. What would they have to say or to hear since the truth is in their battering hands and their lashing whip. You, you're a natural born executioner, the kind that says: 'It's still not too late,' even when your knife has cut the throat of the culprit."

"We also see it in your hands," said the young employee, who had been drawn out of his stupor by the words of his companion, as if they had explained what was ailing him. "There was no need for you to touch me for me to know that they strike hard and handle the rod with severity. But when you strike me, think only of my fault."

"That's quite enough," said Thomas. "I don't know how you might have guessed that I could hurt you badly with my stick, but now you're certainly going to find out." He picked up a piece of wood that was lying on the table and struck the young employee several times; even before the blows reached him, he fainted. "Do you see this rod?" said Thomas to the old employee, who was already screaming. "I only wanted to show you what I would use to correct you if you continue to lie to me. Now answer my questions. Where did the guardian go?"

"We only have one guardian—you," said the employee.

"Watch the stick!" said Thomas. "There is another guardian, the one who brought us here and who must now be walking back and forth in front of some door."

The old man shook his head and said: "He's one of your countless subordinates. It's only natural that you don't know them all. As for myself, I was your servant, and you ignored me until today. It's unfortunate that you remember them only when it's time for a punishment."

"And don't forget it," said Thomas. "What did the guardian go to do?"

"He went to carry out your orders," said the old man.

"And what were my orders?" asked Thomas.

"To prepare the room where you're going to punish us."

"I could just as well punish you right here," said Thomas. "So that is not what I ordered him to do. Think of a better answer."

"You're a hard one," said the old man. "You sent him to get the message."

"That message again," said Thomas. "Why are you bringing it up too? You know then that someone was supposed to bring me a message? Perhaps you saw it? Perhaps you're the one who forgot to pass it on to me? That's no doubt why you're going to be punished."

"You're wrong," said the old man in a whining tone. "We did everything we could. I led you through the room as far as possible, and I even sent an emissary to you in the night to ask you not to take too long. Have I done wrong?"

Thomas looked at his stick, then at the employee, and said: "Wasn't it wrong to keep the message from me?"

The old man took a step back. "But," he said, "no one but you has mentioned it to me. No one has given me the slightest assignment to carry out for you. Who could know the affairs that concern you? The person you should be interrogating is yourself."

Thomas did not answer. He had hoped for something else. So this was all the help he was going to get: an old employee, just today driven out of his post, had, in the dark hours of the night in which he was trying to exonerate himself, reflected on something he had said and had dispatched a messenger who had not even carried out his mission. The messenger's failure could be explained by the insignificance of the message; they had called him with too weak a voice, one that had nothing to say and whose promises were empty. Thomas stared in anger at the old man, as though this man had stripped all value from the message by the simple fact of having gotten his base servant's thoughts mixed up with it.

"Now," he said, "things have become serious. I will not tolerate your equivocations any longer. What is the crime for which you are being prosecuted, both of you?"

"You have no right to interrogate us," said the employee. "If you are really the executioner, you are the one who will show us our crime in your punishment, and we will find out then what your reproach is. What good would the punishment do otherwise? Nevertheless, since in a certain way you have shown yourself to be good to us, since you did not hit us when I spoke of the message, I can tell you a few small things. We are not guilty as you imagine us to be; at least we have no idea about what it could be. Who has ever fulfilled their duties more scrupulously? We worked from morning to night, and when night came we rehearsed in our minds everything we had done, for fear that we might have neglected some order. Perhaps it is this very zealousness that was our undoing. By concentrating so much attention on it, we gradually developed a taste for service; whereas in the beginning we performed our tasks mechanically, not even watching what we were doing, with our eyes fixed on the commandment alone, but little by little we found ourselves attracted by the beauty and brilliance of our gestures, by the value of what passed through our hands, by the dignity of those who worked alongside us. When we were in the kitchen, we never grew tired of staring at all the utensils and implements. Before pouring water into them, we would caress them; we would slowly pass our fingers over their edges as though in search of a breach that would allow us to penetrate them, and from such contemplations we could not tear ourselves away. Likewise, when the liquid had flowed into the cups, we looked at it, wet our lips with it, and satisfied our thirst, and these too had become obligations that gave us infinite pleasure. Should we have resisted? Perhaps; but where was the harm, since it was for the sake of giving a greater perfection to the accomplishment of our tasks that we succumbed to these delights, and since we found joy in them only because we were good servants? And what was our crime, when so many others—who were not nearly as absorbed in their work as we were—gave in to much greater excesses than this? No doubt, this enthusiasm caused us to neglect some of the functions for which we were responsible. After lavishing so much care on the objects entrusted to us for these purposes, we could not bear to lose sight of them, to let them deteriorate in the hands of strangers. It was also our duty to prevent their destruction. Sometimes we hid them; at other times we flatly withdrew them from the use of tenants who were crude and insensitive. It was with deep sorrow that we poured into the clients' cups the beverage they were incapable of appreciating. We followed with mistrust these men who plodded their way through so many splendors without enjoying their beauty. This forced us to live a great deal among them. After spending many hours in rooms whose air seemed sweet with perfume and where everything one touched gave off a glow, it was difficult to climb back up to those dark regions where we could hardly breathe. We were called back downstairs. Serving has no meaning except where there are men to be served. We wanted to see how our work was changing the world, and this desire drew us into an unctuous promiscuity with that world. First, we had to renounce our noble tasks and accept the occupations of the servants that allowed us to have close relations with the tenants. These occupations are very tiring, but since they require great strength, those who go in for them are well nourished and are generally rather plump. That happened to us as well. We could no longer climb the stairs in the evening without panting and straining; sometimes we didn't reach the upper floors until night was over, and it was time to go back down again. What was the point of going up there? Were we not domestics in the large halls? To sleep, now that was what really tempted us, but at the time we had no way of realizing it. All we could think of was keeping close watch over our duties, all the while dreaming of tomorrow's tasks. Unfortunately, the nights downstairs were so hot that it was hardly possible to remain idle there. So we worked without pause. Although our limbs pained us, so heavily were they weighed down with fatigue, we walked all night long. Our ponderous steps could be heard all over. We looked like guardians, and indeed we kept watch over our own sleep. Alas, what can one do against the night? To sleep, that was our dream, and we could not escape it."

"You have told me nothing I did not already know," said Thomas. "Gluttons, thieves, idlers—one can see all that just by looking at you. To what hands, then, did I entrust my message?"

"But you don't know anything yet," replied the employee. "We did no wrong, and there is nothing to reproach us with. Were we not domestics? Even sleeping was not a serious offense; we merely had to take precautions not to be discovered. Our misfortune came from elsewhere. When we resolved to give in to sleepiness, we felt a great joy; finally we would taste this sweet repose that had evaded us. What an illusion! It was to our own torment that we had just given in. The first night we spent in the small room just off the gaming room. Was it emotion, was it desire, or excessive fatigue? We tossed and turned in vain on a crude and ragged bed of our own making. Our eyes received from within a sort of light that woke them like the day. Our limbs snatched at shadows and trembled in a fever that only increased their fatigue without preparing the way to their rest. We

125

heard words being spoken—our own. It was a terrible night. The break of day restored our hope. We could no longer believe that our torture would have no end. Alas, the second night was just like the first, and the third added its cruelty to the memory of the other two. Search as we might for favorable locations, we were only tormented all the more by the rest that eluded us precisely there where it most seduced us. We kicked tenants out of their rooms and took over their beds; a pointless injustice, for the thought of the sleep they themselves had so often found there chased our own away and left us broken and miserable in the morning. Then it happened that the day, far from relieving our sufferings, only increased them by arousing our desire. Hardly had we emerged from the night when fatigue began to weigh us down, and the need to sleep pressed our eyes closed. We would shamelessly collapse into a corner, but here again it was only to knock against that high white wall erected between our sleep and us. What miserable wretches we were! We searched in vain for the rest that the day brought so near to us and from which the night continually chased us away. And yet these were only minor sufferings. Our true distress began when Simon decided to speak to the maidservant about our insomnia. This desire shows how unhinged his mind had become. For he suffered not only from lack of sleep but also from the silence he had to maintain about his long wakeful nights. They condemned him to a solitude that, young as he is, he could only think of avoiding. He, at all costs, had to find someone on whom to unload his burden. It seemed to him that it would almost be the same as sleeping if only he could confide to another the thought of his sleepiness. Obviously I was there, and he was able to talk about it with me. But at the time, he had taken an extreme dislike to me, so that merely to lay eyes on me or to hear my voice threw him into a state of anxious confusion that only increased his discomfort. He said that with me he felt more alone than if the house were nothing but a great void. It's understandable. My face reflected all the pains that weighed on him. I could barely open my eyes, and the look he saw there was so hazy and so obscure that he thought I must have been sleeping on my feet and that I was hiding from him the consolations thus granted me. What would he have said if he could have seen himself? His entire being consisted of sleepiness. If he spoke, it was the beginning of a dream; if he listened, it was through a thick partition that made him mistake what he said for what he heard. He was as much a stranger to himself as to others, as if he had

126

withdrawn from his own body so as not to have any contact with the sleeping thing it had become. So he would continually say: 'Nothing can stop me, soon I will tell.' Whom would he tell? I thought he had in mind some tenant or other, or perhaps, at worst, an employee. He was already long past that. From that moment on, he stalked around the maidservant, and she, with her perverted nature, did all she could to attract him."

"The maidservant?" said Thomas.

"Yes, the maidservant," said the employee. "Don't you know her?"

"Barbe?" said Thomas.

"Yes, Barbe, if you wish," said the employee. "That's one of her names. So—Barbe, far from pushing him away, as her duty would have dictated, made little friendly signs to him and spoke to him whenever he came close enough to hear what she was saying. In other circumstances, he would have scorned such things. But the state in which he found himself led him to judge differently, and this ridiculous coquetry seemed to cause him an incredible pleasure. Or rather it lulled him into mad hopes. These meetings, although they took place from afar, left him upset and anguished. He didn't know what to think of his dream. These distant rendezvous occurred only rarely, and during the time in between he was full of extraordinary thoughts nourished by his fever, thoughts whose bizarre character he had no way of discerning. One of them was that if he could only touch her dress, he would immediately fall asleep. With such fantasies, he was lost indeed. And yet a considerable amount of time passed before things became truly serious. Barbe still did not approach him, and when she shouted at him to wait for her, he could stay for hours and even days right where he was when he saw her, but he waited in vain. So he decided, since this waiting was causing him to lose touch with his reason, to seek her out himself, and he began to wander through the corridors and the rooms, wherever he might hope to find her. Naturally she was nowhere to be found. But was she really? I believe that in his distracted state he often passed her without recognizing her and that, since she cared nothing for him, she herself hardly noticed him and so let him go by. But one day he found her. I was with him. He ran toward her as though he were about to sacrifice her. But he stopped a few steps away, and without catching his breath, in the same breath that his running had already impaired, he told her everything that a confused mind such as his own could express about his confusion, his madness, the void that was choking him. What sense did she make of it?

As she listened, she waved her hands in my direction and greeted me in the most pleasant way. From that moment, so it seems to me, I was the one she was determined to have, I who was older, more reasonable, more difficult to lose—or rather, alas, easier to corrupt. Simon didn't notice any of this, and in any case he would have put up with anything. When he finished his little speech, she smiled at him, called him her sweetheart, and promised to come see him. When she left him, she waved to me again. The strange thing is that a few moments later, while my poor companion had not yet recovered from the agitation these few words had caused him and seemed to be spinning in circles and wrapped in a haze, she came back and led him away. I didn't see him until a few hours later. He seemed even more distraught and miserable, but in answer to my questions, he claimed that he had slept. How could that be? He had the look of a man who had wandered through the woods a whole night long without finding a way out; he was still looking, but now he had no idea what he was looking for; he began his work, and his activity was more alarming than his torpor, for he seemed to have forgotten who he was, and the enthusiasm he showed only testified to his complete absence of mind. He had other meetings with the maid-servant. Sometimes he would come back with a transformed and radiant face, a superb youthfulness; at other times he was ravaged and almost on the point of death; and yet it was his youthful appearance that startled me; one would have thought that he bore the mark of his condemnation and that he was no longer of this world. One day he told me that Barbe wished to see me. I went to meet her in one of the rooms on the first underground floor where she often goes. Hardly had I closed the door when she threw herself around my neck with a kiss and sat me down on the bed. Then she told me she had been waiting for me to come to her for a long time, that I had certainly taken my time in catching on, that she had noticed, however, that I had a weakness for her, but that I was no doubt annoyed by her conversations with Simon. How did I respond to her? I could hardly make out her words; I looked at the room we were in and did not recognize it; it seemed to me that I had been there once before but in very different circumstances, with a heart as light as it was heavy now, and with senses that reached out to things I could no longer touch. But she laughed at my response and said that seeing me from close up, she found me very young, that my age was a question of distance, that if one tried to think of me, it was impossible to form in one's mind a face so obscured by time, but that from now on she would run to me with her eyes closed, waiting to open them until she could see the delicate texture of my skin and the length of my eyelashes. What did it all mean? Alas, what did anything mean to me? This conversation today seems to have taken place in a world I never actually saw, although scarcely a day has passed between now and then. In the end, she asked me to give her a keepsake. 'I don't have anything,' I told her. She didn't believe me and reached into my pockets. 'That's what I want,' she said. It was my employee's badge, a little notebook whose pages had been taken out to pad my dossier. I tried to get it back from her, but she placed it on her knees and contemplated it in silence with a serious look on her face. I looked at it too but made no more effort to take her property from her; it was no longer mine. I said to myself: 'It is done.' I had the impression that I was losing everything but also that I was rid of everything, and for the first time I thought with pleasure of this conversation that up to then had brought me only discomfort, anguish, and distress. She stood up, patted my hand with affection, and gently led me from the room. You can guess what happened after that. She must have said something against me, and I was turned over to the tenants."

Thomas nodded his head, as if in approval. "Where is Barbe?" he asked. The old employee looked at him sadly.

"Do you want to question her?" he said. "It isn't easy to question her. She often refuses to answer, and when she does, it isn't always clear whether what she says bears any relation to what you have asked her. And if you ask her questions about us, there's no telling what she might say. Does she even know our names? Does she remember such insignificant incidents as these? Does she not have a completely different understanding of what happened? There's no way to know what she thinks."

"Are her occupations really so absorbing," asked Thomas, "that she doesn't remember events from one day to the next? She has some influence here, no?"

"Why are you trying to tempt me?" said the old man in a whining voice. "Of course she plays an important role. Any statement to the contrary would be a lie. But who isn't important in the house? I too had a position and wielded influence. Perhaps," he added, after reflecting a moment, "I still do."

"Well, then," said Thomas, "I have influence because I can punish you, if I want."

"No," said the old man, "you really can't do much of anything; you're only the executioner. That's why I fear you."

"Really now," said Thomas, "I'm not so fearsome. I am only asking that you tell me where Barbe is; if you do, then I'll help you."

"That's not the right question," said the old man. "I'm afraid that things are taking a wrong turn for us. Where's the maidservant?" he said, addressing Simon. Then, answering himself, he continued in a deep voice as if he were questioning himself. "Which Barbe is he talking about? Is it the same one? Aren't there several? Do we ever know whom it is we're dealing with? When she was speaking to me, did I not have the impression that there was a confusion of names and that the woman in front of me had neither the figure nor the features of the one who had called to me? And what was it she said? That she never leaves the first floor, that if she strays from the infirmary, even for a moment, all the patients would be lost, that she cannot even look in the other direction without their suffering from some terrible transformation. So someone, or several people, would take her place for the work in the basement. Or she would have a substitute in the hospital. Or else, as others claim, she long ago contracted a deadly disease and has been relieved of all her work."

Thomas interrupted him. "What a lot of foolishness. I saw a maidservant named Barbe who was not sick but was cleaning the rooms, and who worked in the basement, not in the hospital. She's the one I want to see, and you will not dissuade me by turning things around like this."

Straining his ears and pressing his lips together, the old man listened anxiously; he was sitting on the floor and tried unsuccessfully to get up. "But that's the Barbe who spoke to me about you. She also wanted to see you. She asked me if I had met you, what you looked like, if you liked the house. I said yes, without knowing; I had no idea who you were."

"But she had already seen me," said Thomas pensively.

"Perhaps," said the old man, "but she also wanted to see you through the eyes of another."

Thomas did not answer. He turned for a moment toward the door, as if to expel everything he had heard, then he shouted at the two employees: "You're free. Run to Barbe, both of you, and tell her that I want to talk to her right away."

"But," they answered together, "we're not allowed to leave."

"Alright then," said Thomas, "since I'm allowed to punish you, let the punishment begin."

He took up the piece of wood and struck them sharply but without any real cruelty. During the punishment, the guardian opened the door and came in. Without interrupting the beating, Thomas said: "They refused to obey."

Then, since he felt tired, he threw down the stick and waited. The guardian had brought with him three large white gowns that looked like the patients' gowns, although they were more shiny and silky.

"Put these on," he said.

The two employees, subdued by the beating, obeyed immediately; they showed no more signs of the stupefied terror that was so repulsive and seemed irresistibly to invite blows; the younger one, although his face was covered with red streaks, had regained all his vigor. Thomas thought they were just as hypocritical as they were cowardly. The third gown lay flat on the table where the lamplight made it shine with a beautiful golden color. Thomas saw that it was his size, and he put it on, saying to himself all the while—in order to fight off the slight shiver he felt while touching the material—that he would take it off at the first free opportunity. Only Dom kept the same clothes on.

Before leaving, the guardian put out the light and said: "Now keep silent; the patients cannot tolerate any noise."

So they were going to walk through the hospital. Hardly had they crossed the threshold when Thomas, who was in front, stopped short. The darkness was total; it was darker, he thought, than the night he had entered when he left the gaming room. What peace! He had already had this impression with the old man in the basement, but whereas there one remained a stranger to the tranquility that lay all around, here one was a part of the calm, and although it was a calm without hope, it inspired only one desire: to go no farther and to linger indefinitely. Thomas remained motionless only for a few seconds; the guardian called him to order, saying in a voice he made little attempt to soften: "Keep moving please."

Since it was forbidden for him to stop, he stepped slightly aside from the straight line they had formed and went into the little walkways that no doubt led to the patients' bedsides. He walked slowly, his hands out in front of him, his eyes wide open. Finally he knocked up against a small table and raised his voice in surprise. Dom's steady hand held him. Was he trying to stop him from moving forward, or was he pushing him on? Was he, too, lost in the shadows? He then knocked against something himself, and this second shock only increased the strangeness of the first.

"Too much noise, too much noise," yelled the guardian.

Thomas wanted to go back to the middle of the room. Suddenly the light came on. The large hall was visible in all its immensity. The beds were lined up side by side, and at the foot of each one was a small wooden trunk that looked like the first step of a stairway. The beds were empty. Several of them seemed to have been carelessly made, but most of them probably had not had a patient in them for a long time. Thomas looked especially at the trunks. They were large boxes painted in lively colors that hurt one's eyes if stared at too intently. They were used for storing medication. Thomas was absorbed in this contemplation until he noticed again the presence of the guardian, who was undoing Dom's chains.

"Go wait for me outside," said the guardian to the young man, who, free of his fetters, walked toward the vestibule.

Thomas walked away too. He came to the middle of the large space, and seeing that the doors at each end were open, he turned his back to his companions and crossed in a few steps to the other side of the room.

He entered another vestibule, and the first person he saw was Barbe. The maidservant gave him a friendly smile. She was seated at a small table where she had spread out large pieces of cloth. The material seemed rough, and it was difficult to stick the needle through.

"Now that," said Thomas, "is a tough piece of work for you."

Barbe nodded very seriously.

"When do you have a chance to rest?" he added. "I never see you when you're not in the middle of some enormous chore. You don't seem to be like the other employees."

"Everyone here works a lot," she said. "There is so much to do in a house like this."

"But," said Thomas, "I think you work more than the others. What are you doing now?"

"As always, it's work for the sick," she said, with a sigh. "It never ends."

Without speaking, Thomas studied her pretty face: it had a tired look; her remarkably fine features showed no satisfaction; everything that gave her confidence, and even a certain pretension, had disappeared.

"Pardon me," he said. "If I'm intruding into your affairs, please don't hesitate to tell me so. But I can't help seeing how tired your lovely face looks. Do you have many worries?"

The maidservant ran her hand over her face, closed her eyes for a moment, as though to gather her thoughts, and managed finally to smile. "It's always like this," she said, "when there are new patients. Worries? No, why would I have worries? But the work is overwhelming, and one hardly knows where to begin." Nevertheless, she sat there calmly enough, and her fingers negligently pulled through the black thread that fringed the cloth.

"Are there a lot of new patients?" asked Thomas.

"How would I know?" she said. "The staff keeps it a secret. Just try to find out what's happening. All they do is give us commands—and how they bark at us!—commands to put everything in order, as if the entire house were to be transformed into a hospital. Sometimes a dozen patients come, sometimes one, sometimes none. All the while we're working day and night."

"Improper methods," said Thomas. "But," he added, "since I have the pleasure of seeing you here, and we can speak freely, tell me: wasn't there some question of a message for me not long ago?"

"A message?" said the girl in a questioning tone. "Are you sure?"

"Completely sure," replied Thomas. "I certainly didn't dream it. We were on the first underground floor, and you had asked me to leave my room. You were at that moment in the middle of a large cleaning job. I remember your words, more or less; you said: 'I have a message for you.' And then you added: 'Go wait until I'm finished.'"

"I remember our meeting very well," said the girl. "It was even a very pleasant meeting for me. How energetic you were, how strong and determined you looked! But did I really speak of a communication?"

"Not exactly of a communication," said Thomas, "rather a message. But see if you still remember the circumstances of our discussion, because then it should be plain; I was a little afraid that you had forgotten everything. You recall how I followed you around to the rooms, and we stayed a while with a very old man who, according to you, was faking his illness. I lingered there for a moment, and at the time I didn't know how quick you were, and I lost you."

That was not quite the truth, as Thomas himself knew; it was he who had voluntarily left the girl to find his way alone, but there was no need for her to know this.

"Didn't you have a companion?" she asked.

"Yes, I did," said Thomas, annoyed that she was letting her thoughts wander away from what he was saying. "We were just separated."

133

"That's too bad for you, isn't it?" she said. "Now you'll be left to decide and to act on your own. Wasn't he very tall and strong?"

She looked carefully at Thomas; he had the impression that at first she had confused the two of them in her memory. "This message," she continued, "perhaps it was meant for your companion."

"That's impossible," said Thomas emphatically. "Think about it: I could not have made such a mistake. When we were together, the three of us, and despite our good relations, you treated us somewhat differently, my partner and me; it never would have occurred to me to think that something you said to him was meant for me. You would no doubt have put things in a completely different way. How could anyone think you were speaking to him?"

"Yes, I see," said the girl. "I would have said: A message has been submitted to me, which the regulations forbid me to impart to you; I could do so only if it were official business; you must therefore wait until I have terminated my work so that I may confer with you at a time other than my assigned working hours."

"You're joking," said Thomas, although the girl had spoken very seriously. "What language! It might have been necessary to use such solemn expressions with me, insofar as I was a tenant, were it not that we had dispensed with that type of relationship from the beginning. But with my companion! You would have laughed at it yourself. If you will just think about it for a moment, you will recall that it was quite the contrary. I would be glad to repeat to you the words you used. May I do so?"

"Go ahead then," said Barbe, who had stopped her work the better to follow the conversation.

"I'm afraid I may shock you," said Thomas. "Nevertheless, since you give me permission, I will try, for this may not be irrelevant to our discussion. But you must help me. Am I mistaken or did you not call him 'my sweetheart'?"

"Why not?" said Barbe.

"Did you not also say 'this little pet, this little darling'? Of course, in your mind it was only a question of some friendly terms meant to put him at ease, with no other intention. And yet a stranger such as myself, who up to then had only had dealings with very formal employees, could not fail to be surprised by this. Since things do not happen here the way they do elsewhere, I was tempted to find a special meaning in this way of speaking."

134

"But," said Barbe, "there was nothing in any of that to be surprised about. That's the natural way of speaking among employees."

"Among employees?" asked Thomas. He would have liked to leave it at that, but he could not help adding: "Dom—do you remember him? this name was your invention—Dom was not an employee."

This was not a question; it was even, to judge by the categorical tone he had used, a statement that ruled out any possible response; this did not prevent the girl from declaring: "Well, what was he then?"

"I don't wish to elaborate on this subject at the moment," said Thomas. "What I have said to you already is enough to show the unlikelihood of any confusion of language between him and me. In addition, if a moment ago you thought that the message might have been addressed to him— which certainly must appear impossible to you now—then it must be the case that you have not forgotten him and that a little effort will be enough for you to remember him perfectly. Now let me ask you some questions. Was this message from you, or was someone sending it through you?"

"How can I answer you?" said the girl. "In principle, I could only be serving as an intermediary; what could I have had to say, I who did not know you? And even if I had known you better, whether through hearsay or through direct relations, I could never have taken it upon myself to speak with you about something important without calling on powers other than my own."

"From your remark, then, I can draw two conclusions," said Thomas. "First, the message was important. And then, it is likely that some other person had given it to you."

"I said nothing of the kind," answered the girl. "How can you interpret my words in such a way? And yet it is clear that if the communication were really important, and if someone had placed it in my hands, I could not have forgotten it; all the circumstances of the incident would be clearly present in my mind; I would recall every last detail of it. But you can be excused," she added, "for you do not know that I am renowned for my memory. Whatever someone has said to me, I am capable of repeating it ten years later without leaving out a single word."

"A good quality that can be counted among all the rest," said Thomas. "And it will greatly facilitate our little research efforts. Let us admit then that what you had to tell me was not necessarily of very great interest, at least in your eyes—although for me it is a different matter entirely—and

135

that it had to do with a few personal reflections you wished to address to me: does it not surprise you, you who are so spontaneous, so unaffected by your privileges, that in order to announce them to me, you used the rather emphatic term 'message'? In your view, is such an expression suitable for remarks that had to remain outside the scope of your service? Are there not grounds here for reflection?"

Before responding, Barbe took up her sewing again, as if her work would support her during the discussion. She seemed to attach great importance to the conversation; at first Thomas was delighted by this, but soon it began to worry him. After passing the needle through the cloth, she said: "In any event, my words could not have had anything to do with the service, otherwise I would have communicated them to you while I was working."

"Then their value was not as great as I had thought?" asked Thomas.

"On the contrary," replied the girl, with a sad smile. "Unfortunately, they were all the more valuable. After all, we're not automatons; even during work hours we can allow ourselves to make remarks that do not involve our occupation; in general, we are very free to speak as we wish. But of course it is a completely different question if during our work we have some distant thought or memory that we could not express without impropriety; so we save it for another moment, because if we spoke right then, we might risk never getting back to work; we continue to work, and, in the meantime, we forget whatever it was, which is a good thing for all concerned. Now you can understand," she added, with a happier smile, "why this whole affair slipped from my memory."

"I can understand," said Thomas. "But it only makes me wish all the more that it would arise again from oblivion. Mlle Barbe, you used an expression whose meaning escaped me. You spoke of a 'distant thought or memory.' Could you explain what you meant by that?"

"No," said Barbe, "I cannot."

Thomas did not take this answer seriously.

"This refusal," he said, "is supposed to put an end to my curiosity, but it is so aroused at the moment that I cannot rest content with that, and at the risk of being indiscreet, I will ask you another question. Are you thinking of your private life when you speak of things as 'distant,' or are you afraid, on the contrary, of putting your service into question in a way that would run counter to what is expected of you?"

The girl did not answer; she was involved in her work, and Thomas

136

could not tell whether she was too absorbed to speak to him or whether she would have refused under any circumstances to say anything more.

"I will not insist," he said. "Nevertheless—but please do not take my remark the wrong way—it saddens me a little to see how you are pushing me away; I sense that I have suddenly lost your trust and that I will not regain it. I am all the more affected by this in that this trust represented for me something very precious and even a unique benefit; for since I have been in the house, I have only had to do with people who are malevolent, scheming, and, in a word, extraordinarily deceitful. For the first time, I found myself with you as with someone to whom I could say or ask anything. Now I can see that this is finished, and I can only excuse myself for the clumsiness that caused me to lose my last hopes. I should probably go."

"Stay," said Barbe in a harsh tone, as if in losing the girl's trust Thomas had also lost the right to leave. He stayed without saying anything more. He was growing tired again and began to feel the aftereffects of his jaunt through the large hall of the infirmary.

"I have some questions to ask of you as well," said Barbe. "Why does this business of the message mean so much to you?"

"What a strange question," remarked Thomas. "How could it be otherwise? The message was supposed to come from you, and you in turn come from regions to which it is difficult to gain access and which attract me irresistibly. Your thoughts were the only path that could have allowed me to reach these regions. Now here I am cut off from them. Should I declare myself satisfied after all this? If I struggled clumsily, if, at the risk of displeasing you, I insisted on knowing what the message was, it is because its discovery was of great importance to me, and I know of no misfortune more cruel than to be deprived of it."

"You are always exaggerating everything," said the girl. "This message may not have had so much importance; perhaps it was important only to me. What was it, to judge from your point of view? A recommendation, a piece of advice, or else a communication that, as a momentary impression led me to think, had to do with your person. All this was probably not negligible, but that is no reason to torment yourself over not finding out what it was. It would be closer to the truth to think the opposite. You have been in the house long enough to know that there is no great interest in being informed about too many things. You cannot repeat this to yourself often enough."

"I am very touched," said Thomas, "by your efforts to soften my disappointment. But what kind of man would I be if you had convinced me? A piece of advice from you—Mlle Barbe, do you imagine that I could easily accept being deprived of it? And perhaps it was more than advice. Did you not speak of a communication?"

Barbe put down her work and looked at him with a sigh, but without appearing to be angry.

"You behave like a child," she said. "You place too much meaning on certain words, while you completely neglect others for reasons no one can guess. I was already struck by that when I saw you for the first time, and that is what must have made me postpone my remarks. Who knows what great significance you might have seen in them! Such a fuss over a few words! At the same time, in other cases one can spell everything out, and you refuse to pay any attention."

"What then have I overlooked?" asked Thomas.

"Our appointment," said the girl.

"Our appointment?" said Thomas. "Now that's a surprise. Was there ever any question of an appointment?"

"I've caught you," she said. "It was quite useless for me to ask you to wait for me so that we might meet up again. You did not take my offer seriously."

"I took your offer very seriously," said Thomas. "Not only did I wait for you, I even followed you; I watched your every step and did not want to miss a single word of your explanations, and if in the end, despite my attentiveness, I could not keep you from disappearing, I would have had even less of a chance of finding you by standing around passively waiting for you."

The girl shook her head despondently.

"Under such conditions," she said, "it was impossible for you not to lose your way. It was a fatal move. What I had asked of you—and this demand had its price, but you did not want to see that—was to wait for me without any useless exertions, without trying to search on your own for something you could never attain. Was that so difficult? You had only to remain in your corner. But that was probably too much for your strength. Impatient as you are, you preferred to follow me into the rooms, at the risk of becoming absorbed in what you saw, and you let me walk away so as to pursue your path as you wished."

"It wasn't such a bad path to take," said Thomas, "since it has led me once again to you."

"No," said the girl, "everything is different now. Downstairs I could still help you; I was less bound to my service; I did not have to account to anyone for what I did; and you, you were another man; your healthy appearance was attractive, as was the overflowing strength that was so great you hardly knew what to do with it and that made you overlook the danger you were in. However ignorant you may have been, one would have thought that you would stay away from the miserable exertions in which everyone here loses himself. Instead of that, you chose another way, a prideful way in which even I cannot follow you."

"These are grave reproaches," said Thomas, "and they are certainly justified. But since I feel how terribly serious they are, without, however, being able to grasp their meaning completely, and since I now mistrust all my bad interpretations, I would be grateful to you for telling me everything you are thinking. It's true, I was wrong not to wait for you; perhaps a long patience would have been necessary; how much time would I not have given up to live with the single hope of your return! But I continue to believe that the damage is not irreparable; it even seems to be partly repaired. What would that ambitious path have been that would have led away from you and toward my own loss? I see but one path, the one that has allowed me to find you again."

"To find me again?" said the girl. "Do you think you have found me again? That would only be an illusion. You have certainly learned a great deal since our first encounter; you have come to know many people; you have wandered this way and that. What else can I say to you? You know too much about it to listen to me; my warnings could not divert you from the slope you're sliding down."

The girl wanted to take up her work again, but Thomas pushed the cloth aside—the fabric seemed rough and unpleasant to the touch—and he placed his hand on her arm.

"Mlle Barbe," he said to her, "I know that you have decided to remain silent; in vain would I beg you to speak; there is then nothing impertinent in my prayers; they are not meant to change your mind but to make it known to you that you have said everything that could be said to take away my last bit of strength, without saying anything that might restore it to me. In these conditions, it would have been better to leave me to the errors from which—who knows?—I might have escaped with the courage still remaining to me. Do you realize the state you have put me in? Where can I go now? What can I do? If I listen to you, there is nothing left but to disappear."

"For heaven's sake," said the girl, "if only you were really at the end of your strength and my words were able to discourage you and turn you away from everything you have in mind. I could wish nothing better for you. But you still have all too much courage. What I fear in your case is not despair—when it comes, if it ever does, it will be too late—but an unbridled and unlimited hope. What good would my advice do for you? Are you at all inclined to follow it? Have you even decided really to listen to it? Have you not already had enough of this discussion that is keeping you from your plans?"

"This time you are going too far," said Thomas. "I must ask you to reconsider the negative opinion you have formed of me; I don't know what your reasons are. Please think of my situation. Why would I want to abandon the only support I could count on, even though now, despite my supplications, I sense that it too will no longer be there for me? To whom could I turn? Do you know of any other protection I may have? Is there by chance someone watching over me?"

"That way too will lead you astray," said the girl. "It would be better for you to keep silent."

Thomas obeyed the order and said nothing in response; besides, he was tired of talking; each word was diminishing his strength, as if in speaking it, he had to overcome the impression that it would be useless. So he remained there quietly, after taking his hand away from her arm, where he had rested it this whole time, and without even looking up to see if she had begun her work again. It seemed to him that she was much too distant from him and that trying to look at her had no more sense than trying to make her understand him. The girl, after a few moments, tugged at his gown to get his attention; she stared at him with her gray expressionless eyes; then she turned away and said to him: "Where do you think you are right now?"

Thomas wanted to answer: in the infirmary, but he said that he did not know.

"I too," she said, "often have the feeling of not knowing. When I see you sitting there quietly, with no idea of the place where you happen to be, I ask myself if I am not the one who is in error and if we are not together in a peaceful country house amidst the fields, in a foreign land, in one of those

140

distant countries whose memory has faded away. These," she added, "are the dangerous reveries your ignorance drives me to. How could you resist it yourself?"

"So we are not on the floor for the sick?" asked Thomas.

"Please," she said, "don't speak of them to me. Let me enjoy some other thoughts for a moment. What frightens me when I look at you is your conviction that you have traveled a long road and have already arrived somewhere. Even if you were not foolish enough to believe that you were approaching the goal, you still think that the goal has at least come closer. 'How far I have come,' you murmur in silence to yourself, 'since I first met her in the basement!' An error, a tragic error. How can you imagine that you have left your room, how can you think that the decision from above could have been abolished by the mere fact that you have eluded it, how can you attach more importance to appearances than to the ineluctable will of those on whom you depend? Do you have even the vaguest sense of your aberration? On what do you base your hopes? The testimony of your poor, tired senses? The assurance of your perverted and confused memory? You have been reduced to that. Don't say anything: I see on your lips what you want to say, and there is no reason to be proud of it. What are you thinking? That, despite your desire to believe me, you cannot reject as a sad illusion the path that has brought you here. Naturally; who has said anything to the contrary? Don't ascribe such ridiculous ideas to me. But all your walking, your inquiries, your behavior, however real they may be— and they are incontestably real; no one, unfortunately for you, will deny them—all your little personal comings and goings have no importance. You could work your way up and down for years on end and pass through the house from top to bottom a thousand times, and the truth would not be affected in the least. Who would be troubled by any of this? The worse thing that can happen would be if you managed, by some mad turn of fate, to reach those inaccessible regions of which you have spoken with such incredible levity. What would happen then? I have no way of knowing. But one thing cannot be doubted: anyone who saw you there would perceive you in reality to be where you ought to be, where you really are—in your basement room, with the clothes, the countenance, and the thoughts that are associated with that abode and that will follow you wherever you go. That is the truth. You can struggle as much as you like, turn to unreasonable ruses, do only as you see fit, but you will not escape the classification that follows from this truth. No matter what you happen to accomplish, the only result of your exertions will be to exhaust your strength in vain, to debilitate yourself in a morose state of reverie, until the moment when you no longer have even enough force to hold yourself in the last place left to you. You are in danger of meeting with such an end."

Was she finished? Thomas wondered. He still heard the room vibrate from this flow of speech, and it was difficult for him to distinguish, in these words that struck his ear, what belonged to the past and what was still present. To interrupt this whirl of words that was wearing him down, he made an effort to speak: "It is not always clear to me," he said, "whether your remarks are meant to reveal to me the fate that awaits me or to help me turn away from it." Then he added in a low voice: "May I ask you to speak more slowly? It's not always easy for me to follow you."

The girl did not answer, or at least Thomas did not hear her. She had placed the large cloth on her knees and was now busily sewing it; it seemed that suddenly the long neglected task could no longer be delayed.

"So what was I saying?" she said suddenly. "Perhaps I have been too hasty. Things do not always happen as I have explained them to you. There are almost as many different cases as there are people in this house. We who see things from a certain distance, we do not place much emphasis on the details, and to us everything seems to be lost in the same uniformity. But for those who attend more closely to their efforts, and especially for those who really want them to succeed, things are completely different; they are convinced that an abyss separates some people from others, and this conviction shows in their often completely opposite way of interpreting events. This fragmentary and disordered view of things comes from the fever with which they try to seize hold of everything, whereas they can hardly see a few steps in front of them. Who could ever encompass the entire house from within and contemplate it from its heights to its depths in a single glance? Neither you nor probably anyone else."

Thomas watched her anxiously as she continued her sewing work in a rhythm that grew steadily faster; the needle easily pierced the material; the black thread made outlines in beautiful geometric patterns on the fabric. This spectacle both frightened Thomas and reassured him. By staying there and doing nothing, it seemed to him that he was falling under a pernicious influence, exhausting all his courage and making it impossible for him ever to get up and leave; but he also enjoyed a certain mild, pleasant feeling, and he began to have more hope.

142

"I was a witness in a matter concerning the employees," he said suddenly.

"A meaningless affair," said the girl, without interrupting her work.

"Should I not follow it?" asked Thomas.

"Certainly," she said. "But you will follow it in any case."

"How do you mean?" he asked again.

"You must have heard a lot about the staff," she said in a slightly sharp tone, as if she herself had nothing to say about it. "But that is a subject devoid of interest, and there is no need to discuss it at any length. Seen from below, the life of the employees seems extraordinary and gives rise to violent passions. Here, it is something that passes virtually unnoticed. Higher up, there is certainly never any question about it. Do not go creating for yourself worries that would supposedly disappear if you had a different status. The affair you speak of will make use of you as long as you remain within the circle of its influence; it will vanish as soon as you have left it."

"Don't you know these employees?" said Thomas.

"Always more questions," answered the girl, with a look of annoyance. "Don't waste your strength in such a foolish way. How could I not know them? I know them all. It may be true that I remember them individually only when I see them on the lower floors. Otherwise there is no way to think of the staff except as a solid block; they are so similar to each other that it is impossible to distinguish them in one's memory. And why would we distinguish them? Are there hundreds of them, is there only one? If they fulfill their duty, it's as if they don't exist; if they fall back into the common lot, they are always too numerous. Abandon these superfluous problems; it is not by reflecting on them that you will change the course of things."

"But aren't you part of the staff?" asked Thomas.

"What if I am?" said the girl. "It's always possible to say that one belongs to the staff, just as one can always claim to be a tenant. Will the ceiling fall on your head if you assert that you are a porter in the house? Nothing will happen, and bolstered by such an experience, you can confidently display your title to the ordinary clientele."

"I understand what you're saying," said Thomas anxiously. "But in speaking of you, I was thinking of something quite different. Upon seeing you, it does not occur to one to think of how busy you are, of the services you perform, or of your situation, which must be considerable; one's mind is on very different things. There is rather an image of something very new that is not quite clear at first and that, even when one has a sense of it, is never easy to grasp. Perhaps you bring with you an evocation of the world you come from; and perhaps this evocation is not always manifest to us, and our eyes can only perceive it from time to time. Then one cannot look at you without despair; but it is also true that one cannot stay with you without being comforted."

"You are getting lost in illusions," said the girl. "On my face I bring with me nothing but the evocation of fatigue and the traces of a life weighed down by responsibilities. The world you speak of has not left any memories; there is no way to preserve even the smallest particle of something that can only be enjoyed when one remains a stranger to it."

"I am probably chasing after phantoms," said Thomas, "but how could I resist them? I watch you working, and all I have before me is the prospect opened by my recent loss. You spared nothing in taking away all my hope; I am surrounded by misfortune; and yet I make no effort to leave. Something therefore keeps me here with you, and what could it be if not the hope for a more beautiful life that you give to me despite yourself?"

"No," said the girl feebly. "These are mere reveries. I am but a humble maidservant, and you do not see me as I should be seen. It is your own desire to live that you see on my face; here you would search in vain for a true light. Look around: is the darkness not growing? My lamp hardly sheds any light on me, and I, who have very good eyes, I can no longer make out your features. How could you still turn your gaze toward me?"

Thomas did not have the impression that the light had dimmed; he still saw the girl in the same place, her two hands buried in the white cloth—where they worked almost invisibly—her tired but brilliant face.

"Is it also a dream," he said, "that you come from regions not accessible to everyone, regions that one cannot help trying to imagine? Since I will never be able to go there, must I also give up thinking about it? Now that would be rather exaggerated, it seems to me."

The girl shook her head with a look of distress.

"Your words," she said, "are so childish that I have trouble even hearing them. Sit quietly here with me, and banish from your mind all these images that torment it. That is the best thing I can say to you."

"Perhaps I have behaved like a child up to now," said Thomas, "but now it's quite different. I am beginning to see clearly what I have to do. I will make up for lost time."

"Your road ends here," said the girl.

144

"The road I was wrong to follow, yes," said Thomas, "but I will choose another path."

"There is no other way," said the girl. "All the exits are closed. Where would you go?"

"Upstairs," said Thomas.

"That again," said the girl. "Are you trying to force me to reveal what is forbidden? Keep quiet, your words will make me sick."

"No," said Thomas, "I still have quite a few things to say. Let me be the one to give you some explanations now. Mlle Barbe," he continued in a louder voice, "your reproaches were no doubt well founded, and as you pointed out to me, all my exertions have been in vain. But these reproaches, which would be devastating to someone else, do not affect me in quite the same way. I may indeed confide to you that I entered the house only in passing and do not wish to be a tenant. When I was in the street, I thought I saw someone make a sign to me, and I wanted to go look for the person who had called me. After that, things did not happen as I thought they would; I encountered many difficulties, and in the end I have not succeeded. But if I made mistakes through a lack of reflection and through ignorance, I did not lose sight of my plan. It is this goal that I have always had in mind. I am persuaded—you see, I'm being honest with you—that if I found the person who invited me to enter, then all the obstacles would be leveled and the mistakes made good. Now, where is this person? You are the one I am counting on to help me find her."

The girl looked at Thomas with a shiver and murmured: "What insanity do I have to listen to? Why do I stay here?"

"I know, I know," said Thomas. "My manner of speaking offends you, but it is better to speak plainly. I will no doubt scandalize you further by saying that in my opinion, if I could communicate with the higher floors, I would be very near to establishing contact with my unknown stranger. According to what I believe I have seen, she lives on the third or fourth floor, in one of the apartments overlooking the street. With such a reference point, the search should not be too difficult. Of course, the best thing would have been for me to go up and see her myself. But you have proved to me that this is impossible; I will therefore give up the idea. But was it really necessary for me to go all the way to her door? Most likely not. What is indispensable, however, is that I communicate with her so that she may know how things stand for me in the house. One can certainly make objections to such a project, and I already see them rising to your lips; but even though it is a delicate matter, there is no reason to believe that it will encounter insurmountable obstacles, and I believe that with a little determination and tact, it can be brought to a successful conclusion. In any case, I have no choice. Difficult or not, it is to this that I must apply all my strength."

Thomas saw that the girl had pushed away the table and chair and was now sitting a few steps farther away; he tried to move closer. The chair felt too heavy, and he gave up.

"What do you think about my plan?" he asked.

Would she answer him? Would he have to keep up the conversation until the end? Would fatigue not prevent him from continuing? A single word, even a word of refusal, would have given him encouragement.

"You don't want to tell me your opinion? So be it. Then I can only examine for myself the various means at my disposal in order to weigh the difficulties and make a decision. You cannot deny that relations do exist between the various parts of the house. You may as well deny your own existence. For as long as my eyes can rest on you, I will be certain that at least one person has been upstairs and that there is a way to come back from there. That in itself is already an essential point. So I am not overstepping the limits of what is reasonable in thinking that, if I had a message to send, I could find an intermediary who would take responsibility for delivering it. However, I am not naïve enough to believe that, from the moment I found someone I could trust, composed my message, and saw the messenger disappear from sight, I could have much hope for success. Far from it. What goes on upstairs? I know nothing about it. Naturally I have been told a great many things, and it may be that some of them are true; nothing, however, is completely trustworthy. The most serious and the most captivating things I heard have come from you, Mlle Barbe, and it is your presence that continues to provide me with the most precious information. To judge by what you have told me, between the floor we are on and the one above us, there is such a great distance that when one returns, one hardly remembers having been there and can no longer recall what there was to see. Consequently, any effort to imagine what goes on there is useless. Perhaps one's senses do not provide any help; perhaps thought itself remains idle there and can grasp nothing. Perhaps, since there is no way to observe what people do and what happens there, there is nothing

146

in particular to set it apart, and one might find oneself there without even knowing it. All these hypotheses, concerning which I will refrain from asking your opinion, make the following conclusion seem most likely; namely that, despite his good will, the messenger, upon arriving upstairs, will have forgotten his message and will be unable to transmit it; or else, assuming he has scrupulously retained the terms in which it was formulated, it will be impossible for him to understand its meaning, for what has a certain meaning here must have a completely different one there, or perhaps none at all; he will wander aimlessly then, and when he returns, he will simply bring my petition back to me as a categorical refusal that will take away my very last hope. This is assuredly a very serious difficulty, and if it stood in my way, I would be forced to recognize my failure. Is there then no possibility of establishing any contact between the people upstairs and us? I believe there is. For it is a notion proper to this place—which certainly does not have the slightest value anywhere else—that the message would have to be pronounced in order to be understood. A crude and false idea. How could I place any importance at all on words that my mind could dictate, when these words are meant to be heard in a place to which no mind has access? How could I be more intent on transmitting words whose interest depends on the circumstances of my life, than on attaining—in a form that I can hardly conceive, and precisely through the forgetting of these words—the place it is most important for me to reach? Unheard-of luck and good fortune if the messenger has no memory of the message; nothing better could ever happen; if he casts out my thought, then he remains truly faithful to it, has understood it perfectly, and has taken it into his heart. But then how can he communicate this thought that he has totally eliminated because it comes from below, in what way can he make heard in silence the voice translated by muteness alone? Do I really need to know this? He will be there and will simply have to show himself. What he himself will have become, I refuse to imagine, for I assume that he will be as different from what I am as the transmitted message will be different from the one that is received. Everything that distances him brings him closer; everything that makes me fear he is lost confirms me in the hope that he will succeed."

Thomas interrupted himself as if it were better to conclude silently what he still had to say; then he added: "Am I still in error?" He said this not in order to receive an answer—he no longer expected any—but to challenge the girl, who seemed to him to be the last obstacle to his project. What silence surrounded him now! It was true that she seemed to have receded a thousand miles from him, although at times—was this an illusion produced by his tired vision?—this face, from which he never moved his eyes away, seemed larger than it had been at the beginning of the conversation. The lips at which he ardently stared moved as if they personally had something to say but something from which the rest of the body wanted to dissociate itself. Well, what was she saying? He leaned his ear toward her; he was mistaken; she spoke to him in the ordinary way.

"I am trying," she said, "to understand your words; but try as I might, they have no meaning for me. According to the few scraps I managed to catch, I have the vague impression that you are waiting for help and that, so you think, this help should come from someone who lives up above. A strange thought. You are no doubt unaware that there is no one in the upper floors."

"No one?" asked Thomas.

"No one," the girl repeated. "But there is nothing surprising in that. You yourself know enough to guess that the material conditions are defective and that for this reason there is nothing to be found there but emptiness and desolation. Get this into your head: Up above, there is nothing and no one." *NO God*

"Nothing," said Thomas again. "Really nothing?" He thought for a moment, and then he said, as though coming out of a dream: "Naturally. What could I have been thinking? It could not be otherwise. I understand your response perfectly well, Mlle Barbe. For me, having been so deeply absorbed in the life that goes on here—and, after all, even for you who reside at least momentarily in these lower places—there is no other way to put it. You are absolutely right then: There is nothing, and there is no one."

Barbe shook her head. "There you are again out of your depth, and I can no longer comprehend you. And yet I spoke clearly enough, however painful it may have been. Nothing. Do you understand this word? Nothing. Its meaning is simple. Assuming you did have the strength to go up there, well, you could wander around for hours, for months, for your entire life, and you would find nothing there."

"Now wait a moment, Mlle Barbe, you take me for more of a child than I am. It's obvious; I would find nothing. As I am now, poorly dressed, without the least bit of guidance or experience? I would be the first one to be

148

caught if I saw anything. How many transformations would be necessary! How many radical changes in one's habits! It's as much as to say that one must be reduced to nothing oneself."

"But not at all," said Barbe, with anger. "You are uselessly complicating everything. I do not know in what form you would arrive up there; obviously you would be in a fine state; but you would see no more and no less than what there is to see, an empty, deserted apartment, brighter than the others perhaps, covered with dust and uninhabited."

"I like your way of presenting the facts," Thomas said calmly. "You are right to place them before me and to be wary of my unrefined imagination. There is no better way to make a man like myself understand the feeling that would take hold of him in these regions, which he believes he could enter, whereas he must continue to be separated from them forever; in a sense, he would witness nothing surprising; what could be more ordinary than the desolate, timeworn rooms without furniture that he would actually see there, instead of the sumptuous palace conjured up by his imagination? For years he would wander in vain through these spaces; I can appreciate your image; everything would remain as sad, as uninhabitable as it ever was, until the day when he would have to die in disappointment and ignorance, having found nothing of what he had hoped for. As for myself, what else could happen to me, a man from the basement who, as you were kind enough to inform me, will remain attached for his entire life to the humble room that the administration assigned to him once and for all as his residence? I have absorbed your lesson very well and have no fear of falling into my old errors."

"You're even more obstinate than I thought," said Barbe. "Has there ever been anyone so blind? What can I possibly say to make you stop distorting the truth? You speak constantly of yourself, as if everything I told you about the apartments above concerned only you. But there is no question of what you would see or what you would do, and there will never be any question of that. Rather it has to do with me, and with the others, with all those, whoever they may be, who have entered into the secrets of the house. Well, everything we have learned is contained in the word *nothing*; we have seen nothing, because there is nothing, and there is nothing because, between the four walls of each room, no furniture remains, no stove, no useful objects of any kind; likewise the doors have been removed, the paintings taken down, and the carpet carried away. So, please, enough

149

with your childish ideas; your messenger may well accept your message, learn it by heart, and take it up above at the risk of his own life, but he will find no one to deliver it to."

"That's understood," said Thomas, "it is categorical, and your language could not be clearer. Nevertheless, I will make a few more remarks. First, however distrustful I have become regarding the value of my memories, I have difficulty believing that I was mistaken when I saw someone in the window on one of the upper floors. I saw her very distinctly, and although I cannot describe her now—I am much too tired—I believe that I would easily recognize her if she were to appear again. Is it an illusion, a confusion born from fever? I am inclined to admit as much, but I have reason to think that there is a bit too pronounced a tendency here to explain everything in terms of illusions. Besides, the illusions may not all be mine. I was struck, Mlle Barbe, during your exceedingly clear explanations, by certain contradictions—no doubt they are due to my obtuse mind, but they are no less surprising for all that—between what you said to me a while ago and what you later asked me to accept as true. Explain to me, then, how you could have described—and indeed with so many interesting details—the conditions of these famous apartments, whereas, if my memory serves me correctly, you also claimed that no one could retain any memory of the time they have spent there. This worries me. Might there not be a confusion on your part that has led you to express your absence of memory with this word *nothing* that you pronounce with such energy, a word that you then, since it is so easy to use, rendered even more significant by complementing it with the image of a dusty, empty apartment? I cannot pretend that there is nothing more to say on this subject; everything is no doubt different from what one might be able to think using the feeble means at our disposal here. And yet I had the impression, no doubt mistaken, that although you gave up trying to preserve any memory, properly speaking, of your time upstairs, you brought back an extraordinary, inexpressible feeling, something completely unique that could only be experienced outside the bounds of our everyday life. If my impression was justified, should I not conclude from this that these supposedly empty apartments are nonetheless very attractive, to the point of imprinting on a sensibility such as yours traces that anyone can then admire?"

"Where do you see any contradictions?" answered Barbe. She had almost finished her work and poised herself stiffly on her chair without looking up, as if she had to focus all her strength on the final stitches. She spoke in a softer tone, with the very pleasant voice she had had in the beginning. "There are contradictions only between your hopes and this world that does not grant them. Do you want to know the truth?"

"Yes," said Thomas.

"In principle," she continued, "I should keep silent, for it is strictly forbidden to speak of these matters; we fear that words, no matter how carefully chosen, cannot suitably express such delicate facts; it is therefore wrong of me to be discussing it with you; however, if I disregard this prohibition, it is because I cannot bear to see you get lost in these hopes, and because in any case you will have no opportunity to misuse the truth. Most of those who enter the house," she said, "are driven at first by the desires you yourself have experienced. Some feel them so strongly that they cannot make any progress at all. They are nailed to the spot. They exhaust themselves in the first place they light on here, and they offer a sorry sight, for they are still accustomed to the life outside, and their senses are obscured by the fog they cannot manage to penetrate; they burn like unruly candles suffocated by their own flame, and they let off a black smoke and a sickly odor. Newcomers such as these are lost from the very first step. They are locked away so that they will not pollute the atmosphere of the house, which is already so impure. Others, on the contrary, live for a long time in the building without ever coming out of their idleness, which they enjoy without being attracted by the restlessness of change. These are good tenants. They accept their lot. They submit to the rules, these famous rules that people are so anxious to discuss in the grand halls and that most often exist only in the minds of the people who get worked up about them. Gradually, as a result of the relations they develop, and by dint of living in the midst of the perpetual intrigues in which everyone here passionately struggles, the fever seizes hold of them, and they begin to be driven upward. Naturally, for most of them it is only a question of an inner migration. What would happen to us if this crowd actually got it into their heads to begin their journey? But they drift along with their dreams, and these dreams allow them to glimpse great and mysterious hopes that absorb their contemplation and that they project into places they do not know and will never have the strength even to hope to know. The fate that awaits them is therefore infinitely varied, and as I was saying, it is almost impossible to compare the destiny of one to that of another. For some, their desire becomes so pressing that they can resist it only by involving themselves in some febrile and disordered activity; they find it necessary to take care of the business of the house; or they need to create a sense of belonging—even if from afar, from infinitely far away—to the mysterious existence whose center they locate somewhere up above, and from which they receive, so they think, the impulse to continue, as well as a few rules to live by. This applies, if you will, to the bulk of the staff. When they work, they often forget the desire that burns in them, and their service, which is so chaotic and so full of conflict, reflects the vicissitudes of life and death through which they pass, and in which their passion remains just as often unconscious as conscious. It happens in the long run that this desire, which has been unable to triumph over their busy activity, begins to find nourishment wherever it can and takes more and more crude forms, to the point of erasing this hope from above, toward which their desire had directed them. They are then momentarily cured of their torments, and they fall into base and servile occupations from which they sometimes never rise again. But others— who are in truth very rare—escape from this need for miserable activity that drives their companions to flee what had at first attracted them. They resent with great fervor the strange conditions in which they find themselves, and before giving in to the attraction exerted upon them, they are as if indefinitely held back by the vanity of their efforts, and they attach themselves almost forever to the low places they first came to know. In the place where they are, it seems to them that they will never be able to exhaust completely whatever it is they might enjoy there, and despite the bitterness they harbor and the inexplicable sufferings of their very simple life, they patiently wait, persuaded that they are condemned to remain in an obscure and plaintive distress. This wait can last a very long time. It is uncertain whether for some it ever comes to an end. They are seen trying to transform themselves, changing the color of the room they never leave, each day becoming more disaffected and dull, to the point that they are easily confused with objects and come to resemble the house itself. There is really nothing to be said about them; no one knows what becomes of them later. But among the small group of those who have mistrusted their desire, there are some who, one day, receive the order to change places; sometimes they move up, sometimes down, it matters little. The important thing for them, what renews their strength, is that they have been given the proof that in patience and passivity the principle of a blessed action may be found. They have been remembered; they have been pulled from the ditch where they were sure to die. It is true that, as soon as they have entered a new place or a new function, they begin once again to believe they will never get out. They are still distraught at the height of their prison walls, and though their strength may have increased, even if they possessed the keys that opened every door for them, they are incapable of taking the few steps required to attain the object of their wishes. One would think that the passion that ravages them and that grows as they climb higher is only directed against another deeper passion whose fire they will feel when it has been extinguished. As the desire drawing them upward becomes more intense, because its obstacles have been diminished, the more they find within themselves the means to combat it and to detach themselves from it. Thus it is that they alone approach those regions that remain inaccessible to others. I could never describe to you the last stages through which they pass before coming upon that great opening without a door that lies at the end of their aspirations. The torments and delights they undergo there are such that they cannot preserve them in their memory. They are no longer anything, and yet they are everything. They are touched by an intense love that, however, has none of the colors of love and that reaches them through the abandonment in which it leaves them. They are driven by a glorious hope composed of all the hopes they have previously renounced. They are finally so annihilated by the effort required to resist the temptation to go where they desire with all their soul to go, that they are often consumed by it and succumb to the force of their passion. Some never move past the first step; others go as far as the doorway, where they remain lying in a heap; and yet most of them do enter and leave, after realizing, as they take their last steps in utter indifference and in the death of their last desire, that everything was indeed as they themselves had guessed; the apartment is quiet and empty, and there is nothing left to desire because there is nothing. When they return, life begins again; the feelings that remain with a person from such a journey are so fine and complex that what one remembers is liberated from the journey itself, and memory itself retains only the deep and intense ardor that has animated them up to the end. A stronger hope is formed from the particles of images that still burn with a new passion. One aspires to return to these unspeakable places that are tarnished by no disappointment and to which one remains ever near in a patience that is renewed as well. They are the same paths, the same stations where

153

one finds traces of the tears one has shed, and it is the same radiant suffering, the same tragic happiness in progressing so slowly toward a goal that one wishes all the more to reach, since one knows that in attaining it, there will be nothing more to wish."

The girl seemed to have finished her work; she had set the needle and thread down on the table, and she laid her hands on the large cloth that, however, she had left unfolded. She raised her head, and Thomas met her gaze, a pure and candid gaze from which all light had faded away. He wanted to answer her; but although he knew what he had to say, he shrank back from the effort required to search for the words he needed. Yet he regretted his silence when he saw that the girl still wanted to speak to him. No matter how gently she might address him, he was oppressed and fatigued by all this talk.

"What could you have seen at the window?" she said. "The shutters are closed, and no one can open them onto the outside and lean out. If a ray of light happens to slip between the cracks, it is so feeble that no one notices it, and only later, when going back down, or even much later than that, does one perceive it, as though it could only illuminate you when you have come back into those dark rooms below. No, you have been the victim of an illusion; you thought someone was calling you, but no one was there, and the call came from you. Now," she said, standing up, "it's getting late; you are very tired; you should think about getting some rest. What a mess here," she said, looking at the shreds of fabric and loose thread on the floor. "I'm going to clean up after my work."

Thomas watched her intently. She was small and agile; he had not been mistaken when, downstairs, he had been struck by her childlike face, full of kindness and charm. She stepped lightly across the room. In a few moments everything was put back in order. She stopped near Thomas, touched his shoulder, and said: "I'm going to open the door. You can look out for a second; it's nice to have some open space out in front of you after being closed up in this room."

She went to the door opposite Thomas and then turned back to add: "I am disobeying the orders, so look quickly."

Through the opening, Thomas saw a long vault held up by short, thick columns that came together in arches. He was able to see clearly the first columns, which were lit on each side by a shimmering light like the fire of a distant star, but in the other two-thirds of the nave he saw nothing more.

154

"Close the door," he said, realizing he could not penetrate the shadows. "That's enough for today."

The girl closed the door, and Thomas stopped paying attention to her. He thought about what she had said, but he could not overcome his fatigue. So he stood up to leave, putting off until later the conclusion that he would have to draw from this conversation. He stood motionless for a moment; the room seemed to him surprisingly low and cramped; thus it seemed to him, now that he was standing, that he was contemplating it from high above, and that his head had gone up through the ceiling, and he could no longer tell what was happening down at his feet. When he tried to look up, his eyes grew dim, and he fell ponderously to the floor.

After this fall, Thomas sank into a long period of illness, and he could no longer remember anything that happened. Only during the course of his convalescence did he look around at the room that enclosed him and at the bed where he lay. The room was large and bright; several paintings hung on the walls, and on the table there was a carafe next to a glass half filled with water. Thomas sat up and drank the fresh water with pleasure; his lips still burned; his eyes were aching. He had certainly been very ill. Nevertheless, he left the room, and surprised by the calm and silence that reigned in this part of the house, he hesitated to go any farther. Across from his room he saw a half-opened door; someone must have been in the room, for he heard footsteps now and then. He crossed the wide hallway and went in, but when he saw a woman half hidden behind an armchair, he hastily excused himself. Yet he remained standing in the doorway. The room seemed immense. It was divided into three sections, separated from one another by two sets of steps that ran the width of the room; at the far end, there was a narrow bed, hidden by a curtain, whose miserable appearance clashed with the rest of the furnishings. After observing these details, Thomas thought that he had lingered too long to go away without saying a few polite words, and he asked if there were not a domestic somewhere nearby whom he might call on, since, having recently been ill, it was still difficult to do without the service. The young woman turned slowly, and her gaze, sad and lovely, fell on the half-opened door. Would she answer him? While he listened intently with a slight apprehension, not knowing whether after the silence of a long illness he could bear the sound of another voice, the young woman, as if she had guessed what fear was troubling him, turned away, walked a short distance in the other direc-

155

tion, and sat down on a stool next to the first steps. At first, Thomas did not know how to interpret such an attitude. Finally, he took a few steps himself and saw that the room was even more vast than he had thought. The ceiling was very high; it was supported by columns built into recesses in the wall, and it rose in the form of a vault that soon vanished into the heights. After looking upward, he had difficulty, when he lowered his eyes, estimating the limits of the large room; he was as though lost in an infinite space; he looked around in vain for the objects that had served as points of reference for him. To escape from this impression of emptiness, he sat down on a beautiful chair covered with velvet, and he felt how much his illness had deprived him of his strength; he was exhausted, and this rest, far from relieving his fatigue, weighed down his limbs and made them ache. After a few moments, he fell into a brief sleep that only intensified his feeling of confusion, for he dreamed of the vast room he had entered, in which he wandered alone, threatened at every moment with being driven away. When he woke, he felt stronger, and he walked out.

He was glad at first to be back in his room. Its atmosphere was mild and pleasant. But when he called out in a loud voice, he went back to the doorway to see what kind of person would be sent to him. The hallway, though high and wide, was dark; it was lit only by a few rays of light coming through large sliding panels on each side. He waited for a long time, leaning his back against the wall, his head bent forward, as if he had fallen asleep while on guard duty. Then the door across the way opened, and the young woman said, without leaving her room: "Why don't you answer? I called to you several times."

Were these words really meant for Thomas? They sounded like words addressed to a servant, and their tone was harsh and contemptuous. He did not move; avoiding her question, he said: "I myself am waiting for a domestic."

The young woman paid no attention to this remark and turned back into her room without closing the door. Thomas, for his part, went back to his room. But hardly was he on the threshold, when he noticed that it was far from being as comfortable as it had appeared to him during the long hours of his fever. There was no chair, the table was ridiculously small, and the too spacious bed was covered in black-and-white sheets that forced one's eyes away. It was a sick person's room. He therefore gave up trying to find any rest there, and, greatly worried, he went to see his neighbor. She was standing in the entrance to the room, her arms calmly at her sides. She was quite young, but her youth did not make their relations any easier; as near as she was, she remained distant.

"There you are at last," she said to Thomas. "Your service leaves much to be desired."

Surprising words.

After giving him a little time to acknowledge and to understand her reprimand, she added: "What you can do now is make me forget your lapse. Get to work and don't waste any time."

With an authoritarian gesture, but without any real severity, she dismissed him. Then she withdrew into a corner of the room, slightly behind the little stool where she had sat down at the end of their first meeting.

Thomas hurried from the room and went down the hall to find the equipment he needed. He had to walk quite a distance. As he had imagined, this corridor was monumental. Almost completely covered in darkness, he noticed as he went that it did not in any way resemble an ordinary hallway; rather it had the appearance of a huge underground tunnel whose ceiling was invisible and which numerous recesses, enormous pipes, and deep holes carved out of the floor—revealing wooden pillars and iron beams—transformed into a silent catacomb. In a small side room Thomas found a broom, a bucket, and a dust cloth, and he set to work. The floor was paved with stones, but it was covered with a thick crust of dirt that could only be removed by scraping it with a shovel or a pickaxe; since Thomas had no such tools, he settled for sweeping it with heavy strokes, casting to either side the largest and most visible detritus. He raised a lot of dust; a sort of red mold with an acrid smell permeated the atmosphere and slowly drifted back down, sticking to everything. Although he put great care and attention into his work, he soon came to the end of it, reaching the spot where wooden planks replaced the paving stones and the dirt. A little farther along was the room. He could therefore consider his task complete. Nevertheless, not wanting it to be known officially that he was finished, he continued to sweep in front of the doors of the two rooms, without paying attention to the red streaks he was leaving on the wooden floor. What he feared, though it was the direct result of his efforts, soon occurred. The young woman, drawn by the noise—Thomas was violently knocking his broom against the wall—came out and shot a look of silent disapproval at him. He must have presented a sorry sight: the dust he had raised had stuck to his clothes and probably covered his face and hair as well; the bucket lay overturned on the floor—fortunately it was empty—and the rag, made of two pieces ripped from a morning coat, was lying soaked in slimy mud. Thomas therefore expected a harsh reprimand. But the young woman did not deign to pass judgment on a piece of work that spoke so clearly for itself, and after going back to the room, she said to him through the door, as if he were no longer worthy of being addressed face to face: "During your absence you were the subject of a communication concerning the affair in which you are a witness. It has been made known to you, then, that for the time being you will have to fulfill the functions of the two employees."

What an unpleasant tone of voice! While listening to this voice, he sensed in its words an inexorable meaning that was perhaps not contained in the words themselves; but at the same time, he was glad that the judgment had been pronounced by her, in all its truth and all its force, such that once it had been expressed, it seemed there was no longer anything to fear from it. Thomas reflected for a long time on these words. Then, taking up his work again, he tried to clean up the mess he had made. Seeing that his efforts had little result—the moldy dust had become encrusted in the slats of the floor, and the more he scrubbed, the more they turned black—he went to put the broom and the bucket away and returned to his room to shake off the dust that covered his clothes. Coming back out into the corridor, he noticed that the door opposite was closed. That was something new. The door was hermetically sealed. He pressed his ear against it without hearing the slightest noise. He bent down to the floor to look for a ray of light, but a large rolled up cloth blocked every crack. As with many doors in the house, there was neither a latch nor a lock, and it could only be opened from the inside. He stood with his forehead pressed against the doorframe. Hours passed, but he could not resign himself to knocking; nothing drew him into the room; nothing drew him outside it; he had a feeling of emptiness and distress that came over him more painfully than any illness and that made him wish he could bury his sorrow and forget his very name. How forbidding everything was here! What strange colors things had, how heavy was the silence! He would have liked to push it away and at the same time to find nothing other than himself. After a long while his knees gave way, and he fell to the floor.

He could no doubt be heard from inside, for the young woman—it could only be her, though he did not recognize her voice—asked who was there. How could he answer her?

"Open the door," he said, without going any further.

Before he had time to get up, the door was open.

"You again," said the young woman in her disdainful voice, and she looked at him very attentively, as if to convince herself that he had not changed.

Thomas thought that, yet again, he was not showing himself to his best advantage; he was partly lying on the floor—the door had made him lose his balance when it opened—and he had fallen so clumsily that he was unable to raise his head to look at the person in front of him. He struggled, and in his disarray he asked for help, forgetting whom he was addressing. The young woman held out her hand to him, and he managed to rise to his knees.

"Could I stay here a few moments?" he asked her boldly.

"Your service is limited to the vestibule," she answered evasively. "Perhaps later you will also have to take care of the rooms."

Thomas made a motion to straighten up, but he was so bruised from his fall that he still needed help, and once he was standing, he had to lean against the door for support. So he remained there, uncertain and miserable, without leaving the room, and his hesitations only succeeded in making the woman more impatient. After backing away a few steps, she approached again and asked if there was anything in particular that he had to tell her.

"No," he answered.

"In that case," she said, "I must ask you to return to your service."

Thomas did not raise his eyes; he only noticed that the floor was marked with the dirty stains he had left from falling and climbing to his knees.

"I have," he said, "a little more work to do here. These spots outside need to be cleaned away. I will return momentarily."

He went to get his cleaning equipment and began to scrub the floor with the rag. But the marks would not come off. Attributing the ineffectiveness of his efforts to a lack of energy, he took off his long work coat and threw himself into his task. The floor began to shine; the spots were still visible, but they seemed more like points of gleaming brightness than unpleasant remnants. Encouraged by these results, he went on to scrub the entire room, to which he tried to give the same shining appearance.

It was quite a piece of work! The room only appeared to be well kept. If one looked closely at the furniture, it was clear that it could benefit from being scrubbed and polished. So he continued his efforts, first by taking on a writing desk. It was only a lounge piece, made of a fragile wood that had been finely engraved, and it was impossible to reach the dust that had settled into the small grooves. He had to pull from the broom a thin stalk that he used to scrape out the lines sculpted into the wood; but the work was even more delicate than he thought: as he cleared out the thin grooves, he would find still others that were even finer, which he had at first overlooked, and when his eye could no longer distinguish anything, the needle-shaped stalk in its turn found invisible etchings that it slowly brought to light. This little piece of wood soon became unusable. Since he did not want to lose his place to go get another one from the broom, he asked his neighbor to please lend him a needle. The young woman, who seemed to be right next to him—probably bent over the desk to survey the progress of his work—placed in his hand a tiny point that was so small he could hardly take hold of it; its shiny reflection was the only thing to keep him from losing sight of it altogether. With this new tool, he continued to cut out the lines on the table; their elaborate interlacing seemed to become more and more dense; he strayed farther and farther from his point of departure, and the circles he traced were like the many paths of a labyrinth with no way out. At times he thought he had made a mistake and would have to start everything over, then the point that looked like the sparkle of a diamond led him into another path whose curling movements passed around the obstacles, leaving a bright mark that shone like a beacon, It was impossible for him to gauge the time required for the work. At times he thought he had spent hours and days cutting out a single groove; at other times it seemed to him that he was only in the very first stages, and he still had all the courage that comes at the beginning of a task. Thus he had no idea how long he had been working when the young woman made a remark. Was it a compliment, a reprimand? Absorbed as he was, he could not say. Suddenly, he realized what she had said: "The work is done." Well, then, he was finished; there was some satisfaction in that after all. He moved back a little, and the entire design that he had traced according to the model appeared to him in a soft, sweet light; each line had received from the diamond point a few particles of light that made them sparkle. This drawing did not, strictly speaking, make much sense; it was a tangle of threads that had not yet been unraveled and that drew one's gaze ceaselessly in every direction in search of the image they were meant to construct. Perhaps it was a map, perhaps a simple work of embroidery; it hardly mattered.

Although it was an equally minute task, he cleaned the other furnishings without difficulty, relying on his experience to avoid errors and finding again the ornamental motifs—always the same ones—whose enigmatic character took the monotony out of his efforts. Soon he had transformed a large part of the room, and he looked around: everything was in order, and now he was able to look directly and without discomfort at the space where not long ago he had almost fallen into a faint. In a corner he saw a small sliding window that struck him with its ruined appearance. The boards in which the frame was mounted were in a very bad state; they were broken in several spots; the dampness had badly cracked the runners, and to keep the shutter from falling, it had been clumsily nailed onto two diagonal crosspieces. Thomas tried to pull it open, but of course since everything was nailed down and screwed tight, it would not open, and he could only shake the whole contraption in frustration. Then he leaned his ear against it, hoping to hear a noise from outside. He even drew the curtain behind him, and from that moment on he forgot about the room, the young woman, and all the rest. He waited for quite a long time. He neither saw nor heard anything, but this silence seemed to be the prelude to a great effort that was destined to break down every barrier and lead to someone who was out of reach. Soon enough a voice did indeed make itself heard; it was still very weak, although it appeared to be quite close; a sort of faith was necessary to hear it, to follow it without confusing it with the sound of his own voice, of which it seemed the very echo. It evoked for Thomas the shouts he heard when he first entered the house. His heart beat fast as he listened to it, as if it reproduced a moan that he himself had uttered in some very distant past. After remaining with his ear pressed to the apparatus, he realized that the voice was coming from inside the room. He quickly raised the curtain and saw the young woman standing on the steps leading to the second part of the room.

"I beg your pardon," he said, "I did not know that you had called me."

"I didn't call you," answered the young woman. "But since I have the opportunity to speak to you, I will point out that the item you are so interested in is no longer in service. It is therefore useless for you to try to repair it."

"Not in service?" said Thomas, with a look of surprise, although he himself had already seen that this was so. "I was under the impression that you had used it to receive the communication concerning me."

The young woman shrugged her shoulders.

"In any case," she said, "it's not in use now. So leave off worrying about it. If you would really like to make yourself useful, there is other work here that requires your attention."

"What work?" asked Thomas, still looking astonished.

The young woman did not answer directly, but pointed to the room he had just cleaned in such a conscientious manner. What had he forgotten? He reexamined the floor, the furnishings, the drapery, the columns; he saw no signs of negligence. Obviously, the vaults of the ceiling could not have been very clean, but he could hardly see them, so high and indifferent were they, and he had no way to reach them.

"Are you referring to the ceiling?" he asked.

He immediately regretted his words, for at that very instant he saw hidden in the curtains, which hung along the walls, a rope ladder that was probably used for cleaning the higher parts of the room. The ladder was far from new, some of its rungs had been eaten away by moisture and mold, but next to the ladder there was a sturdy rope with knots that could be used for support. With one hand holding the broom and the rag, and the other grasping the rope, he slowly climbed up, keeping his eyes all the while on the drapery with its bright silvery color. Having gotten about halfway up, he looked up and noticed that the ladder did not rise all the way to the top of the structure but was attached by two hooks to the capital of the column, above which there was another column that went farther up. This very obviously settled the matter. Nevertheless, he held it as a point of honor to climb as high as he possibly could. He continued his ascent, and when he reached the cornice, he looked up again to see where he was. This time the vaults seemed very near. He was some thirty feet from the first arches, perhaps a little more. As for their highest point, he could not tell how far it was, for the stone was so white and shone with such brilliance that one could only feel far away from all this light. There was some cleaning to be done, no doubt about that. Thomas grew dizzy at the thought of his task.

To regain his balance, he grabbed onto the column and sat down on the entablature. There was something icy and frozen in the light that fell from above. It did not force one's gaze away, on the contrary, it attracted it, but then it gave nothing back, and this gaze, after rejoicing at the splendor to which it had been admitted, felt disdained and returned from this upward surge with nothing but bitterness and disgust. And where were the vaults? Was there really any stone behind this sparkling powder, with its innumerable drops that constantly broke apart and reformed without forcing one's gaze away? It was possible to think that the arches, reaching their highest point, had been broken and that what seemed to be the key element of the structure was only a large opening through which poured the light of day. Thomas would like to have spoken to this light. Was it possible that it shone on him in vain? Could he not say to it that no man can be lost this way, without a sign, without a word of explanation, without understanding anything about the infinite efforts he has made to come this far? Again he looked up. Absurd, foolish thoughts. Who could hear him? Who knew anything of his story? Without thinking of whether or not he had completed his task, he climbed back down the ladder, and as soon as he placed a foot on the ground, he was addressed in a loud voice by the young woman.

"Well, now, there you are," she said. "I kept my eyes on you the entire time, and I was very pleased by your enthusiasm. The way you carried your work through to the end deserves nothing but praise."

Thomas, still out of breath, answered her calmly: "Your praise is no doubt ironic, and it probably disguises a sharp rebuke. But if my work has not corresponded to your wishes, I am only partly responsible, for I did not receive all the instructions that could have clarified this task for me. What should I have done?"

He stared at her intently and saw that, still motionless on the steps, she hesitated to go down into the first room and seemed rather ready to leave. Was she not about to go away for good? Should he try to hold her back? Perhaps he ought to walk over and speak to her. In an attempt to satisfy her, he began his work again. He hid the ladder in the curtains and went around the room wiping away the footprints that marred the shiny floor. When he came to the door, it still stood open, and he could feel a little air from the hallway; he wanted to lean out, but at that moment he heard the young woman moving around and saw that, regardless of his renewed efforts, she was preparing to leave him. He angrily threw all the cleaning equipment into the hallway and said in a stentorian voice: "Please stay."

His words resounded like thunder through the entire room. He was as terrified as if he himself had been the object of some tremendous order.

He dared not turn around; he gently closed the door and began to walk back and forth, wanting neither to look at what was going on around him, nor to form any idea of what would happen to him. Nevertheless, after a few moments, surprised that no one had come to take him away, he looked down at the lock and remembered that the door could not be opened from outside. How forgetful! He hurriedly tried to push the bolt to and turn the key, but either he had somehow jammed the mechanism or he had become so clumsy that he could not carry out the simplest operations. He was unable to disengage the handle and was hurting his fingers for nothing. He examined the door more closely without being able to find the cause of the problem. Then he stood quietly, understanding finally that the door was closed from both sides and slowly realizing the misfortune that this situation represented to him. Hanging his head, he went to sit down on the armchair and, closing his eyes, gently slipped into a dream. He saw the room just as it was, but instead of peacefully enjoying his rest, he noticed that the floor was slanted and that it was causing everything to slide toward the steps and into the second part of the room. He too was undergoing the effects of this inclined plane. It seemed to him — strange vertigo! — that he was being pulled along in a slow movement that forced him to stare into immense empty spaces.

The young woman drew him out of his dream by asking him to bring over the little stool. He stood up quickly and, despite his aching body, swiftly climbed the steps. His neighbor was half hidden behind a larger and more imposing desk than the one in the first room. She was bent over a notebook and was leafing through it, her feet covered with beautiful white rugs. Slowly straightening up, she said to him: "You are not authorized to be here."

She approached, and he looked at her with extreme pleasure. "Such a serious attitude," he thought. "At least with her, there is no point in wasting one's time begging and pleading. I'm lucky; she's completely inflexible." She came right up next to him, and he had to raise his head to look at her. She was really very young; but her strict attitude was all the more pronounced because of it. "Finally," he thought, "here is a fine soul who will not leave me to my despair. Everything will quickly be taken care of." But she did not seem to be in any hurry. Her gaze fell on him from time to time, but then she forgot him. So, using all the strength he had left, he rose up and almost pressed himself against the young woman; her face seemed immense, and he recognized none of the features he thought he had seen before. She bent over abruptly and threw herself at his face, which her mouth lightly touched, like a young animal trying to soak up all the water from a spring with a few laps of the tongue; then she squeezed him with rage, pressing his face with one hand, holding him by the back of the neck with the other; although her hands were rather small, they were very strong, and they held his head in a veritable vice. "Obviously," thought Thomas, "there is nothing very pleasant in any of this, but it is better to have done, even at the price of a few inconveniences." This thought gave him courage, and when the young woman began to chew furiously at his mouth, as though to exhaust this source of false words, he even pulled her against him to show that he was in perfect agreement with what was happening. To him, these were moments that seemed endless. He struggled desperately not for this life but to find the limit of this life. At times they stopped and looked at each other with a grimace. Then they rolled again on the floor, knocking against the stool and then against the desk, attracting each other and repelling each other with moans that were only incomprehensible words; both of them were lost, wandering among loathsome punishments they could not quite reach, with no hope for light, in deeper and deeper shadows, now with neither hands nor body to touch each other, pulled along by a shattering transformation into a world of misfortune and despair. Finally, Thomas heard the sound of the heavy desk as it fell, after a shock more violent than the rest, and he thought with terror that, given their blind struggle, it could only end like this: from the moment when they had strayed so far, they could just as well have rolled to the bottom of the steps. So when he opened his eyes, he had a feeling of satisfaction at seeing that there were no other signs of disorder in the room; the stool had simply been knocked over, and the rugs, the precious rugs, had escaped unharmed from the furious destruction.

Right away he tried to get up and to eliminate these vestiges of the struggle—was he not still a domestic?—but the girl placed her hand on his arm; he felt like a prisoner and abandoned himself to a strange feeling of sleep and peace. This rest could only last a moment; his eyes closed; his body relaxed; he said to himself that he had returned from a great distance and had nothing more to seek; he too placed his hand on the girl's arm, and in this restless peace, he tried to think of what it was he could have done during such a long journey, unknown to all; then he thought that it didn't matter after all because the journey was over. Looking at the arm he gently touched, he thought: "Why could she not be a woman like any other, with whom I could forget my cares, rest in comfort, and become once again the man I used to be? But what is it that distinguishes her? Can I not hold her wrist in my hand? Is she not my own? Will I not, in a moment, fall asleep by her side? Who could take her away from me now?" All these thoughts were very relaxing. He had not felt such calm in a very long time. "Likewise," he said to himself, looking at the room again, "how could I complain about such a beautiful dwelling as this? It is a magnificent structure, and I never would have dreamed of finding such a grandiose residence. When it comes to quiet and calm, it too is perfect. No one contests my right to stay here; no one asks me to leave; on the contrary, I am welcomed and smiled upon; if there have been a few disapproving comments here or there, they had no practical consequences, and it was all soon forgotten. Why then am I so anxious?" Half closing his eyes, he looked at the fingers on her hand; they were smooth and pink but a little plump, as if they had never done any hard work. It was a very pretty hand, and it was a pleasure for him to hold it.

The girl did not seem to mind this admiration.

"I don't want to trouble you," she said to him, "but I must ask you a question. Have you stared at Barbe's arms with the same look in your eyes? Did you not find them pleasing? What was your impression?"

A strange question.

"Barbe," said Thomas absently.

"Yes," said the girl, "Barbe, the maidservant. You certainly know her; she was your friend."

Thomas did not want to answer; he had the impression that if he turned toward this memory, he would suddenly lose his footing and would see everything disappear that still made it possible for him to live.

"It would actually be very helpful if you remembered her," continued the girl. "The moment has come to compare the present and the past, and it is an important choice to make. But perhaps," she added, "you prefer to withhold judgment."

Thomas made an effort to recall the features of the maidservant. It was not easy. She had shown herself in very different guises, and in addition there had been the story from the two employees who had given a memorable description of her. How to sort out all these memories?

166

"The decision does not appear to be easy," said the girl. "You are certainly right not to commit yourself lightly. Take your time. The essential thing is to judge well."

Thomas wanted to ask if it was really necessary; would his choice change the situation? Would it give him the means to return to the place from which he had set out? No, of course not. But since he could not make his explanations clear, and since he was not free to say no to anything at all, he answered in a low voice: "My choice is here."

"Perfect," said the girl. "Of course I will take your word for it, and if it were only me, I would refrain from asking what your reasons are. But, unfortunately, we must do things according to the rules. A few words, then, to justify your choice, and we will never speak of it again."

Thomas was very embarrassed. Not only did he have no more than a vague image of the maidservant, he also did not know how to describe the impression on which his preference was based. There was no way for him really to speak of it. The girl was beautiful, but it was not because of her beauty that he preferred her; was it her seriousness that seduced him, this air that gave her smallest gestures an extraordinary value? No, for this rather frightened him. Then perhaps he liked being with her simply because she was there, because she benefited from the grandiose surroundings, from his fatigue, his abandonment? How foolish it all was.

The girl, probably displeased by the prolonged silence, moved away and crossed her arms. No longer feeling her body in contact with his, Thomas said to himself: "Well that's no good. Now I'll have no point of comparison at all." So he was obliged to declare: "Don't move away. I'll give you all the explanations you want."

He was glad to see that she accepted his request. For a few moments, the calm and even some of the intimacy returned, and in his state of absorption, he really believed that the girl was held in place by his contemplation and that he was forgetting all other cares. He was therefore surprised when he heard her say, in a very gentle voice, and without the serious tone she had used before, as if such gravity were insufficient to bring out the seriousness of her words: "I am far from believing that it is a sign of ill will, but all the same, your silence is surprising. Anyone else would interpret it as a real insult. How to explain your hesitation to speak a few polite words without much importance, words that you are free to choose, on the condition, of course, that you provide assurances that the past is dead? Do you have memories that still trouble you? Does my presence prevent you from seeing clearly what your thoughts are? At least tell me the reason for your embarrassment."

Thomas could hardly overcome the confusion these words caused him. Such consideration! How nicely she was speaking to him! He had never heard anything so pleasant, so persuasive. He would have liked to merge with these words so as to know all their sweetness; he would have liked to be as true and as perfect as they were. He turned to the girl and wanted to express his satisfaction to her and to make it clear to her, by a gesture at least, that he was in agreement with her. Certainly a gesture would be enough; words were superfluous; a gesture or even a facial expression, a simple wink, would bring everything into the clear. It was impossible that she would reject his prayer, that she would not read on his face how much he needed her and how in the heart of his distress he had chosen her since always. As he pulled himself toward her along the ground, she stood up, saying: "The hours are passing, and we are getting nowhere. You know, we will have to reach a decision. I interpret your silence as a desire to give me the initiative and to avoid any more errors. Confide in me then; I will make things easier for you."

She took a few steps, hesitantly at first, then with more confidence; she put the room back in order, put the desk back in its place, set the stool down next to it. After picking up the notebook, she sat down and attached a label to it, on which Thomas read the name Lucie—the name of its owner, no doubt. He stared at her continuously, as if losing sight of her at this moment would have led to incalculably serious consequences. She was seated now at some distance from him, and he no longer had the protection that her contact and her proximity had brought him; this only made it all the more necessary for him to keep her in view. After tearing a page out of the notebook, she began to write in a dark and miniscule handwriting. From what he could tell, it was not the choice of the words or the structure of the sentences that preoccupied her; rather, her efforts were directed at the details of the letters—as though she were drawing rather than writing—and she placed great emphasis on the downstrokes and the upstrokes, the punctuation signs, and all the various accents. This work took time. Although Thomas knew that she was working for him and that a decisive advantage would result from this effort, he wondered if the help he would find in it could ever compensate for the displeasure of such

168

a prolonged separation. Already his eyes looked at her less intently; his contemplation of her, instead of appeasing him, became mechanical and sterile; what he saw did not bring her closer to him; rather, it made him more conscious of the distance that divided them. Finally the girl set down her pen, and after glancing at Thomas, as if to reassure him that she was still there, she said: "There now, that settles our problems."

It was good to hear this, but it was perhaps premature, for she re-read under her breath the page she had just written, and after finishing, she remained silent, as if she were weighing both sides, without quite knowing how the scales would fall. Was she satisfied with the final impression? Thomas could not tell. She only said to him, gently and somewhat reticently, in the tone that is used to prepare a sick person for bad news: "I will read out the declaration I have composed for you; if you approve, you will sign, and the incident will be closed."

Hearing this, Thomas was very disappointed. He had hoped she would bring the page over and that they would read it together, that not only would the separation come to an end but also would be replaced by a greater intimacy that these lines would seal; instead, he was being offered more postponements, the prolongation of the same state of things.

Paying no attention to the disillusion she was causing, the girl began to read: "In order to resolve the misunderstandings that could result from certain incidents of my past life, and to dismiss in advance any incorrect and malicious interpretations, I believe it necessary to make the following statement, which alone should stand as an accurate representation of the truth. Of course I am speaking in your name," said the girl, interrupting herself, then she continued: "I entered the house with the explicit intention not to interfere with its customs, to remain here for as long as it was desired that I be kept on, and, if possible, to die here in accordance with its principles and in harmony with its people. From my very first steps, I recognized that all the regulations of this imposing edifice were inspired by order and justice. I neither observed any negligence in the staff nor any discontent among the tenants; I was charmed by the welcome I received, which was unwarranted for a man of so little merit. Each time I exchanged words with any person unknown to me, I admired the value of their advice, and I can only congratulate myself for having always followed it. Thus, considering the benefits I have received from my stay among such virtuous men, with the conviction of having lived modestly, simply, and correctly, certain, in addition, that it would have been impossible for me to do any wrong in the presence of such examples and under the direction of such august laws, I have the duty, at a particularly important moment in my life, to thank all those who have granted me so much favor, by communicating to them a solemn testimony of my gratitude."

When she had finished reading, Thomas saw that the girl was not thinking of coming to him but was resting from her work, with her hands on the desk, saying nothing; he tried unsuccessfully to get up. During the last few moments he had lost a great deal of his strength, although a little while before he had already been very weak. It was quite unfortunate, but there was no reason to be sad about it; instead of going to the girl by walking straight ahead, with his head high enough to keep it on her level, he would drag himself along the floor, and perhaps this painful position would convince Lucie to come to him. He set off immediately but realized that his legs were half paralyzed. He pushed on the floor with his arms to move the rest of his body along, but he had to keep raising his head to see if he was moving in the right direction. Nevertheless, despite these difficulties, which he had not foreseen, and despite a dull anxiety about the future, which the thought of his semi-paralysis caused him, he felt so full of hope that he completely disregarded his fatigue, and soon enough he had crawled up next to the desk. Still out of breath, he said with a stutter: "Here I am," not only to make known his arrival but also to convince himself of it — as if it were something utterly incredible — to taste all the joy of success, and to put an end to his adventures. The girl held out the paper to him and said: "Write your name at the bottom and make the characters as legible as possible. One can never take too much care with one's writing."

That was easy enough. The text filled an entire page. At the bottom, in an empty rectangle, there was a large space for a signature; an arrow began at the top of the sheet on the right and crossed the page diagonally, leading the eye directly to this spot below. Thus, whoever had this paper in his hand could not doubt that this was the most important part of the text. To show how highly he estimated the importance of his task, Thomas asked whether, before providing the definitive version, he might practice a few times. "Naturally," said the girl, and she quickly tore several sheets out of the notebook and gave them to him. On a page that already showed several finely executed words intersecting one another, he set about drawing the letters, one by one. The first letters were almost illegible, for his hand was still numb from the recent strain, and it trembled and shook as it traced out the confused characters; but his attempts quickly improved, and soon he found himself quite enchanted with the results. After receiving approval for the example he displayed, he immediately began to inscribe his name. The first letter, in a magnificent calligraphy, stretched across a large portion of the rectangle. It was then that, wanting to involve the girl in his enthusiasm and wanting also to be certain that she would appreciate it, he asked her if she knew his name.

"If you worked more quickly," she said to him, "I would know it already."

Thomas heard the response as nothing other than an invitation to do better, and Lucie's haste seemed to him a good omen.

"Fine," he said. "I won't waste any more time. But would you mind spelling out the letters for me one at a time? That would help me, for when I write one, I no longer think of the others, and the whole escapes me."

Lucie shook her head. "I meant what I said," she replied. "Your name has not come this far. So hurry and sign."

Thomas thought for a moment and took up his pen, as he had been asked; but then he suddenly realized that his task had become ludicrous and impossible. Why should he sign now? She did not know who he was, and this was a sorry comedy. Any other name besides his own would have done the job. He handed her the sheet on which he had signed the first letter of his name, a monumental letter that in itself had the importance of a word, and as she tried to pronounce it in a quiet voice, lending it the significance that the presence of the other letters should have given it, she only increased his regrets, for he sensed how much she could have consoled him simply by naming him.

"I cannot be satisfied with this incomplete signature," she said, "but time is passing, and we still have a number of things to clarify. Your statement relates to the past and protects you, *grosso modo,* from the demands through which the various floors of the house might make claims on you. So now you are a little more free. Nevertheless, the primary difficulty remains, for you still belong to the staff, and, in this capacity, your stay with me will be tolerated only within strictly defined limits. If you do not find a way to escape from the rules, I will be obliged to send you away."

Thomas expected this, too; but since he was too weak to reflect on this dreadful prospect, he declared with all the strength he could manage: "I am not a domestic."

"Good," said Lucie. "I thought so. When I saw you struggling with my furniture, it was clear that a mistake had been made, or perhaps that the employees had played a joke. Consequently, your situation is much clearer, although not necessarily better. Indeed, I no longer have any reason to ask you to leave, but as for you, you no longer have any grounds for staying. Your entry here was illicit, and although the abuse of confidence was not directly committed by you, you associated yourself with it, calling down upon yourself and accepting in advance any consequences that such an action may bring. Therefore, we must separate."

"And if I really was a domestic?" asked Thomas.

"Are you or are you not?" said the girl. "How can I respond to you, since my response depends strictly, as is natural, on your situation? If you were a domestic, I do not know what would happen and what decisions your presence would necessitate, for you would most likely have a completely different appearance. In principle, however, there need not be any absolute impossibility in letting you stay in some dark corner of the room, on condition that nothing brings your presence to my attention, but all relations between us would be strictly forbidden. In any case, this hypothesis is no longer conceivable; there is no going back on a statement as categorical as yours."

"What should I do?" Thomas asked feebly.

"Unfortunately," said the girl, "I see but one solution: you must leave. The fact that you would not submit to servile tasks eliminates, in a sense, the greatest obstacles between us; no bond is possible with a man who is already bound to a task. As for you, you are free; in that sense everything would be fine. But this advantage—and you should know that it is considerable and that it can console you for a great many things—deprives you of every pretext that would allow you to stay here, even illegitimately. You yourself understand this. With the freedom you have earned, how could you seriously invoke any duty or obligation whatever in order to prolong your stay? By virtue of what constraint could your presence be justified, a presence that could not be accounted for in any other way? Can you say: 'I must stay'? Obviously not. The situation appears to me to offer no other choices."

Thomas, half turned toward the desk, could not look at the door that would soon open on him once again, perhaps, but it remained in his thoughts.

"I cannot leave the room," he said, pointing to the paper, which the girl was folding and unfolding dreamily. "After the statement that I have just signed and that makes it impossible for me to go back, the other parts of the house have ceased to exist for me. Everyone would refuse to receive me, and there would be no place for me. Everything has, so to speak, collapsed in the wake of my passage. Have you thought of this difficulty?"

"It's glaringly obvious," said Lucie, "and you have probably not grasped how serious it really is. Not only have you made yourself undesirable in the rest of the building, in that you have politely and definitively taken leave of everyone you have encountered here—this past has disappeared, and it is best never to refer to it again—but you have likewise nearly been driven from this room, which cannot be separated from the other rooms or floors. By now you have but one foot on the ground, and when I look at you somewhat distractedly, I see you half suspended in the void and barely hanging onto the tip of a cornice. Rest assured," she added, noticing how her words were terrifying Thomas, "that is only an image; you are in no real danger. And yet that is how it stands with you, and there is no need to get upset about it. Such a situation is all to your honor."

"Really?" said Thomas timidly.

"Your statement is very beautiful," said the girl, tapping the paper gently on the desk. It powerfully attracts me to you. Thus, whatever problems it may cause, it should remain in your eyes a source of pleasure and satisfaction. Contrary to custom, I will even let you hold it for a moment. It will bring you comfort. On the other side of the paper, I can feel the imprint of the letter you traced. You inscribed it in the most magnificent way. It establishes a true point of contact between us."

The girl laid the document on a corner of the desk and placed a large inkwell on top of it, forgetting to give it to Thomas. He was on the point of reminding her of her promise when she leaned toward him and touched his shoulder with the end of her penholder.

"Would you," she said, "take a look behind you? It seems to me that night is coming on."

Thomas had to lie down on his back; raising his head a little, he looked at the first room and noticed an intense ray of light falling on the ornaments of pearl and silver decorating certain pieces of furniture, giving them a resplendent glow; but the wall hangings remained very dark. "Not at all," he said, turning back around, "night is still far away. The day has not dimmed."

Lucie listened attentively, then asked him with a troubled look: "Could you, if it came down to it, justify your presence in this room?"

"Certainly," said Thomas, "nothing could be simpler. Even though I am not a domestic, I am nevertheless attached to you."

"You are?" she said. "I am also very attached to you. Your eyes are bright, and you have large, beautiful hands. I would like to look at you more closely. Could you stand up?"

Thomas thought that with her help it would be possible.

"Wait," she said, seeing that he was already trying to move. "You must first know what you are getting into. Feelings are always very simple, but if one gives in to them without reflection, it is easy to lapse into dangerous and careless things. If our relations ever became serious, you would have various obligations to fulfill, obligations that you can only accept with joy, since they prove the solidity of your attachment. Do you wish to learn about them?"

Thomas nodded yes.

"Perfect," she said. "Naturally I have no intention of explaining to you in detail all the conventions concerning which we must first be in agreement. That would be tedious, and my pride could not bear it. On your side, you may have some suggestions to make. A few examples then; that is all I will tell you about for the moment. First, I will ask that you speak as little as possible; words are of no use between us. For you it would be a cause of fatigue, for me a source of anxiety. Since the house is nothing but an immense sonorous cage, in which everyone hears what everyone else is saying, I would always have the impression that we are still exposed to the general throng and that when you tell me the secrets you keep for me, you want at the very same time to let your old acquaintances take advantage of the opportunity. Nothing could be more unpleasant. As for myself, I would end up thinking that you are still down below, and of course that would not be conducive to our relations. Second point: I will ask you please not to look at me. We still hardly know each other, and however much you may wish to please me, you cannot see me as I am. When your eyes turn to me, they are caught by one or two details, which they observe with a jealous care, and of the rest they grasp only a vague resemblance, which they fill out with imperfect recollections. Thus I am sure that right now you have a completely false image of me. You think that I am tall and energetic and that my bearing is majestic, whereas I am quite short and endowed with little resistance; my face is not oval or elongated, as you imagine it, but bony and large. Likewise, if my mouth is small, in accordance with your impression, my lips are thick, fleshy, and very red, which you do not seem to have noticed. As for my hands, I will say nothing about them; you saw them more or less as they are. These errors, for which you are not responsible, can only cause misunderstandings if, instead of eliminating their causes immediately, you stubbornly attempt to correct them. You would then be falling from one mistake into another. I have sometimes been told that right next to me there is a second, more easily approachable person on whom I have placed the burden of welcoming my friends and to whom their eyes are naturally drawn. I am sure that this is a legend, but it shows you the kind of explanation a person may be driven to by the desire to see me and by the feeling that this vision does not do justice to the truth. Since, if you continue to observe me, you will soon admit that I am not always the same, you too will be tempted, in the long run, to doubt my presence, and your suspicions will intensify our disagreements and will make me suffer for nothing. Even now I feel them in the most painful way. Your gaze constantly gives me the impression that I am absent for you and that instead of contemplating me, you are forming relations with someone else, relations from which I am excluded. To whom do you direct your admiration, your need for sympathy, your friendship? Alas, to all those you have seen before me; despite your promise, it is their images that you unconsciously seek with your eyes."

Lucie stopped for a moment; Thomas continued to look at her.

"It distresses me greatly," said the girl, "to reproach you with this when I see how much you like to look at me. But it is necessary and precisely in the interests of this vision that you want to preserve at all cost. If it is too unpleasant for you to lower your eyes, you can begin by looking only at my shadow; it will still be visible for a little while longer; night will not be long in coming, but if it leaves you only a few moments, I will light a lamp, and even in the darkness you will know that I am here. Now I would like to draw your attention to the third item in our contract. Are you ready for me to tell you?" she asked, as if she needed Thomas's assent in order to bring this question to her lips. "Good," she said, seeing that he was still listening. "A few words and I will be finished. Beginning from the moment when our union shall begin, you will be obliged not to think of me. This is a strict obligation that will suffer no relaxation. This prohibition applies above all to any friendly thoughts that you may wish to address to me and that may show through on your face, giving your presence a kind of reality completely at odds with the already precarious situation that you must come to accept. It is necessary, if circumstances require it, that I be able to claim that you are not here and even that I do not know who you are. For this purpose, your legal absence must to some extent coincide with your real absence. A few precautions will therefore be useful. If you continue to murmur my name within yourself, or if you wonder at every moment what I am doing, you will not be able to prevent your features, your gestures, and even your clothes from betraying the impressions to which you are subject and which will reveal to any well-informed observer that if you are thinking of me, then you are also close to me. I myself cannot disagree with this opinion. On the contrary, what will happen if you strictly follow my recommendations? I can see nothing but advantages to be gained. First, materially, your situation will be greatly improved. By emptying your mind, you will gradually eliminate from your person whatever is still somewhat rough or even crude. Your features will be refined and will take on an appearance that better suits them. Your eyes will become softer and grayer. Everything that makes it such that no one wants to see or hear you anymore—because when one saw and heard you before the impression was too strong—these excrescences, this brilliance devoid of delicacy, these violently emphatic contours will disappear. Your physique will be perfect. It will then be very pleasant, especially for those who, like me, will not look at you, to know that perhaps their senses have registered you but that they were neither harmed nor affected by your presence. Yet another advantage, and I will be quite certain that you belong to me and that our intimacy will not be disturbed in any way. Not to think about me: that will mean thinking about me without there being anything to separate us. By refusing me the gift of a few particular thoughts, you will be offering me not only all your other thoughts, not only your thought and attention as a whole, but also your distraction, your absence, and your distance; you will absolve me of all that is yourself, and you will open up to me all that is not you. That, then, is what I ask of you, because I want to remain as close to you as possible. Neither silence nor night nor the deepest repose will stand in the way of our friendship, and this room will be for us a favorable place for sleep."

Thomas renewed his efforts to rise by holding on to the foot of the desk. He was very frustrated with his legs, which would not bend, but he thought that if he could reach the board that served as a writing surface, he could grab onto it, and even if it fell on him, he would not let go of it until he was completely upright. The desk was heavy, and if the girl held him steady, it would have been enough to make the maneuver much easier, but, on the contrary, she moved farther away, so as not to risk being struck by the repercussions of these dangerous oscillations; then, having stood up, she merely flashed a friendly look in Thomas's direction. Contrary to all reasonable expectations, the desk did not fall; it was more solidly attached to the floor than one might have believed; perhaps the girl had screwed it down when she put it back in its place, and the oscillations no doubt had another cause—such as the wind that was violently blowing outside and that gave rise, in this part of the house, to some considerable shaking and trembling. Once he was standing, Thomas thought about what Lucie had just said to him, but a moment later he thought he had begun to fall asleep, for he jumped with a start upon hearing the girl say in a loud voice: "Who's there? Who knocked?"

Yet it did not seem to him that anyone had knocked at the door. The silence was even more complete than before, when at times there seemed to be distant sounds of people coming and going in the house. Now there was absolute peace.

"No one is there," said Thomas, after listening intently for a moment. "Are you expecting a visit?"

He asked this question only to emphasize the extraordinary quality of such an idea.

"But there is someone. Listen," said Lucie, "someone knocked."

Thomas listened again, but no more now than before was the slightest noise to be heard; it is true that, turned toward the desk, he was better situated to hear what was happening in the bedroom than to pick up the muffled sounds from the hallway. Since there was no use in contradicting the girl, he remained silent but without appearing to take any part in her waiting, and soon Lucie too abandoned her expectant attitude, saying in a promising tone, in order to forget these few moments of distraction: "Now the night will not make us wait much longer. There is already a thick fog in the vestibule, and the stained glass windows are beginning to shine with the first flames lit by the guardians. I will go draw the curtains and close the doors. Stay here until I return."

Thomas wanted to say to her: Do not bother with the room; it needs no care; there will be time enough to watch over it later. But he thought that such suggestions would not be sensible and that, since he could no longer fulfill his functions as a domestic, he should be grateful to the young woman for performing them in his place. As for the night, that was certainly a mistake. There was, on the contrary, more light than when he arrived, and the presence of the fog could be explained by many other causes, particularly the bad ventilation of the building. Besides, if it really was almost night, the wind would not be rising in such gusts, to the point of shaking the roof and rattling the vaults; everything would have been much more calm. After moving a few steps away, the young woman abruptly turned around and said: "Our conversation has been most useful. You have understood perfectly what I wanted, and I feel that we are in agreement on every point. So do not lose confidence. Your fidelity will be rewarded."

Thomas heard her walk away and listened to her footsteps until the onslaught of wind had drowned out their last echoes. The racket that shattered the silence from time to time — making one think of demolition work being carried out by bungling laborers — seemed deeper, more desolate, more foreign to all efforts at comprehension than the calm, already so empty, that it drove away. "I am probably lost," he said to himself. "I no longer have the strength to wait, and if I could hope to overcome my weakness again for a short while, as long as I was not alone, now I have no more reason to make any new efforts. It is of course a very sad thing to come so close to a goal without being able to grasp it. I am sure that if I reached these last steps of the stairs, I would understand why I have struggled in vain to search for something I have not found. It's a stroke of bad luck, and I am dying of it." He fell clumsily to the floor and was unable to protect his head with his hand. When he regained consciousness, he heard through the beating of his heart the distant sound of clanging metal; it sounded like the grating of a lock. He attributed this noise to the rattling of the room's framework as it was shaken by the wind. Was someone opening the door? He lifted his head, which he had buried in his arms, and saw that his fall had landed him next to the first step of the little set of stairs. There was no consolation in this. It was rather the supreme insult, this invitation to take the last steps, whereas he was already digging a pit for himself in the floor. At this moment, the door opened with a clatter, and although it was far away, he smelled the icy humid air from outside. "It looks like I didn't have the right key," he said to himself. "How could I have fulfilled my task as a domestic without the necessary tools? I really have no reason to reproach myself." The door did not close again, and he thought that the young woman had not left the room and was hesitating to pass through the doorway. There were several possibilities to consider: perhaps she had no intention of leaving and only wanted to ventilate the room; or else she wanted to chase away the intruder who had come to knock a moment ago, and she was giving a sign that she would remain loyal to her commitments. He stayed with this thought and was not surprised to hear the sound of voices. The negotiations were beginning, and they continued for a few moments. This prospect encouraged him; he tried to use this delay to gain a few inches by grasping onto the edge of the steps. First he reached out his arm and took hold of a piece of wood, which he pulled toward him with all his strength; he struggled tenaciously and managed to bring his head close to a round carpet covered in thick, rough hair that gave off a strong bitter smell, similar to the smell of pepper. He pressed it against his cheek and was relieved no longer to feel the cold, hard floor. "How is the discussion going?" he said to himself with a certain detachment, thinking of the girl. He still heard voices, the halting and combative voice of a man, and the voice of Lucie, which sounded remarkably deep. Important interests were no doubt at stake, and he followed the back and forth movement of the responses, which resembled the chaotic calls of the wind. The girl shouted to him, as though forcing him to participate in the conversation: "It's someone to visit you."

Then she quickly returned, followed a few steps behind by the visitor who had been delayed by closing the door. Thomas waited until she came up next to him before worrying about this extraordinary news, but first she called to the man walking behind her, and holding his arm, she again took up her place by the desk. Thomas made a great effort to recognize this visitor, who was arriving at such a bad moment; he was a young man, strongly built, with an imposing presence, a man who held his head high and seemed to be conscious of his dignity.

"I am your former companion," he said to Thomas, without giving him the time to draw his own conclusions from the examination.

"Yes," the young woman interrupted, "he has come to verify that everything is happening according to the rules." And she added, anticipating an objection: "It's the customary practice."

Thomas asked him to kneel down next to him so that he could observe him more easily and, if need be, speak to him. A great deal of negotiation was required to arrive at this result. The young man thought that Thomas was asking him to go away, and serious about his role, he refused by shaking his head irrefutably. When he finally understood that he could reconcile Thomas's request with his assigned duties, he made up for his delay with an exaggerated haste, and as if leaning over were not enough, he lay all the way down on the floor. Thomas considered him for a moment with surprise.

"You find me changed?" inquired the young man, looking annoyed. Then, so that the question would not long remain without an answer, he added: "It's quite natural. When you met me, I was coming out of a serious illness and had not entirely recovered. Now that's an old, long-forgotten story. Besides," he added in a flattering voice, "you have certainly changed as much as I have."

Despite these explanations, Thomas continued to look at him all the same. He seemed like a man who later in life had undergone a phenomenal development, who had from force of thought molted and transformed into the model of vigor and strength he was bound to become one day. His scars were no longer visible, except around his mouth, which, when he spoke, lifted up toward his eyes a little. Through a mysterious association of ideas, Thomas thought about that woman seen by some to hover next to Lucie and who alone communicated with them.

"If you are looking now to see if there really are any resemblances between me and you," said the young man, "you are making a mistake, and I must warn you about the illusion you may let yourself fall into. It is a well-known fact that when people have lived for a long time together, they come to have identical mannerisms and common expressions. But the resemblance goes no further. I advise you not to linger over these remarks, whose superficial character will not stand up to serious consideration."

"Where do you live now?" asked Thomas.

"I have not yet left the old room on the first underground floor," he said. "It's a temporary assignment that will be modified as soon as the tenants have re-assembled."

Thomas asked another question in a weak voice, but since the young man could not understand him, Lucie had to kneel down to listen to him as well.

"This is the customary practice?" repeated Thomas.

"It's more than that," said Lucie, "it's an obligation. The agreements we have discussed, to the extent that they are of a personal nature, must be guaranteed by a third party who oversees their execution. This supervision is indispensable because, with the feelings that draw us together, we would be incapable of mutually overseeing ourselves in a sufficiently rigorous manner, and from this there would result problems that must be avoided. The intervention of this young man is therefore an excellent sign; soon, nothing will stand in the way of our intimacy."

The former companion thought it useful to complete the response: "My role is very important," he said. "I have the responsibility of serving as a mouthpiece for you when your weakness no longer allows you to express yourself and when there is something particularly important that you need to say. I am also supposed to facilitate your knowledge of events that you could no longer experience directly or that you seem especially inclined to misinterpret. Since no one in the house has been more closely associated with your existence, I was especially suited for this role, and I hope that the way in which I carry out my duty will give you complete satisfaction. Now," he added, turning to Lucie, "everything seems to me to have been clearly specified; would you be so kind as to take down what I say? A simple formality," he shouted for Thomas's sake.

"One more word," said Thomas, as the young man was about to stand up. "The thought never occurred to me to compare myself to you, and I find that we do not resemble each other in any way at all. For me, you are only a former companion."

"Really?" said the young man incredulously. "Well, then, it's all for the better. So we are all agreed and ready to begin."

He quickly stood up, as if he were afraid that Thomas might have something more to add, and touching Lucie lightly on the shoulder, he drew her attention to the vestibule where there was something he wanted her to see. They both stood there staring in that direction. Thomas, annoyed by the silence, also wanted to look at whatever it was that so aroused their curiosity, but he only succeeded in troubling the young man.

"Night is coming," said the latter. "We are only waiting for the moment to light the lamps; when the last reflections of light have faded from the furniture and the floors, we can consider the day to be over. Have a little patience, it will only be a few moments."

Thomas thought that his work was not completely wasted, since the furniture he had polished so well was still catching the light and prolonging the day; he said to himself, thinking of all the facets of the desk: "They are mistaken to think they will soon be done." But the two observers probably did not have the stamina to wait for the darkness to be complete, for it seemed to Thomas that he had hardly had the time to close his eyes and open them again, when he saw on the steps several lamps whose red light was very different from that of the twilight. They had a glass ball on top to serve as a lampshade, and on each one was inscribed short sentences that glowed from the fire. Three of these sentences struck him in particular; the first was written in gothic letters and carried these words: *The lamps of love are lamps of flame;* the second, more drawn than written, said: *I lit up his ignorance;* as for the third, it was so long that the words he read seemed to be only a small part of it, although the deciphered text needed no complement: *The day sings praises to the day, and the night teaches knowledge to the night.* These lamps shed a pleasant light, and Thomas, while remaining convinced that they had been lit prematurely, did not ask that they be taken away, which in his opinion, he would have been right to do. But realizing that the mottoes he had just read probably had a much more important continuation or reply on the side facing the bedroom, he asked the young man to tell him what they were. The latter looked over at Lucie for a moment and said: "In the uppermost sections of the vaults, some of the panes of colored glass are no doubt broken and are letting the light of day pass through, for at such an hour we should be in complete darkness, whereas only the vestibule is filled completely with shadows. This is surprising, but we can do nothing to counter this phenomenon. For as long as the night is not yet complete, you will have the right to remain in the room, and you can choose between prolonging your stay here another few moments or disregarding this unexpected delay and withdrawing to the bedroom right now. You are therefore free to decide. Nevertheless, since it is not always easy to judge the exact moment when night falls, there is every reason not to wait until the last minute, which would oblige me to act swiftly and would deprive you of the precautionary treatment that will be indispensable to you."

Thomas noted with pleasure that he was not mistaken in his sense of the day's long duration. To emphasize this advantage, he said: "I wish to claim the fullest extent of my rights."

"Of course," said the young man. "I cannot act against your will."

Lucie walked over to the lamps and bent over them with her tall thin form; Thomas thought she was going to turn the glass balls around so that he could see the other sentences, but either because the lampshades were too hot, or because she had never intended to do this, she overlooked the desire he had expressed, and stepping past the line of light, she entered the third room. The young man did not want to remain behind; he indicated with a few gestures that he was not responsible for the decision, and in a single stride he had climbed the two sets of stairs. But his absence was brief. If they had gone to prepare the room, their work could not have been very meticulous. Thomas said as much to his former companion, and he added: "Why was it precisely you whom they sent to me?"

The young man thought about this question for a moment, then he slipped his hands under Thomas's arms and, with an abrupt movement, stood him upright, holding him tightly against himself. In this uncomfortable position, the two of them climbed the stairs; Thomas was squeezed against the chest of his guide, shoulder to shoulder, and was walking backward, able to see only the vestibule and the room he was leaving. "Of course," he said to himself, "it is still the middle of the day," and he protested the abuse of which he was a victim by resisting with all his might. To his great surprise, he was less weak than he thought, and he succeeded in paralyzing his opponent by tightly clinging to him; he was the same size, his shoulders were almost as large, and he was able to prevent him from moving around by pressing hard against the steps. In the course of this struggle, he looked closely at his old companion; he tried to determine what resemblance there might have been between them. If there was any resemblance, it was not very striking. Perhaps his eyes were the same color, and the shape of his face might well be identical, but there were little spots here and there on his skin that made any confusion impossible. He was discouraged nonetheless by the analogy between certain features, and holding off his resistance, he let himself be carried away by the young man, who took him straight to the bed and laid him down on it.

"Now," he said to Thomas, "rest peacefully. I will keep watch in your place and will inform you of any important events."

He drew the curtains, leaving only a narrow gap through which the room could be observed. Then, sitting on the bed, he took a piece of bread out of his pocket and ate it ravenously. Thomas, happy at first to be lying on a real bed, soon grew anxious. The bed was narrow and short, and although its dimensions were perfectly adapted to his body, it gave him the impression of being meant for a much smaller man; there was also a large hole in the middle, formed no doubt by the thousands of bodies that had already been there, and Thomas had great difficulty keeping himself from slipping into it. The young man paid no attention to this uncomfortable position and made it even more cramped by sitting across the whole width of the mattress and gradually forcing his companion into the hollow spot that threatened to engulf him. As he ate, he said, no doubt out of politeness: "I will always have good memories of the time we spent together. Your company was a pleasure, and I appreciated your way of living. I will reproach you with one thing only, which is that you did not follow my advice more closely. In my opinion, this dwelling did not suit you; you were made for life in the open air, and your organism could hardly tolerate a long reclusion in these rooms that are insufficiently ventilated, overheated, and contaminated by the frequent presence of the sick. Your bad physical condition is what hindered you in your searches, and in the end it has been responsible for your failure."

Thomas merely replied: "But I have succeeded."

"Most certainly," said the young man, "you have succeeded; I am not here to contradict you; but you know very well that one always succeeds and that that is not what's important. I simply wanted to point out to you that you chose the wrong path and that you would have been well advised to stay in a climate that is more appropriate to your temperament. The success you have gained, however laudable, will not leave any deep traces; it will not be recorded in the annals, believe me."

"I know," said Thomas in a low voice.

"And yet you were not lacking in fine qualities," the young man continued. "You were industrious, persevering, sensible. You made enormous efforts that should have put you in the foremost position and earned everyone's esteem. I regret that all this strength was squandered."

"What was I lacking, then?" asked Thomas.

"You didn't recognize your own way," said the young man. "I was placed with you in order to enlighten you whenever you wished. I was like another you. I knew all the pathways of the house, and I knew which one you ought to have followed. All you had to do was ask me. But you preferred to listen to advice that could only lead to your loss."

Thomas tried to remember whether he had not turned to Dom several times without ever receiving an intelligible response; but these things were too old, and he was too tired; so he said: "What was the way?"

"You turned your back on it," the young man answered in his quiet and somewhat fatuous manner. "Your ambition was to reach the heights, to pass from one floor to another, to advance inch by inch, as though, simply by walking on, you would necessarily come out on the roof and stand in the midst of nature's beauty once again. A puerile ambition that quite simply has killed you. What deprivations did you not force on yourself! What weariness in this pestilential atmosphere! And these stories that were as deceptive as they were depressing, these contacts with men already eaten away by vice! Anyone would have succumbed in your place. Yet the true way was already laid out; it was a gentle slope requiring neither effort nor consultation. In addition, it took you toward a region where you would have led a life that would have been worth the trouble. There, truly, you were at home."

"And where was it?" asked Thomas, his eyes half closed.

"In the underground floors," said the young man in an unctuous voice. "I cannot speak to you about it as long as I would need to, and it is not with words that one can explain the inextricable beauty of the basements and the cellars. You must judge it for yourself. You are a man from the country, and you would see immediately what a feeling for life one has in these places carved out of the earth; there one breathes a warm intense odor that inspires disgust for the more enclosed rooms. The layout is very curious: despite the maze of hallways that intersect, bifurcate, and turn back on themselves in complex, dizzying circuits, it is not possible to wander astray, and you see perfectly clearly where you are at every moment. Enormous signs, employing a system of arrows and dashes, show every thirty feet which route to follow in the section where you think you are lost; go to the right, and you descend ever farther beneath the foundations; go to the left, and you approach the basement and the entrance. That is the only rule that remains; as for the rest, you are perfectly free."

"Free?" Thomas repeated.

"Yes, free," said the young man. "You cannot imagine how shocking is the contrast with the life of the house. They constitute two modes of living so opposed that, while one can be compared to life, the other is hardly more desirable than death. Down there, the tenants cease to depend on the rules whose power, already weakened at the approach of the great doorway, is completely suspended when one passes through it. This great door, contrary to its name, is only a barrier made of a few pieces of wood and a little latticework. But against it, the forces of custom are shattered, and the imaginations of the tenants depict it as an immense carriage entrance flanked on every side by towers and drawbridges and guarded by a man whom they call Aminadab. In reality, access to it is very easy, and a sudden downward slope is the only thing that indicates to those who pass through that they are now under the earth."

"Did you say 'under the earth'?" asked Thomas, trying to raise himself up to hear better. "How curious."

"That's exactly right," said the young man, looking around with an air of triumph. "Have you never thought of the advantages there would be in living underground? They are many. First of all, you are no longer subject to the alternations of night and day, which are the cause of endless difficulties and the principle source of all our anguish and worries. Thanks to an installation that costs very little, you can, as you wish, remain continually in an agreeable light or—and this is preferable—in a gentle darkness that leaves you absolutely free in your actions. I hasten to add that there are many absurd prejudices concerning the darkness underground. It is completely false that the darkness there is total or in any way distressing. With a little adjustment, one succeeds very well in distinguishing a sort of clarity that radiates through the shadows and that is deliciously attractive to the eyes. Some claim that this clarity is the inner truth of objects and that it is dangerous to contemplate it too long. Do not believe it, for it goes without saying that once one has decided to set oneself up in these regions, it is not in order to find the atrocious furniture or the jumble of objects and implements that make up one of the torments of life in the house. On the contrary, it is yet another advantage not to have within reach these uncanny objects that are supposedly so useful but concerning which it is at bottom impossible to know what they are, what they're used for, what they're supposed to mean. The earth—this is a well-known fact—is a medium for nourishment, in which each body finds its subsistence, in which breath too is a sort of food, and which offers extraordinary possibilities of growth and duration. As soon as you enter into these underground spaces, you are stunned by the impression it makes, which is like the end of a bad dream. Until then, you have always hoped to escape from the worries and the responsibilities of existence, but you lacked courage,

186

and you could not renounce the desire to continue. Down there, hardly have you descended into those long tunnels that pass through hundreds of feet of earth, when you feel as if you have woken up. First, you are free. The room you thought you would never leave has disappeared; you are at home wherever you happen to be, and you no longer live in fear of violating instructions that are unknown to you. Next, you soon understand that the earth aspires to a profound union with you, that, far from reducing your efforts to nothing through the action of a law that is unsuitable to you, it works slowly, with a delicate art, to shape itself to your form, and at the same time it tries to draw your breath to itself and adjust it to its rhythm. What you feel is so gentle and pleasant that you think it is a dream; but you are not dreaming; nothing is more real. On the contrary, you begin to rise up and to seek out new underground spaces that you have never seen and where you come to a stop, holding yourself upright, with your arms spread, against the wall of earth. Then you look across the layers that form enormous heaps of dust, and you are surprised to notice that your vision has been altered, for your gaze—and this phenomenon appears odd and even humiliating when one speaks of it at these heights, but down there it seems much easier to explain—your gaze makes you think of fine crystal plants that have rapidly grown from the moldy earth on which your eyes have opened. This is no miracle, despite what simple-minded people may believe. But it is a manifestation to which some importance can be attached. These arborescent shapes, although—need it be said?—they in no way resemble real bushes or trees, are a sign of the elevated form of union that exists between you and the milieu in which your life is fashioned. Just as the night makes one's eyes sparkle in order to draw truly nocturnal images from them, so does the earth bring them to fruition in the only forms it is allowed to propagate and in which it places all its love. Some like to use a comparison to explain this phenomenon: they say that this earth with which you are surrounded is pure night and that plants and umbels are born from your eyes so that nature might take greater pleasure in the act that passes through every part of it, just as it sometimes happens that a man who has studied the law sees judgments and sentences leaping from the eyes of the woman most dear to him. But that doesn't matter. The fact is that you feel a great satisfaction. It seems to you that such a change announces the return of a totally bygone era, which you no longer even remember, so far has it receded into some fabulous distance. Your hope is that these light vegetable forms will live and prosper, these forms that are still so fragile that most often they wither and fall apart. But you are patient; from your breath you extract your food and your sleep—a small part of the reserves allotted to you—and this is a sacrifice you make with all your heart, in order to nourish this seed that holds on by a mere thread but within which you feel the strength of stubborn memories. Naturally, for someone from here who lives in a feverish haste, the wait would seem exaggeratedly long; but that is not the case with you; from time to time you make exciting discoveries, and these are enough to occupy your time. For example, you notice that your fingernail is split down the middle and that through this small breach something that had disappeared from your memory has reawakened and is returning to life. Of course, it is still too small for you to be sure that you are not mistaken, but the hope it gives you is no less great, and you endlessly examine the minute specks of dust that scatter when the least little breath falls on them. During this time, your eyes too have undergone a transformation, and far from being hindered by the obstructed view and the triple branches proliferating through the earth, they become larger and deeper, and their roots extend down the back of the neck to the top of the shoulders. You begin to be somewhat frightened by this unexpected development, then you feel that your strength has magnified tenfold and that soon the hole in which you think you are contained will not be able to hold you. For your fingernails are now open; at the ends of your fingers, you see tiny flowers, almost imperceptible but already well formed, which look like the buds of a heliotrope. Where have they come from? How could the seed have persevered enough to sprout under the nail? It is only a small mystery, but you are passionately absorbed in it, and you come to believe that during your great journey, you carried a grain of pollen under your fingernail; this is probably only a fanciful idea that you yourself do not accept, for you know very well that your entire past life has perished; nevertheless, you cannot help staring at these little leaves gently rising and swaying. Their growth is much more rapid than you expected; it even becomes quite bothersome, and since the roots are very fragile and have not gone any farther than the tips of the fingers—how could they have?—you are obliged to keep constant watch over these delicate shoots. At times, everything appears to be dead; it seems that you have judged your own strength too hastily, and the earth itself hardens as if ancient suspicions were being revived. But these are only moments of dis-

188

couragement, no different from those that occur in all serious endeavors. One day you notice a curious fact: from time to time, the plants feverishly move about; one would think that the clay was no longer enough to satisfy them and that somewhere far away, in the distance of distances, an event had taken place toward which they are forcefully drawn. You see the trembling of the miniscule petals, and you too ask yourself if you may not have heard, through the silence of the underground spaces, a message or at least the echo of a message. Perhaps it is only a meaningless noise; perhaps the attempt is worth the trouble; soon you have decided, and taking up your shovel, you courageously set out to open a hole in the earth. This is the beginning of an immense task. You must dig for a very long time and accumulate mountains of silt on both sides of your path. Fortunately, you have become very strong; far from being threatened by the shock of the work, the plants continue to grow and begin to look like small trees that, it's true, lack all color. They spiral firmly, and with authority, into layer after layer of earth, without letting you choose your direction; you need only wait until they have grown deeply, and since, after all, this takes a long time, it seems to you that it takes months and years for your eyes to pierce this dense night and to light the path you are to follow. But why would you be worried? You are heeding the call, and if the difficulties are great, they are no more insurmountable than the ones encountered in an ordinary existence, and they are certainly less petty. So you continue on your way; dirt covers your face completely and almost envelops your entire body; but one of your hands remains free, sinks all its fingers into the thick crust, and furiously scrapes open the passage; although it works unassisted, it gets through more work than a whole team of ditchdiggers; with such help as this, you will not be long in finishing. One day, the earth caves in, and beneath the mound that surrounds you, you perceive a thin sliver of light that hovers around the edge of your vision. This was no doubt bound to happen; the day is not far; although the idea of beginning a new life frightens you a little, you turn with pride toward the past, now buried for good, and you realize that there is a way out; you have managed to escape the inevitable, the only one among countless thousands, for you recognized that the true path did not lead toward the heights but lay deeply buried under the ground. Now a thin crust separates you from the end of the nightmare, and only one problem remains: what will happen up there? Obviously, you are forced to think about the appearance you have taken on and the habits you have developed, and you are not unaware that one does not journey for years under the earth with impunity. Would you not do better to remain where you are, joyously waiting for the air and the sun to make your memories grow and to lead you toward your new existence? That is the question now, and you must answer it."

Thomas sat up in his bed as if he really did have to answer this question. He looked at the young man and saw that he was questioning him in a most urgent manner that did not allow any escape or even any delay. The strange air of his former companion had struck him already during the course of the conversation. To make his words more lively, he had stood up to mimic the various scenes he recounted. Of course, his gestures were very discreet, and since they often related to events that were difficult to represent, an inattentive person would not always have understood how the anguished force of his movements — the swaying of his body, his way of quickly passing his hand over his face, as though to erase its features, the sly expression with which he moved his fingernails toward his eyes, and many other gestures besides — exhausted the attention of his interlocutor and obliged him to accept everything in this conversation. Thomas was no less disturbed by the efforts his companion made to hide the resemblance between the two of them. The care he took to avoid all of Thomas's habitual attitudes only ended up accentuating this resemblance and increasing its threatening quality; his immobility itself was a reproach, and it humiliated both of them.

Thomas continued to stare at him for a long time; then suddenly thinking of Lucie, he said: "Please excuse me; I am not ready to answer your question; I must prepare for an important visit, and I need to be very calm."

The young man went to the curtains and distractedly looked out between them; he was probably very frustrated.

"I would be happy," Thomas added, trying to soften this disappointment, "to demonstrate my gratitude, for your account greatly interested me. But you will understand that, in my present situation, it would be impossible for me to give any useful consideration to the extraordinary life change you have proposed. I am afraid that it is much too late."

"I know," said the young man, "I know that."

Then he called Lucie in an impertinent voice that Thomas found extremely tiresome. The young woman came carrying one of the lamps that had been shining on the steps of the stairway a few moments before;

upon entering, she put out the light; daylight continued to stream through the curtain. After a few moments, Thomas, who was trying to determine whether this brightness was coming from the other lamps or from a nearby window, was astonished to hear his companion speak for him in a melancholy tone: "I have long been waiting for this interview. Unfortunately, it will not be possible for me to pay close attention, for my strength is lacking, and I have difficulty following a conversation. Come, then, and stay next to me."

Lucie approached Thomas.

"I am much weaker than you might suppose," the young man continued. "You neglected me in the beginning, and now I am just lucid enough to listen to your words. The end awaiting me is not enviable."

These last words shocked Thomas, who said immediately: "I am not happy with this language. I would like to express my thoughts myself."

Dom turned around, surprised and somewhat annoyed. "That is not possible," he hastened to say.

The young woman interceded. "Don't be too quick to condemn him," she said to Thomas in a new tone of intimacy.[1] "He is acting with good intentions. Tell me, what else would you like to communicate to us?"

"It is certainly true," said Thomas, "that my end does not merit such a sad judgment. On the contrary, I feel very happy to have fulfilled my duty and to have lived long enough to meet you."

"And yet he is the one who is right," she said, pointing to the young man. "Now you see only the superficial signs, but your last moments can only inspire pity."

"But," said Thomas, "I did everything you said to do. I trust you, and I am waiting for my efforts to be repaid. Even though many things were refused to me, I would consider myself satisfied."

"Don't commit a final error," said the girl.

"And what error would I be committing?" asked Thomas.

"Let me give you a piece of advice," said the girl, as if this were the answer. "I am very attached to you, and it pains me to see how badly things have turned out for you. Lie down on your side and lift your head to look through the curtain. There is a window with a black frame that stands out

1. Here Lucie begins to address Thomas with the familiar *tu* form, rather than the formal *vous* that she has used up to now. — Tr.

from the wall; despite the drapery covering it, it lets in a little air from outside. Can you see it?"

Thomas turned over painfully. The girl was directly in front of him. Since the bed was very low, she seemed to dominate him more than ever, and her shape almost towered out of sight. With great effort he saw two intense rays of light.

"This window," said Lucie, "gives you an idea of the darkness that will fill the room when the moment has come for our union. Right now your eyes still discern the shadows that slip through the cracks, but soon the darkness will strike your senses, and you will fall into a state in which you will see nothing more."

"A window?" said Thomas. "That's curious. Would you go stand next to it and raise your hand as if you wanted to make a sign to someone outside and were asking him to enter? That would give me some relief."

"No," said Lucie, "I am not allowed to leave you now."

"Well then," said Thomas, "send the young man. He too has played his role."

"You're asking for the impossible," said Lucie impatiently. "Listen to me instead."

Thomas looked toward the window again and was still surprised to see the bright light coming into the room. It seemed that the drapery, though made of a thick velvet, could no longer block out the daylight pressing in from the outside.

"That's it," said the girl. "Don't lose heart, and look with manly courage upon the coming night. As I speak to you, you will stare more and more intently at the shadows, and the darkness will help you to understand me. Indeed, I have some unpleasant news to tell you. Contrary to what you have thought, I do not know you, I never made a sign, and I did not send any message. It is only thanks to the carelessness that reigns in the house that you have been able to come this far; but no order called you here, and someone else was expected. Of course, since you are here, I must take account of your presence, and I do not want to send you away under the pretext that you are a stranger to me. You will stay, then, as long as you like, but it was my duty not to allow you to delude yourself any longer."

Thomas listened to the girl, as if she would necessarily have to take back what she was saying.

"I cannot believe you," he said. "I do recognize you."

192

"Don't be so stubborn," said Lucie. "You have committed an error; I am not the one you are looking for, and you are not the one who was supposed to come. This is very aggravating for you, but I cannot change the truth."

"All the same, I don't believe you," said Thomas. "There are many things that you too do not know. I have been searching for you longer than you think, and I cannot lightly abandon all the proof I have gathered. Long ago—this, at least, you cannot deny—I met you in a large building where you lived in a room next to mine. You knocked at my door; I opened, and since it was late, and I had some urgent work to finish, you sat down at the table where I was writing, and I dictated several letters to you. We became very absorbed in this work; you barely had enough time to grasp my words and to write them down as you recalled them. It could be, then, that you were unable to look carefully at me and that my features, fleetingly glimpsed, were erased from your memory. But I, I could not forget you; I recognize you; I know it's you."

Thomas put all his strength into these last words, and it seemed to him, after he had said them, that there was no longer anything that he could really believe; his statement had been too categorical.

"I would like to spare you the pain I am causing you," the girl said sadly. "It is a dreadful thing for you to have followed this long road and not to find yourself in the presence of the person you wanted to see again. It's a terrible misunderstanding."

"No," said Thomas shaking his head, "I am not mistaken. The resemblance is too great. But something has happened that I cannot understand and that I have no time to explain. Do you resent me for not being very friendly to you back then? The work claimed all our attention. We had no time to look at each other. It was wrong. Now we will have all our lives to ourselves."

"Why do you persist?" said the girl. "As we speak, you are losing precious time. Look rather at the darkness that rises and gathers behind the curtains. Night will be here, and we will be reunited. When darkness has come, what else is there in the world? So lay your thoughts aside."

"No," repeated Thomas, "it is still day, and the day cannot be long enough for my distress. Understand what I say: I began to search for you everywhere as soon as you left me. On the roads I sometimes saw young women who resembled you; I looked at them, and I touched them, but it wasn't you. So I went farther, despite my fatigue, I visited all the streets and all the houses: no one had seen you. Later I no longer dared speak of you, so afraid was I that my questions made you flee. I hung my head as I walked and saw only the stones of the road. 'Then whom,' I said to myself, 'shall I find?' It was not even worth the trouble to know; my weariness left me with only strength enough to find my way. But when I saw you from the street, and you made a sign to me, I entered the house and slowly made my way to you. It was mad, no doubt. Is it possible to find anyone in this world? But I searched for you all the same, and here you are next to me."

"No," said the girl, "you're deluded. I had never seen your face before you came in here, and I remember nothing that would confirm your claims. There might be others besides you who could make me doubt, and if I rummaged through my memory, perhaps I could succeed in finding an image that would enlighten me. But with you, that is not the case; I do not need to question you to know that we have never yet been in each other's presence."

"It's frightful," said Thomas; he made an effort to turn away from the window and to look at the young woman; but she dissuaded him and caressed his hair. "Whom else could you remember? We were always alone, and you have known no one but me. Nothing will shake my conviction."

"So be it," said the girl. "Since you are so sure of what you say, I surrender to your words. You have convinced me."

She turned to Dom and addressed him in a harsh voice, as if she were reproaching him for letting himself be interrupted: "You can speak now."

"Just a moment," said Thomas. "I would like to clarify one detail. Although all the features of your face are the same as those I hold in my memory, there is something, however, that does not correspond: your voice has changed."

"My voice?" Lucie repeated.

"Yes," said Thomas. "Don't you remember that your voice was very weak? It was hardly audible. Now, it still has some very gentle intonations, but at times it resounds with such force that one fears being unable to bear it. This is only a small detail, but it worries me."

"I can speak more softly," said Lucie, and she said a few words in a whisper.

"To whom are you speaking?" asked Thomas.

"To you," said the girl. "Do you want that?"

"Yes," he answered, but a few moments passed while he listened attentively, as if he were waiting for Lucie to try the experiment again in a more satisfying way. Since she hesitated, he spoke to the young man. "Perhaps," he said, "my illness has altered my organs and is causing me to hear voices in an abnormal way. Would you say a few words as well?"

The young man hesitated, then said with a certain ill humor: "With regard to the conversation we had a moment ago, I fear that you may have been too hasty in reaching a conclusion. In my opinion, my proposal ought to have interested you, and it was not too late."

"Really?" said Thomas. He thought for a moment, then added: "I hear your voice perfectly well; it seems to me that even in times past I would not have heard it differently. This forces me to be less categorical."

He abruptly raised his head and stared at the girl's face, less to judge its character than to find in it a confirmation of his hopes. He did not appear to have regained any calm.

"In considering your features one by one," he said finally, "I can only maintain my first impression. They correspond at every point to those of the person I knew. In terms of the resemblance, it is equally as precise, although one cannot be so sure about a simple analogy. But one thing that requires more caution is the expression of your eyes. You do not look at me as you did back then. It seems to me, when you stare at me, that you are not the one I see. I no longer know then on whom my eyes are resting, and I am afraid of making a mistake. I am obliged," he added, as if he were apologizing for contradicting the girl, "I am obliged to take this remark into account."

He waited for a response, but since Lucie said nothing, he asked her: "Do you hold it against me? It is very important to me."

The girl still remained silent.

"I have only reported my impressions," Thomas continued. "Might you have something to say perhaps?"

But no response came.

"I did not want to alter the truth," said Thomas.

The girl then bent down to him and shouted: "You won't listen to anything; you're incorrigible."

She violently took his head in her hands and forced him to turn toward the window; since Thomas tried to see something new that would have explained her gesture, she said to him furtively: "You must wait for the night; it is slow in coming. I do not know if anyone pointed this out to you, but the darkness is easily driven out of the house. Although the sun does not directly illuminate it, hardly does the light seem to have left when it has already returned, and the eye that closed on a sleepy world reopens onto an intense brightness. Only in this last room, situated at the very top of the house, does night fall entirely. It is generally beautiful and soothing. It is pleasant not to have to close one's eyes to be freed from the insomnia of the day. It is also very charming to find in the darkness outside the same shadows that long ago struck down the truth inside oneself. This night has its particularities. It brings with it neither dreams nor the premonitions that, at times, take the place of dreams. Rather it is itself a vast dream that is not within reach of the person it envelops. When it has surrounded your bed, we will draw the curtains that enclose the alcove, and the splendor of the objects that will then be revealed will be enough to console the most unhappy of men. At that moment, I too will become truly beautiful. Whereas now, this false day takes away many of my charms; at that auspicious moment I will appear just as I am. I will look at you for a long time; I will lie down not far from you, and you will not need to question me, because I will answer every question. And at the same time, the lamps whose inscriptions you wanted to read will be turned around the right way, and their sentences, which will make you understand everything, will be indecipherable no longer. So do not be impatient; at your call, the night will do justice to you, and your worries and your weariness will sink out of sight."

"One more question," said Thomas, who had listened with great interest, "will the lamps be lit?"

"Of course not," said the girl. "What a foolish question! Everything will be covered in darkness."

"Darkness, night . . ." said Thomas with a dreamy look. "Then I will see you no more?"

"No doubt," said the girl. "What did you think? It is precisely because you will be lost for good in the shadows, and because you will no longer be able to see what is going on around you, that I will immediately tell you about it. You cannot hope to hear, see, and rest all at once. I will therefore warn you about what will happen when the night has revealed its truth to you and you are fully at rest. Is it not good for you to know that in a few moments everything you have wished to know will be legible on the walls, on my face, on my mouth, in a few simple words? That this revelation does not touch you yourself is a drawback, to be sure; but the essential thing is to be sure that you have not struggled in vain. Imagine the scene right now: I will take you in my arms and will murmur words of the greatest importance in your ear, words that are so important that you would be transformed if you ever heard them. My face, how I would like for you to see it; for it is then, then but not before, that you will recognize, that you will know you have found the one you think you have been seeking throughout all your journeys and for whose sake you miraculously entered here, miraculously but uselessly; think of the joy that will bring; you have desired above all to see her again, and when you entered this house, where it is so difficult to be received, you said to yourself that you were finally nearing your goal, that the most difficult part had been overcome. Who else could have had such a stubborn memory? I admit it: you were extraordinary. Whereas all the others, as soon as they set foot in here, forget the life they have led until then, you held on to one small memory, and you never let go of this meager sign. Obviously, since you could not prevent so many memories from fading, it is as if for me we were still separated by a thousand miles. I can hardly see you at all, can hardly imagine that one day I will know who you are. But in a moment we will be permanently united. I will stretch out my open arms; I will embrace you; I will roll with you through great secrets. We will lose each other and find each other again. There will never be anything to separate us. What a shame you will not be able to witness this good fortune!"

Lucie stopped for a second, as though to give Thomas a moment to think, and then she added: "Are you satisfied?"

Before answering, Thomas wanted to look at her. He was surprised to see that she no longer looked the same. She seemed taller and stronger. Dom approached then and said in a timid voice: "No, I am far from satisfied. Night is falling fast, and I cannot breathe. In a moment, I will not even be able to find words to express my discouragement. Who can console me?"

Thomas thought about this, and then looked again at the girl. It was odd; now she looked like the house.

"Why would I consider myself satisfied by this night that I did not desire?" the young man continued. "On the contrary, I would like to remain eternally awake, awake while all of creation sleeps and while everything rests in universal midnight, awake even when the truths I would like to know have been changed into peace. Could I not then leave the house?"

"A useless question," thought Thomas, seeing that the girl looked more and more like the silent and tranquil façade of the building and that she was slipping right into these shackles of stone and cement, which, in truth, did not transform her appearance but rendered her more reserved and distant. He should have suspected long before that the girl, by dint of living in the house, had taken on its aspects, and at certain moments, when one could best discern what she was, the sad and enigmatic body of the building seemed to merge with her own. While he reflected on this transformation, his companion no doubt continued to speak, for when he began to pay attention again, he saw that the conversation had taken another turn.

"I thank you for letting me leave," said the young man, "but my mission is not completely accomplished, and I have a few more words to say. Strange shadows," he added, "they are very deep, and they are very empty. If I did not trust you, I would make another effort to rise, and I would return to retrace my steps, saying: Where is the village? Could I not be turned toward the outside so that I might receive a last ray of light, in case the night is not complete? Help me, I do not want to commit any last fault."

At that moment, the young man approached Lucie and addressed a few tired phrases of politeness to her. He took hold of her in an odd way by squeezing her tightly, as if he wanted to become one with her. There was an unpleasant confidence in his gestures. He did not take account, properly speaking, of the girl's nature, but he knew who she was, and he was showing Thomas how, with a little decisiveness and presumptuousness, one comes to the bottom of secrets against which others collide in vain. Thomas watched the couple sadly. It was for him alone to squeeze in his arms this cold and beautiful dwelling that rises against the sky and that was now closer to him than ever before. A great silence reigned there, as always, but this time the silence was calm and benevolent; one had only to look in order to experience an extraordinary sensation of deliverance.

Thomas asked her to come close by making an imperceptible sign. Both of them moved forward, for they were still tightly squeezed together.

"You are right," said the young man. "It is time to leave. This time no one will come anymore to explain why I am alone, among these leaf-covered trees, in this country that spreads before me like a desert. I must renounce the house; I will go."

Thomas understood that these words were meant for him; he had to submit to them; he could not — after maintaining his role to the end — he could not rise up to revolt at the last minute. And yet, he raised his hand in order to obtain a reprieve for a few moments. The girl certainly had something to tell him, only one good call for help was enough. So he threw himself forward, but at that moment the last glimmer of light disappeared. He opened his eyes wide and extended his arms. His hands opened timidly and groped in the night. He thought then that it was time to receive an explanation.

"Who are you?" he said with a voice full of calm and conviction, and it was as if this question would allow him to bring everything into the clear.

Blaise Cendrars
*Modernities and Other Writings*
Edited by Monique Chefdor
Translated by Esther Allen and Monique Chefdor

*The Cubist Poets in Paris: An Anthology*
Edited by L. C. Breunig

René Daumal
*You've Always Been Wrong*
Translated by Thomas Vosteen

Max Jacob
*Hesitant Fire: Selected Prose of Max Jacob*
Translated and edited by Moishe Black and Maria Green

Jean Paulhan
*Progress in Love on the Slow Side*
Translated by Christine Moneera Laennec and Michael Syrotinski

Benjamin Péret
*Death to the Pigs, and Other Writings*
Translated by Rachel Stella and Others

Raymond Queneau
*Stories and Remarks*
Translated by Marc Lowenthal

Boris Vian
*Blues for a Black Cat and Other Stories*
Edited and translated by Julia Older